BATTLESHIPS AT WAR

HMS *Royal Sovereign*
and Her Sister Ships

BATTLESHIPS AT WAR

HMS *Royal Sovereign* and Her Sister Ships

Peter C. Smith

Pen & Sword

MARITIME

See all Peter C. Smith's books at www.dive-bombers.co.uk

A CIP catalogue record for this book is
available from the British Library

Typeset in Palatino by
Phoenix Typesetting, Auldgirth, Dumfriesshire

Printed and bound in the UK by
the MPG Books Group

Pen & Sword Books Ltd incorporates the Imprints of Pen & Sword Aviation,
Pen & Sword Maritime, Pen & Sword Military, Wharncliffe Local History,
Pen & Sword Select, Pen & Sword Military Classics and Leo Cooper.

For a complete list of Pen & Sword titles please contact
PEN & SWORD BOOKS LIMITED
47 Church Street, Barnsley, South Yorkshire, S70 2AS, England
E-mail: enquiries@pen-and-sword.co.uk
Website: www.pen-and-sword.co.uk

Contents

Acknowledgements

In recounting the story of a famous British battleship in peace and in war I was conscious of the fact that, sixty years after her demise, even the youngest of her former cruiser members must now be of considerable age. As the years pass the opportunity to record for posterity the last eyewitness glimpses of a way of life now extinct becomes increasingly difficult. My thanks and gratitude are therefore all the more sincere to those gallant gentlemen who have kindly allowed me into their lives and homes and who have patiently recounted their experiences for me to set down. Cross-checking the facts from official records, signals and battle reports, the essential dry stuff of an historian like myself, is made less of a burden by the contributions of those who both knew the *Royal Sovereign* and loved her.

My thanks then to the following for all their help and assistance in the preparation of this book. Whenever possible I have let their words tell the story: Admiral Peter Skelton CB, RN; Lieutenant-Commander E.S.W. MacClure RN; Lieutenant-Colonel C.L. Price RM; Major I.F. Wray MBE, RM; Len Thomas; Harold Jago; B. McDermott; H. 'Buck' Taylor; Lawrence Dixon; W.G. Mills; Stanley Terry; James H. Clayton-Pearson; Dorothy Parker, widow of the late C.H. Parker; Des Whitby; E.C. Moore; Tom Pope; Stan Amesbury; Fred Troughton; Stan Smith; S.E. Crouch; K. Simmond; E.B. Mackenzie; Lorna Darley; Bill Heffernan; J.A.C. Yendell; Robin McGarel Groves; and many others who, regrettably, have asked me not to name them, including 'ARFBH'. Also to Russian Naval Historian Alex Bolnykh for his invaluable assistance in researching the short career of the *Royal Sovereign* when she was on loan to Stalin as

1

the *Arkhangelsk*. And to Mr J. A. Cunningham for useful additions.

My thanks, also, to David Higham Associates Ltd, London, for permission to quote from *The Bismarck Episode* by Russell Grenfell; to Collins Publishers Ltd for permission to quote from *Operation Neptune* and *Men of Action* by Kenneth Edwards; to Mrs H.M.B. McKendrick, Carnoustie, Scotland, for permission to quote from *A Sailor's Odyssey* by Viscount Cunningham of Hyndhope.

Peter C. Smith
Riseley, Bedfordshire

Explanatory Note

It is a measure of the gap 'sixty years on' that I feel the necessity to explain to younger readers just what the nickname 'Tiddly Quid' meant. Following the restoration of the monarchy after Oliver Cromwell, it became practice to reaffirm loyalty to the Crown by prefixing warships' names with 'Royal' or 'Loyal', or renaming them to commemorate some act of allegiance or an event, such as *Royal Oak*, *Loyal London* and the like; and *Royal Sovereign* was in this tradition. However, ships of the Royal Navy have also been named *Sovereign of the Seas* as a mark of their great size and majesty, or just plain *Sovereign* for a variety of reasons. A more recent ruling (contained in the Appendices of this volume) has confirmed once and for all that all these variations are but different manifestations of the same continuity of lineage.

So much for proud tradition down the centuries; and as such warships' names perform a valuable function in forming a bond between the wooden walls of the sixteenth century and the nuclear submarines of 2008. But of course 'Jack' will have none of this. The lower deck has always come up with affectionate names of their own for the ships they fought and served so well down the centuries. Thus *Bellerophon* became 'Billy Ruff'n' to the common sailor, *Penelope* was invariably 'Pennyloap', and more recently the 1930s sloop *Weston-super-Mare* was immediately dubbed 'Aggie-on-Horseback' after Dame Agnes Weston, founder of the well-known sailors' homes. *Royal Sovereign* was always a smart ship – more than that, an *extra*-smart ship – in an age when burnished brasswork and holystoned white decks marked the outward manifestation of efficiency and pride. To the sailors such a ship was a 'Tiddly ship', the best, the smartest,

3

the top-notch ship of the fleet. A sovereign was also the mark of coinage: the Imperial British Pound was a 'Sovereign', and so the transition of *Royal Sovereign* to 'Tiddly Quid' was a natural. From that to Marine Major Wray's inspired 'Regal Rouble' was but a short step for mankind!

But to a whole generation of naval officers and seamen from 1916 to 1949 there will always be only one 'Tiddly Quid'. May this book help preserve her memory for future generations of fighting sailors.

CHAPTER ONE

The Early Years

Our story begins in Portsmouth Dockyard in the last days of peace before the onset of the First World War. Here, on 15 January 1914, the keel of another mighty battleship for the Royal Navy was laid down. This was at the period of the intense naval rivalry between the ambitions of Imperial Germany, as decreed by Kaiser Wilhelm, and the traditional ruler of the waves, Great Britain. That rivalry culminated in the Great War, but was not the cause of it.

Ordered under the 1913 Building Programme, with a waterline length of 580 feet and an overall length of 624¼ feet, a beam of 88½ feet and a mean draught of 28½ feet, the *Royal Sovereign*, as first built, had a designed displacement of 28,000 tons, or 31,200 tons full-load displacement. She was engined by Parsons direct-drive steam turbines developing 40,000 hp which drove four shafts and gave her a top speed of 21½ knots as designed. She was thus slower than the preceding Queen Elizabeth-class battleships, but fitted in with the rest of the battle fleet of Dreadnought and Super-Dreadnought types. Her slow speed was always to dog her down the years, but at the time of her construction this speed was the norm and not exceptional. None the less, the Royal Sovereign-class ships were always rated lower than the Queen Elizabeths for this reason.

She was fitted with eighteen Babcock and Wilcox boilers in

three boiler rooms, and all their funnel uptakes were trunked below decks into one, thus allowing them to have one single funnel rather than the more normal two in most contemporary battleships. This gave them a dignified silhouette, quite unique for the period. In later years battleships were modified thus, and some were built to give a better all-round field of fire for the AA guns, but in 1916 the *Royal Sovereign* and her four sisters were quite special in this. Unfortunately, as in many of the ships influenced by Admiral 'Jackie' Fisher, the proximity of the bridge structure to the funnel led to problems with smoke. The ship's gunnery control top was sometimes made almost untenable in a following wind. The *Resolution* was fitted with a clinker screen in 1922 to overcome this problem, but not until World War Two did *Royal Sovereign* herself follow suit.

They were originally designed to have been coal-burning ships, like most of the battleships of that period. Fortunately, the benefits of oil-fuel having been grasped with the Queen Elizabeth class, the courageous decision was taken to convert the Royal Sovereigns in the same manner while they were still on the stocks, so they were completed thus. Initially they were fitted with tanks with a capacity of 3,400 tons, but they also carried 140 tons of coal for other purposes. For her crew this had one obvious benefit and one unexpected one. They were to be spared the horrors of coaling ship after long patrols at sea in ghastly conditions, and the ship's company's bathrooms were built below the waterline in what were originally to have been coal bunkers.

Launched on 29 April 1915, she had as her motto, *Ducere Classem Regem Sequi* – To lead the Fleet to follow the King, and she was the eighth ship of the name.

There were originally to have been eight ships in this class, but three were cancelled, and Admiral Fisher had determined on extra battle-cruisers for his hare-brained Baltic Expedition. Thus the *Renown* and *Repulse* became different warships altogether, of the same vintage, but much swifter. In compensation they carried hardly any armour (a fact which had to be hastily rectified when they joined the fleet in the aftermath of Jutland) and two fewer 15-inch guns.

Royal Sovereign's armament comprised eight 15-inch, 42-

calibre guns, paired in four turrets, two forrard, 'A' and 'B', and two aft, 'X' and 'Y', each set super-imposed to give all-round firing coverage. Her secondary armament was of fourteen single 6-inch, 45-calibre guns, designed to sink attacking enemy destroyers while the main guns slugged it out with the enemy battle-line. These were disposed in two batteries, port and starboard amidships. The total number of these secondary guns was reduced to ten when two on the main deck aft were suppressed. As a concession to the infant air services two single 3-inch HA guns were fitted, along with four 3-pounders for saluting purposes.

The naval 15-inch gun was one of the great success stories of the period, and it became the 'standard' British battleship mounting, reliable and trustworthy. Initially, however, it was designed to fulfil the role envisaged for it of battle-lines pounding each other at 10,000 yards' range. It therefore had an elevation of only twenty degrees. As the battle ranges doubled and then trebled as the years went by, this was to be another crippling limitation of their power as they became progressively outranged while foreign battleships were modified. Apart from 'A' and 'B' turrets aboard the *Resolution* in 1941, the 'Royal Sovereigns' never had their twin 15-inch turrets modified to 30 degrees to extend their range, although it was often mooted. Lack of funds prevented this being done, and this was the second limiting factor which brought them such a bad press in the Second World War.

But this was twenty years in the future. In 1914, when they began to take shape, they were the ultimate in battleship design, far superior to the equivalent German designs of the time, and, in their internal armour protection, actually *superior* to the Queen Elizabeths, a fact often overlooked or ignored in reference books.

They had a main belt 13 inches at its maximum thickness, with 10-inch maximum barbettes and 13-inch maximum turret armour. Deck armour was similar to the Queen Elizabeths, but an additional 2-inch-thick deck was built on top of the 13-inch main belt at main deck level instead of a 1-inch deck on the waterline.

Anti-torpedo bulges were coming into fashion. These were

appendages built outside the main hull and designed to take the main blast effect out of a torpedo hit and prevent it penetrating through to the real hull itself. The *Ramillies* was actually constructed with this feature, but *Royal Sovereign* had to wait until a refit in the 1920s before she received hers. It had the effect of increasing the beam of the ship to 108 ft, but surprisingly had little effect on the ship's speed, reducing it by perhaps half to one knot.

It is often forgotten that battleships of this period also carried torpedo tubes. It was thought that opportunities might present themselves for the *coup-de-grâce* to be delivered in this fashion after a naval battle, a thought that proved largely illusory. None the less, at the time of her completion, *Royal Sovereign* carried four submerged 21-inch torpedo tubes with twenty torpedoes.

As for seagoing qualities, so essential for Royal Navy ships, which, unlike other navies, were usually at sea, the Royal Sovereign class, although shorter than some, proved themselves to be the steadiest seaboats of all the various Dreadnought classes, and the best gun platforms.

The names of the five ships as finally allocated were, as befitted the time and the might of the navy they were built for, both stirring and traditional: *Ramillies, Revenge, Resolution, Royal Sovereign* and *Royal Oak*.

Captain T.A. Hunt RN, who had commanded the battleship *Thunderer* in the Grand Fleet, was appointed in command of the *Royal Sovereign*, and he therefore travelled the full length of Great Britain, from Scapa Flow to Portsmouth Dockyard, to take over the great vessel in the early spring of 1916. With him went his navigating officer, Lieutenant James Troup. He gave this record of his captain, the takeover and her first voyage north to join the Grand Fleet through submarine-infested waters:

> Our ship was commanded by Captain A.T. Hunt, whose fearlessness brushed every difficulty aside. He was reputed to have shot five lions before breakfast. We had a small billiard-table aboard and he could beat everyone playing only with his right hand and with his left behind his back.
>
> I had the privilege of following him to HMS *Royal Sovereign*, which we took over from Portsmouth Dockyard.

I had to sign my name under his on a receipt for this ship – rather a large transaction for me!

We sailed from Portsmouth with a large company – all the ship's complement, naval 'passengers' joining other ships at Scapa and numerous experts and workmen to ensure that the machines from their firms and the dockyard worked correctly – perhaps 1,400 in all.

We were not long away before I observed every time I came down from the bridge that the same civilian was always hanging around on the boat deck near the bridge ladder. He got into conversation with me and his only topic was the prospect of a submarine attack. Indeed, I heard that when he was absent he had a workman stationed to give instant, personal warning.

'I suppose we're in the worst part now for submarines?' 'Yes.'

'How soon will we get clear?' 'I wish I knew.'

Then, next time:

'I suppose we're getting clear of the submarine area now?' 'I'm afraid not.'

So it went on all the way round Cape Wrath to the Pentland Firth, any sadism I might possess having full play. Poor devil!

The ship had commissioned in May 1916, and was still at Scapa working up due to a hitch in her gunnery trials when the Battle of Jutland was fought on 31 May 1916, so she took no part in this great sea fight.

After joining the 1st Battle Squadron on 25 May 1916, they were often at sea from that time onward, in all weathers, constantly hoping against hope that the Germans would venture forth once more to try conclusions with them. It was a vain hope. Crow as they might about a 'glorious victory', both the German admirals, Hipper and Scheer, knew in their hearts that they had only escaped total annihilation by the onset of darkness. Their one aim was to get home as quickly as they could, and once home their great fleet stagnated. Their battle fleet became truly mere floating barracks, the seedbeds of discontent and eventually mutiny and the overthrow of the state from within.

So for *Royal Sovereign*, as for all her contemporaries, the war years were weary and monotonous days of sweeps across the North Sea, days spent in foul weather covering the Norwegian convoys and in long hours on patrol in submarine-infested seas, all for no reward. The submarine remained a vague threat, which, though often spotted, rarely if ever inhibited the work of the battleships. During one sweep in August 1916, for example, two submarines were reported from *Royal Sovereign*, but no attacks were made.

Captain H.M. Doughty relieved Captain Hunt on 24 July 1917, but the pattern of their life continued much as before.

With the coming of the Armistice itself, the whole of the mighty Grand Fleet went to sea on 21 November 1918, to meet and escort the German fleet back to Britain. It was '*Der Tag*' all right for the German Navy, but not in the manner that they had foreseen when they first built it to challenge British seapower. Admiral of the Fleet Lord Chatfield left this impression of the mutinous and sullen High Seas Fleet at its nadir and the Grand Fleet's supreme triumph:

> The surrender of the German Fleet was to many of us a highly painful if dramatic event. To see the great battle-ships come into sight, their guns trained fore-and-aft; the battle-cruisers, which we had met twice under such very different circumstances, creeping towards us as it were with their tails between their legs, gave one a real feeling of disgust. These ships that had fought so well, that had been such doughty opponents, what must they themselves feel? Surely the spirit of all past seamen must be writhing in dismay over this tragedy, this disgrace to all maritime traditions. The surrender of their Fleet, one felt, could never have been agreed to by a nation, which had a naval tradition or history.

The Commander-in-Chief, Admiral Sir David Beatty, summed it all up in one sentence at the end of that day. Turning to his flagship's company assembled on the quarterdeck, he acknowledged their ringing cheers with, 'Didn't I tell you they would have to come out!'

The overpowering arrogance of some Germans, even after this humiliating display, was very apparent in the dealings that the Royal Navy had in the aftermath of the German ships' mass surrender. Lieutenant-Commander Troup remembered the various encounters they had with the surrendered High Seas Fleet thus:

> After escorting the German Fleet into Rosyth and then north to Scapa in 1918, it was my duty to pilot one of the German battleships to her berth.
>
> I understood that the crew to do duty for the occasion on the bridge had released the captain from arrest in his cabin. The committeemen who headed the mutineer crew expected to be shown the berth on the chart and gave their futile approval. The movement was completed without trouble.
>
> Our final transaction with them arose when they sank their fleet at Scapa. We set off for Rosyth that night with 400 Germans aboard.
>
> Accompanied by these prisoners, it was an eerie experience to be on that run, which we had done so often during the war. Some of them were a little troublesome, especially officers. They expected more to be done for their comfort, and asked for cushions. The provision was reasonable, and by the time they came to leave next day our men had had enough of them, and gave rather short shrift to troublemakers.

As far as possible normal fleet routine was maintained to keep the Grand Fleet alert while the negotiations leading to the Versailles Treaty dragged on their weary course. *Royal Sovereign*, like many of the big ships of the fleet, had been fitted with 'flying-off platforms' atop 'B' and 'X' turrets from which fighter aircraft like the Sopwith Camel could be flown off to deal with Zeppelins, and in later years the Hawker Osprey floatplanes for spotting. *Royal Sovereign* also had catapults of the McTaggart type fitted to her quarterdeck. All these aeronautical appendages were only possible to use in very good weather with calm seas, and were therefore of only very limited value.

Although they were to linger for most of the ships' lives they were considered fire hazards, and by 1939 'Tiddly Quid' had discarded hers.

The opportunity was taken in 1919 to dock the ship, and this involved de-ammunitioning. They entered the drydock at Invergordon in September. The Royal Marines took the opportunity to land their detachment at Houston Bay on 21 June to carry out exercises.

By now a commander, James Troup was also to recall the difficulties encountered by the demobilisation of the fleet in 1919:

> We had over 500 men due to leave in my ship, many of them receiving letters from employers telling them that their posts could not be kept open if they could not come at once.
>
> As might be expected, the 'last in' were the most vocal about being the 'first out'.
>
> They were due for warmer climes but first they recommissioned at Portsmouth.
>
> After these troubles were resolved, we got a very young but long-service ship's company. I had given up navigation for a time and remained in the same ship, *Royal Sovereign*, as Executive Officer, second-in-command. We served for some months in the Mediterranean.

Although now part of the 1st Battle Squadron in the newly named Atlantic Fleet between 1919 and 1926, they went to the Mediterranean Fleet in 1920, and after a stay at Malta sailed from there in April 1920 for the eastern basin, where trouble was brewing again with the Turks and Greeks. As F.C.M. Anderson recollected, 'With HMS *Resolution*, the *Royal Sovereign*, in which I was serving at the time, was rushed from Gibraltar to deal with a spot of bother at Gallipoli.'

Commander Troup later recounted his experiences in Turkish waters:

> Early in 1920, we visited Constantinople, where some show of force was necessary, and we marched in large numbers

through various districts and occupied the War Office for one night.' It was the Royal Marines' No. 9 Platoon that carried out this particular operation:

Eventually [wrote Marine Anderson], an Army force, the 'Buffs', took over, their colours being handed over to the Tiddly Quid for safe-keeping. Nine months later, when the affair was settled, there was a ceremony on the quarterdeck when we trooped the colours and handed them back – perhaps the first occasion that a regimental colour had been trooped aboard a British battleship. I was one of the colour guard.

On one of our marches it was decided that the commanders should be mounted, and I was 'teed-up' in front of my company on an animal, which was more of a mule than a horse and had seldom, if ever, been ridden before.

To the delight of the sailors, the animal did his best to get rid of me by rearing. Then it tried walking backwards on its hind-legs towards the edge of the jetty. The prospects were poor even though I had learned to ride. However, an expert explained the dynamics of the dilemma, namely to hit hard whichever end came up, and the beast came under control, perhaps somewhat to the disappointment of the audience.

It was a moving experience to walk all over the Gallipoli Peninsula, the scene of great heroism, the graveyard of many heroes.

The fortunes of the White Russians fluctuated wildly at this time in the Crimea, where the Civil War against the 'Reds' was still raging, but eventually the tide of war turned finally against them. Many eminent Russian refugees now fled their homeland aboard British battleships. *Royal Sovereign*'s most distinguished 'guest' in this chaotic period was Princess Galitzine, whom they embarked at the port of Prinkipo on 31 July 1920.

Commander Troup continued:

By this time I had been a commander for a couple of years and had turned from navigation to executive work.

It came, therefore, as a shock when early in 1920 I was given the opportunity to become Master of the Fleet. The use of the Nelsonic title of this post had been resumed at the beginning of the war, the Master of the Fleet being the navigating officer of the Senior Commander-in-Chief's flagship.

It was a post which carried heavy responsibility for the safe navigation of the Fleet and berthing of perhaps, 60 ships or more in harbour. I had become tired of navigation, but every previous Master of the Fleet had been promoted to captain. In my slight affairs, I realised that this was the tide 'which taken at the flood, leads on to fortune', and I compelled myself to accept this generous offer.

Troup therefore took farewell of *Royal Sovereign* to join the fleet flagship, *Queen Elizabeth*.

The policy of the Royal Navy in its reduced post-war circumstances was to rely on cruiser squadrons on the more distant stations (South America, China, East Indies and West Indies), while keeping the two main fleets, Atlantic and Mediterranean, and using them to reinforce the others in times of stress. From forty Dreadnought battleships in 1919, Washington had cut down the Navy to a mere fifteen, and other types of warship had suffered the same severe pruning. A battle fleet now only had sufficient ships for one or, at best, two squadrons of battleships, and therefore in order to exercise properly the two fleets met annually to carry out combined exercises, either in the Mediterranean or the Atlantic, following which they assembled at Gibraltar to assess the results.

In between times they carried out lesser exercises, gave 'flag-showing' cruises around the British Isles and the Empire and assimilated new equipment and doctrines. The severe cash shortages prevented all but a very modest modernisation programme or the construction of anything but a handful of new ships, and the further complications of the London Naval Treaty only made things worse. Therefore if ideas were slow in percolating down, the crippling effects of lack of Government interest and Government spending limits were the major factors. In the main, therefore, the battleships soldiered on with what they had and hoped for better days.

In the smaller Royal Navy of only some 100,000 officers and

men, it was cosy enough for almost any 'character' to quickly become known throughout the fleet, and all manner of personalities and larger-than-life individuals, from admirals down to ABs, made their indelible mark on that happy band of brothers. Naturally stories abounded about their deeds and misdeeds, and were told and retold from Plymouth Hoe to the furthest reaches of the Yangtze river.

As for armament modifications, these were small in this period. The 3-inch HA guns had already been replaced by single 4-inch guns in 1925. In 1921 it had been proposed that four sets of multiple 2-pounder pom-poms be fitted, but there were only two prior to the Second World War. In May 1925 *Royal Sovereign* became part of the 2nd Battle Squadron, still with the Atlantic Fleet, and in October 1926 she was flying the flag of Rear Admiral D.T. Norris CB, CMG, in the 1st Battle Squadron, Mediterranean Fleet.

One young cadet who joined her as his first ship at that time is now Lieutenant-Commander E.S.W. MacClure RN. One of his uncles had served aboard the old *Royal Sovereign* in 1895, so the young Winton MacClure felt he was perpetuating a family tradition:

I am now aged 78, and it seems a long time since I and four of my fellow Naval cadets embarked from Cornwallis jetty, resplendent in our shell jackets ('bum-freezers') and midshipman's dirks on 1 September 1925 to join HMS *Royal Sovereign* in the picket boat that forenoon.

The Captain at that time was Captain B. Domville. His career in the Royal Navy ended, I think, in the mid-thirties, when he was President of the Royal Naval College at Greenwich. The big Naval Pageant was held at Greenwich, which suited him down to the ground, as he and his family were very much interested in theatricals and stage work.

On 3 September the ship sailed for a courtesy visit to Wick, the fishing port in the north of Scotland. Wick had not received a visit from a battleship since HMS *Iron Duke* visited the port in 1912. My main recollections of Wick are of the overpowering smell of herring gutting and the dance laid on for the officers in the city hall. Captain Domville insisted that all the young officers should dance the Lancers – a favourite of his youth, no doubt, but certainly few of us knew very much of how to perform it.

The rest of the autumn's cruise centred on exercises off Invergordon. The main incident that I can recall is when the *Royal Sovereign*'s first picket boat collided with and holed the flagship's picket boat from HMS *Revenge*, the latter sinking just off Invergordon pier. We lost our second picket boat, which had to be transferred on loan to the flagship. Fortunately I was not in charge of *Royal Sovereign*'s picket boat at the time of this disaster.

Another incident that reflects life aboard a battleship in the mid-twenties is well worth retelling. MacClure again:

It so happened that at that time the Admiralty was considering the introduction of steam laundries to capital ships in the Royal Navy, and HMS *Royal Sovereign* was chosen to receive an early prototype model, a somewhat fearsome structure, I recall.

Battleships and cruisers in those days carried their own detachments of Royal Marines on board, and with the reputation held by the Royal Marines the captain and commander decided that who better could handle this latest equipment in the Royal Navy than the Royals. Accordingly, a ship's laundry crew was appointed with a Royal Marine NCO in command and a young lieutenant RN as ship's laundry officer in general overall charge.

I fancy the drill book for operation of the laundry contained little other than general instructions. The days of commercial brands of soap powders, etc., had not yet arrived. The laundry crew wasted no time in raising steam true to Royal Marine traditions, the laundry became operational and loading of the officers' and ship's company washing got under way.

I myself possessed a caring mother who insisted on equipping me with the best Chilprufe underwear, flannel pyjamas, etc., when I was first released to sea. Regrettably, it was my new flannel pajamas that proved to be the fly in the ointment. Once the laundry was operating at full pressure, most articles for the wash were loaded in with scant regard for individual materials. I considered myself of normal stature at the time, but both the laundry staff and I were more than surprised when my flannel pyjamas emerged from the wash. Flannel does not take kindly to boiling, it would appear. Somewhat unwisely, I sent my pyjamas back home, where they proved almost a perfect fit for my young sister's teddy bear.

My father was far from pleased when he saw the result of the ship's handiwork, and did not hesitate to send a letter of remonstrance to the ship's commanding officer. This, of course, passed down the line, ending finally with the lieutenant in charge of the laundry. By some miracle of fortune there the matter stopped, as had it reached the midshipmen's gunroom I feel sure that the sub-lieutenant in charge would have awarded me summary corporal punishment.

I recall some years later reading an article in *Punch* about a somewhat similar incident abroad, when it was alleged that the Admiral's white uniform had emerged from the wash a delicate shade of light mauve. Clever detective work established that the Admiral's laundry and that of the Sergeant Major Royal Marines had entered the same wash, but accidentally the indelible pencil from the breast pocket of the Sergeant Major's tunic had not been removed prior to washing. I think this tale is fictional, but strange things *do* happen at sea!

We did not remain very long aboard the *Royal Sovereign*, as she sailed in October to Portsmouth for docking and a short refit prior to proceeding to the Mediterranean.

On 4 October 1927, the *Royal Sovereign* returned to Portsmouth and reduced to reserve complement in order to undertake a major refit, as she was now ten years old. Four new rangefinders were fitted, along with eight searchlights. Normally she would be looking for newer battleships to have taken her place in line, but in the aftermath of the disastrous Washington Naval Treaty, when Britain had thrown away her age-old dominance of the sea, only two new battleships were built. These, the *Nelson* and *Rodney*, arrived on the scene while 'Tiddly Quid' was refitting, and they remained the only new British battleships for thirteen years! It was clear therefore that the *Royal Sovereign* and her sisters would have to soldier on for a long time yet.

CHAPTER TWO

The Sands Run Out

Following the London Naval Conference, the *Royal Sovereign* was rerated under the new displacement rules as being of 29,150 tons, standard. The refit was completed on 15 May 1929, when *Royal Sovereign* was recommissioned once more in the 1st Battle Squadron, Mediterranean Fleet. Here she remained until the following year. In August 1930, the young Ernle Chatfield, son of the C-in-C, took passage for home in the gunroom of the 'Tiddly Quid' by the kindness of Captain Washington.

Royal Sovereign was one of the four battleships of the Mediterranean Fleet in January 1934, the others being the fleet flagship *Queen Elizabeth* and the *Revenge* and *Resolution*. They were under the command of Admiral Sir William Fisher, a very wise and thoughtful leader who brought the fleet to the acme of readiness and perfection in time to face Mussolini's threat to Abyssinia only to see the Government back down in appeasement. *Royal Sovereign* remained part of the Mediterranean Fleet, and among her leading seamen was Stanley Terry:

We were part of the 1st Battle Squadron between 1932 and 1935 and she was always Portsmouth-manned. One of the interesting things from this period was that *Royal Sovereign* carried a 'Queen Bee' wireless-controlled target plane. It was berthed on a catapult on our quarterdeck and we used it for AA gunnery practice. During this commission *Royal Sovereign* was a very happy ship and we won all the trophies in the fleet for gunnery and sport. The only one we couldn't get our hands on was the 'Cock of the Fleet' trophy for the Fleet Regatta.

Most of our time in the Mediterranean was spent 'showing the flag' on various cruises. We were sent to various trouble spots in the Mediterranean as they erupted, Palestine, Athens and Cyprus. We thought we were the finest and most efficient unit in the fleet and certainly the cleanest, as it was all 'spit and polish' to the last degree. We really earned our nickname as we were the most 'Tiddly' ship in the most 'Tiddly' fleet in the most 'Tiddly' navy in the world!

We finally came home in April 1935, and after being given leave we took part in the big Jubilee Review at Spithead in honour of King George V. We entertained aboard Ramsay MacDonald and Mr Runciman during this time, and then we went into dock for a major refit and paid off, thus missing the Abyssinian War confrontation.

James H. Clayton-Pearson remembers joining the *Royal Sovereign* for a few months in 1934:

I was a Boy, 1st Class. We had to make do on twelve shillings per month, which was our total wage. We were at Split in the Adriatic and manned the ship's guardrails when the King of Yugoslavia was murdered and his body brought home from Marseilles by the French fleet.

Exercises that year were held in the Bay of Biscay in a full gale, during which even the battleships were dripping their bows and 'taking it green' across the fo'c'sles, but it was a good practice for what was to come in later years off Greenland. By contrast the fleet regatta was held at Navarino Bay in Greece under a blazing sun. It was in the following year that she anchored at Spithead for the Jubilee Review of the Fleet by King George V.

By now, although the old peacetime routine was still being

followed, the world was a very different place. The Fascist dictatorships had arisen unopposed in Italy, Germany and elsewhere in Europe. In the Far East Japan had been changed by the Washington Treaty from a loyal ally into a potential enemy of great power. The world was rearming, save for Britain and the United States. The halcyon days were coming to an end.

In August 1935 *Royal Sovereign* recommissioned as the flagship of Rear Admiral C.G. Ramsey CB, in the 2nd Battle Squadron, Atlantic Fleet. Walt Mills and Harold Jago both recall that she was serving as a training ship and had some 600 youngsters embarked. Walt Mills:

> At that time we joined the Atlantic Fleet as Boys' Training Ship. We leading hands were responsible for the signal and wireless boy trainees. At Reveille it was our job to rouse them, and the routine was once through the messdecks with the usual 'Wakey-wakey' calls, then a second trip to check, and any boys still found in their hammocks had the hammock clews cut. During my time aboard *Royal Sovereign* corporal punishment was eliminated. One of our yeoman signallers, who was awaiting promotion to signal boatswain, was disrated to leading signalman for striking a junior rating. To my knowledge he was the first victim of the abolition. We instituted our own methods of punishment, such as standing on top of 'B' turret or out on the bridge wing on the weather side in heavy seas.
>
> Capital ships were allocated a drifter; ours was the *Halo*. Our signal bosun had a brainwave, and on passage from Portland to Portsmouth transferred me, with ten signal boys, to the drifter for signal exercises. We had barely cleared Portland harbour when the boys began being seasick, and they ended up hanging over the side, with the heaving line rove through their belts, presenting their breakfasts to the fishes *en masse*! The drifter's 'Bunts' and I did all the exercises possible, which wasn't much, as our best speed was nine knots.

One such youngster was Fred Troughton, and he has vivid memories of the 'Tiddly Quid' as a training battleship:

I left HMS *Ganges*, the boys' training establishment, in early January 1937, to join the *Royal Sovereign* at Devonport along with a large number of other boy seamen to complete our boys' sea training. We were isolated from the rest of the ship's company in boy's messdecks, with a leading seaman as boys' instructor. During working hours we scrubbed decks (bare feet!), polished brasswork, provided working parties and the like. I remember we exercised 'coaling ship', a thing not done since before the Great War twenty or more years earlier. It was our ship's galleys which still burned coal, so we boys were in the coal lighter filling the sacks. We also did a certain amount of instructions as part of our sea training.

Our first sea trip was a cruise to Madeira in the Canary Islands, very nice for us in our white duck suits. Or so we thought! In practice we hit a real howler of a gale in the Bay of Biscay (where else?) and many of the boys had as part of their initial training the true meaning of seasickness! However, the weather at Madeira and onward made up for it, although most of us suffered agonies with our first inoculations.

I recall the ship's padre organising a boys' trip ashore and doing the run down to the harbour over cobbles in the sledges; also manning the pumps as diving party alongside in the launch while the ship's divers got in some practice.

Then on to Santa Cruz and Las Palmas in the Canaries. Very hot, tons of cheap bananas. We went ashore and played football. On the next pitch were new recruits for Franco's army doing squad drill.

We then sailed to Gibraltar and joined up with the rest of the Home and Mediterranean Fleets, and I was very impressed with the might of the Royal Navy. We lay astern of the *Hood*; sadly a couple of her Marines had been killed earlier when a berthing wire parted and whipped back. Then came the combined fleet manoeuvres in the Atlantic. We boys took part in gunnery drills, bridge lookouts and streaming paravanes for mines.

Eventually the fleets split up and we made for the UK with the rest of the Home Fleet, arriving back at Devonport in time to take Easter leave. A number of us Portsmouth ratings left the *Sovereign* after a mere three months to join HMS *Nelson* at Pompey. Years later, during the war, I was serving in HMS *Howe* and we were at Scapa Flow when I next saw my first ship, *Royal Sovereign*, flying the Hammer and Sickle on loan to Russia. I did hear – after the war – that she came back in a much worse and dirtier condition than she had left us.

Royal Sovereign remained on this duty until 2 June 1937, when she again reduced to reserve for another major refit This one lasted until 18 February 1938, when she recommissioned for the 2nd Battle Squadron, Home Fleet. As always this meant the crew were fully extended in storing and ammunitioning ship. It also meant getting the ship cleaned up to her former 'Tiddly' condition after many months in the uncaring hands of the dock-yard workers, in time for her to pass her C-in-C's inspection before joining the Home Fleet. This meant long hours of work if you were on duty, working into the dogwatches, getting in last-minute stores and clearing up in general.

Tom Pope relates how this affected the *Royal Sovereign* on this occasion:

C-in-C Inspection was in three parts in those days: first, Action Stations. When we were closed up at our action stations he would walk round the ship thinking up different drills for the guns' crews and asking awkward questions. Second, General Drill. This time he would have us doing exercises such as towing forward or towing aft, collision mat over the side, drop anchor and weigh them again by hand, walking the ship's capstan round with capstan bars. This was a very hectic day. One was always rushing from one exercise to another, the decks being cluttered up with ropes and wires. Very often you finished up not quite sure what one was supposed to be doing, as there could be two or three different exercises going on at once. I, for one, was very glad when the day came to an end and I could crawl into my hammock, utterly exhausted. Still, no doubt the 'great man' felt satisfied with himself at the end of it, although what relevance it had for actual combat conditions I could never ascertain!

The third phase was inspection of the ship herself with the ship's company at 'Divisions'. On that day you were up before the crack of dawn, scrubbing, cleaning and polishing the ship from stem to stern. You were almost frightened to walk on the deck, and often a shout would go up: 'Get that so-and-so off that deck, I have just scrubbed it!' It was a case of 'Walk on your eyebrows'. After fully inspecting the ship, it was the turn of the ship's company to stand intense scrutiny. We all fell in by divisions and wearing our No. 1 uniforms, with those who were entitled to, their medals.

As the C-in-C went round the ship's company, he would detail men off at random to lay out their kit or hammock for inspection. This would often cause a bit of a panic, especially if the man's kit or hammock was not quite up to scratch.

After passing this ordeal *Royal Sovereign*'s crew could settle down to the normal routine of a Home Fleet battleship. The summer cruise that year included a visit to Greenock in conjunction with the Glasgow Exhibition, when 'the Second City of the Empire' put on display what was, in those distant days, a huge range of manufacturing and shipbuilding industries. Tom Pope:

> During our stay we were made most welcome by the people of that city. Entry into the exhibition itself was free for us, and on their trams more often than not we were also allowed to travel free. The Royal Navy was held in high esteem then.
>
> *Royal Sovereign* herself repaid the courtesy by throwing herself open to the public, and we quite enjoyed showing people around. In fact a good time was had by all. But all good things come to an end and we said farewell to Greenock and set a course for Scapa Flow.

The old Grand Fleet base was then still being run down, and teams of workers and servicemen were still hard at work demolishing the defences and guns from 1918, even though the threat of a new German war stared everyone in the face twenty years on! The islands looked as bleak as ever, but no opportunity was ever lost to test the men's mettle, as Tom Pope recalls:

It was while we were in Scapa Flow that the Captain thought it would be a good idea to exercise a landing party on the island of Hoy, and just to make it more interesting it was to be a night attack by the Royal Marines, while the seamen were to act as the defence force. So, on the day, the seamen were landed with rifles, webbing gear and some blank rounds of ammunition, plus food and water to last for 24 hours.

I was with the section which was in support of the Headquarters, which had set up their post near the oil tanks. The gunnery officer had a 3-pounder saluting gun brought ashore, along with OA, carpenters and gun's crew, and he had this weapon emplaced at the end of the jetty, facing seaward, with the intention of firing blanks should the attacking force try a frontal assault. However, when they fired a blank round the gun unseated itself without more ado, and that was that. End of experiment, end of defence capability and red faces all round!

Later on we got the word that the 'Royals' had landed and were on their way. We were therefore marched off to defend, of all places, the cemetery! This I think must have been the Naval cemetery at Lyness, as when it got lighter we found one or two headstones with German names on them, also some British. We remained there, sitting behind a wall until the morning, when, feeling very cold, tired (a night out at Scapa, even in summer, is not reckoned to do one's health much good), we returned to the jetty and embarked in the drifter and returned to the ship in time for our tot of rum. We never did see the attacking force. What happened to them I am not sure, but I did hear that some of the 'Royals' got lost. Still, once more, a good time was had by all.

Their next port of call was to be Portland, where they were again to spruce the ship up to perfection in readiness for a visit by His

Majesty King George VI. This meant a lot more bull, but this was wasted as, in fact, the King did not come aboard *Royal Sovereign* herself. In the event the ship's company were landed and were inspected by the King ashore. He then embarked aboard the fleet flagship, the *Nelson*, and went to sea with the whole fleet. The highlight of the day was a full-calibre shoot at sea. Also, the fleet carried out AA firing against one of the 'Queen Bee' radio-controlled target aircraft. Although the combined ships put up a barrage with their 4-inch and pom-poms, it flew serenely on through it and was not shot down! It was certainly a fore-warning of just how effective the fleet's defences against aircraft were – or rather, just how useless. Norway and Dunkirk were only to confirm numerous peacetime examples, but no lessons were heeded until it was too late.

While at Portland, the ship's company also competed at soccer for the King George V Cup, which was an annual competition in the Navy. Many considered the standard of play quite worthy of that played by the professional clubs. Certainly it was widely supported by the ships' companies. The biggest football match, the Royal Navy's equivalent of the Wembley Cup Final, was the game played between the Home and Mediterranean Fleets, which took place at Gibraltar during the spring cruise. Regardless of who won, everyone retired afterwards to the 'wet' canteen, where the usual congratulations and 'inquests' were held over a few pints of beer.

Another event which took place at Portland at this time was the Fleet Regatta, when all the ships in the fleet, which had been training and working hard for months, displayed their best crews. It was regarded as an unofficial holiday, for apart from cleaning the decks there was no work done, all free time being taken up with cheering on the crews pulling the boats, cutters, gigs, whalers and skiffs. Some of the crews dressed up for it and ended up swimming across the harbour. At the end of the day the ship with the most winning crews was known as 'Cock of the Fleet' and proudly carried the cup around the assembled ships to the cheers of all the matelots. A huge model cockerel was made out of plywood and, gilded with gold paint and other embellishments, mounted atop 'B' turret for all to see. Boxing was another favourite competition held in the fleet, a cup again being fought for by all the different weights. There would also be ships' dances held on board from time to time, and a ship's concert with the Royal Marine band and many female guests. In the evenings, there being no cinemas aboard at that period, the crews had to make their own entertainments, so there would be card schools under way throughout the ship, and another popular game was Mah Jong. Time was taken out for writing letters or doing one's dhobying.

The King also paid a state visit to Canada in 1939, sailing in one of the 'Empress' liners, with the Home Fleet escorting him part of the way and meeting him again on his return. *Royal Sovereign* was to become very familiar indeed with this particular stretch of ocean in the years ahead.

In between these duties the 'Tiddly Quid' paid a visit to the French naval base of Brest. The French Admiral Taub paid a visit to the ship with his staff. Again they were made most welcome by their hosts, and some of the ship's company were invited to the homes of the inhabitants. After returning to Portland once more, the *Royal Sovereign* left for Sheerness at the mouth of the Medway, and gave leave. They also embarked new crew members to bring their complement up to war standards. Among those who joined her towards the end of 1939 was James Clayton-Pearson again, now an ordinary seaman.

> I was drafted to her in the spring of 1939. I left her again to go HMS *Vernon* at Portsmouth to undertake my LTO course, but, halfway through it the crisis came and I was sent back to Chatham, where we were urgently needed. I was next drafted, for the third time, to HMS *Royal Sovereign*. We all had to have our kit ready to be sent to Chatham if we had to at the end of our leave. When in the last week we did have a travel warrant sent to us to report to Chatham, our kit didn't arrive until eight days after we had left the Depot. Aboard ship we could not be given any work to do as we only had our best suits to wear! Then I was sent back down to Eastbourne and another training unit, HMS *Marlborough*, to finish the course and pass for LTD. Thus my job on *Royal Sovereign* was LTD of the Battery Room and

Low Power Supply Panel and maintenance of the Low
Power Generators. But no rise in pay!

The Home Fleet was concentrating at its war stations by the last
weeks of August, and *Royal Sovereign* herself sailed north up the
east coast in the closing days of peace to Invergordon. Here she
anchored in company with HM Ships *Repulse, Resolution, Rodney*
and *Royal Oak*, the 2nd and 18th Cruiser Squadrons, *Belfast,
Edinburgh, Glasgow, Newcastle* and *Southampton*, and eight Tribal-
class destroyers of the 6th Flotilla, *Ashanti, Bedouin, Eskimo,
Mashona, Matabele, Punjabi, Somali* and *Tartar*.

By 31 August the bulk of these ships had joined the C-in-C,
Admiral Sir Charles Forbes, with his flag in HMS *Nelson*, back in
the famous land-locked anchorage of Scapa Flow in the Orkney
Islands. The following day came the news that the German army
had crossed the Polish border, despite warnings from Britain
and France, and the deadline set by them for a declaration of
war, 1100 on 3 September, was steadily ticking away.

The men of the *Royal Sovereign* were as ready as they could be
for the great test. The old ship, now more than twenty years old,
was none the less prepared once more to play her part in whatever fortunes of war were to come her way. Few could have
envisaged, as those last days of peace ticked away, just how long
that conflict was to last, to what strange waters and climes the
dictates of war were to take her and just what unique fate
awaited the 'Tiddly Quid' before that war was brought to a
conclusion.

CHAPTER THREE

Home Fleet

The Second Battle Squadron of the Home Fleet comprised the battleships *Nelson* (flying the flag of the Commander-in-Chief, Admiral Sir Charles Forbes), *Rodney*, *Royal Sovereign*, *Royal Oak* and *Ramillies*. They lay at Scapa Flow, in the Orkney Islands. Thus 'Tiddly Quid' returned once again to the old Grand Fleet base she had known in the first German war.

Also present were the battle-cruisers *Hood* and *Repulse*, the aircraft carrier *Ark Royal*, three cruiser squadrons totalling twelve light cruisers, two destroyer flotillas and a minesweeping flotilla. Veterans looking back two decades and recalling the waters of that great anchorage covered with line after line of battleships, cruisers and destroyers could only compare this much reduced force and past glories with regret and apprehension. It was in such a setting that the enormity of Britain's decline as a seapower could be clearly seen. Truly the politicians had much to answer for.

Ironically enough, one of those politicians who, as Chancellor of the Exchequer, had done so much to reduce the Royal Navy's strength, now returned as its political head. The fleet heard the news in the form of a signal from the Admiralty: 'Winston's Back!' Whether this news was received with satisfaction or apprehension depended on one's knowledge of the man. The lower deck took it cheerfully as a sign that someone with guts and determination was at the helm at this moment of grave crisis. Others, the more knowledgeable or thoughtful officers, who had experience of Churchill's petulant and arrogant ways, were less enthusiastic. They were soon to experience his influence for good or ill, and the 'Royal Sovereigns' in particular became his particular *bêtes noires* throughout the war years.

In addition to the main fleet outlined above, other naval squadrons were under Admiral Forbes's command and could join his flag if needed. Both *Resolution* and *Revenge* lay at Portland with the aircraft carriers *Courageous* and *Hermes*, three more small cruisers and another destroyer flotilla, while there were two cruisers and another flotilla at the Humber and the aircraft carrier *Furious* at Rosyth. Apart from ships refitting, the bulk of the Royal Navy's remaining heavy ships were in the Mediterranean. As it became clear that Mussolini was staying dithering on the sidelines for the moment, many of these latter ships made their way home during the next few months and relieved the older ships there for other duties. Thus *Royal Sovereign*'s time with Britain's premier line of defence was very brief indeed.

The fact that the Germans had sailed two of their pocket battleships, *Admiral Graf Spee* and *Deutschland*, out into the Atlantic prior to the outbreak of hostilities was not then known to the Admiralty. These two vessels lay at their 'waiting stations' with their accompanying oilers and supply ships ready to pounce on Allied convoys. There is little doubt that they could have inflicted considerable carnage had the Germans unleashed them right away, but for the time being Hitler ordered that they stay their hands until he had crushed Poland. No doubt he hoped that once he had scored his quick victory in the East the British and French would recognise his *fait accompli*. For once his famous intuition let him down, and so the German raiders lost a good chance. When they did begin operations their victims were for the most part isolated merchant ships, lean pickings indeed. When these began reporting their attackers by radio signals, the priceless advantage of surprise was lost to the Germans. The Allies quickly formed hunting groups to bring them to battle and destroy them, but in the meantime it was essential that the most important Atlantic convoys, especially those bringing in the Canadian troops, be given heavy ship protection.

The 'Royal Sovereigns' would never be able to match the pocket battleships for speed, but they easily outweighed them in hitting power and armour protection, eight 15-inch guns against six 11-inch guns, and no German skipper would pit his vessel against a convoy with a 'Royal Sovereign' as part of its escort. The deterrent value of even the oldest battleships was therefore made manifest right at the beginning of hostilities. It was a quiet and low-profile job, but so vital and essential. Perhaps it was *because* it worked and the Germans never dared to challenge them that their very success has been ignored, overlooked or belittled by post-war historians. None the less, even if they had done nothing else at all, the old battleships justified their existence by performing just this one essential duty in the first two years of the war.

This then was to be the pattern of the first months of the Tiddly Quids' war.

The Home Fleet had concentrated in the Flow by 1 September, the day Hitler's dive-bombers and tanks had been unleashed on Poland, and the world held its breath to see if Britain and France would honour their obligations. The ultimatum was duly delivered, the deadline 3 September. In the tense and expectant days before Prime Minister Neville Chamberlain's hesitant and feeble announcement of the commencement of hostilities, the officers and men of the *Royal Sovereign* got on with the job of making their ship as fully efficient as possible while there was still time. One young sailor, T.W. Pope, remembers how that momentous broadcast was received aboard the ship:

Sunday 3 September at 1100 hours found us gathered around the wireless speaker, divisions and church having been held earlier so that we could listen to the Prime Minister's speech. Afterwards one or two ratings made remarks on what they thought of it and what they considered should now be done to the Germans (none of the suggestions were very complimentary and some physically impossible to achieve!). But on the whole I think that most of us took it rather quietly and thoughtfully. I think at this stage we were all wondering just what it meant to us and what the future held. The duty watch was turned to in the dogwatches and they were employed painting over all the brass fittings on the upper deck, and the gun muzzles, which had been highly polished, these too were covered with paint. The old 'Quid' didn't look so 'Tiddly' after that!

The first requirements were obviously to top up with both fuel oil and ammunition, and it was to these two tasks the crew duly applied themselves in the few remaining hours of peace. Two fleet oilers, *Petronel* and *Belgol*, took it turns to secure alongside the battleship during the daylight hours of 1 September, and their cargo of liquid black fuel oil was pumped aboard. Soon after midday, in between the oilers' visits, the ammunition ship *Horizon* came alongside and heavy shell was hoisted out from her holds and swung inboard to be stacked in the battleship's capacious shell rooms. These vital tasks completed, the 2nd Battle Squadron lay expectant and ready as the sun set over the surrounding islands.

Away to the East, Polish cavalry were charging the German *Panzers* with heroism and futility, while trainloads of their infantry *en route* to the front were being massacred by precision Stuka attacks. It was a new kind of war, the long-awaited unleashing of the *Blitzkrieg* tactics: fast-moving armour columns spearheaded by dive-bombers, against which neither the obsolete forces of little Poland nor, seven months later, the complacent Allied armies in France and Flanders, had any effective answer. But back in the Flow the great grey bulks of the British capital ships lay swinging at their buoys, the very embodiment of Britain's latent power, ready and willing, but as yet unable to bring their influence to bear on these momentous events.

One enemy ship which British Intelligence had not failed to keep track of was the luxury liner *Bremen*. She had sailed from New York for home prior to the outbreak of war, and was thought to be trying to reach German waters relying on her high speed. Admiral Forbes therefore decided to take the fleet to sea on 4 September, both in the hope of intercepting such a valuable prize and to sweep the northern half of the North Sea in full strength to show whose ensign ruled those waters. They were already far too late to catch the German liner, for she had steered north and put in at the Soviet port of Murmansk until such time as she could make the final dash home. The ironic fact that the two bitter enemies, Hitler and Stalin, were now formally allies and friends, and were to carve up Poland between them, has often been glossed over since June 1941, but the plain truth is that for the first two years of the Second World War the Communists and the Fascists marched in step against the neutral states of Europe, and conducted virulent propaganda against the Allies.

While Germany smashed the Polish army, Soviet troops occupied half that country without any effort on their part, on the pretence of 'protecting' it. The little Baltic nations Estonia, Lithuania and Latvia were also obliterated by the Russian giant while Germany was preoccupied in the West. Finland was also on Stalin's menu, but gave the aggressor a bloody nose before finally going down to sheer weight of numbers in the Winter War of 1939–40.

Meanwhile, back at Scapa Flow, the *Royal Sovereign* weighed anchor at 1335 on the 4th, and passed through the anti-submarine boom at 1410 in company with *Royal Oak* to join their screening destroyers outside. Admiral Forbes had sailed the day before with the other three heavy ships, and *Ark Royal* and the two 'Royals' set a course to join them north-east of the Shetlands. At dawn the next day the destroyer *Whitehall* joined their screen as an extra escort, and by noon on the 5th, they rendezvoused with the C-in-C in position 60° 02′ North, 00° 25′ West. Word had been received aboard the British flagship that the German fleet had put to sea from their anchorage in the Schilling Roads, and Admiral Forbes therefore turned his big ships eastward, passing through the Fair Isle Channel. He planned to linger in the predetermined 'cutting-off position' between the Shetland Islands and Norway to await further information. Several of the crew remember sighting the elusive *Bremen* at this time as she sped south safe in the neutral coastal waters of Norway. The Germans used these waters, the 'Inner Leads', with impunity until Winston's patience ran out with the *Altmark* incident several months later. Royal Marine corporal Bill Heffernan told me, 'The most vivid memory I have of that time was when we passed Germany's largest liner but could not touch her as she was in neutral waters.' T.W. Pope gave me this detailed account of their first wartime sortie:

> The next day, Monday 4th, saw us at sea with *Royal Oak* and two S-class destroyers, sweeping down the North Sea in an attempt, as far as I can recall, at stopping the German liner *Bremen* from reaching her home port. This we failed to do, although we did pass her, but owing to the thick fog which had come down we failed to see her. No radar in those days so it was a case of keeping a good lookout. There were lookouts in the Air Defence Position (ADP) just above the bridge, whose main task was to spot enemy aircraft approaching, and others in the 15-inch guns' spotting top looking out for surface ships, torpedoes and such. I think that at this stage, our first war patrol, nobody really knew quite what to expect from the enemy. As one of these lookouts myself I half expected to see torpedoes coming at us from all directions or aircraft diving down on us, but none of this happened and we arrived back in Scapa Flow a few days later. While we were at sea the ship's company were closed-up at cruising stations, the high-altitude (HA) director and close-range guns being manned. At night we were at action stations all the time. Although the 15-inch guns were our main armament it soon became clear that the 4-inch guns and close-range weapons would become our most used weapons, and therefore the defence of the ship was based on the manning of these guns.

As related, while off Norway the fleet was soon enshrouded in thick fog, through which it groped its way hesitantly. It quickly became obvious that there was no hope of carrying out any interceptions in such conditions, and at 0800 on the 6th, in position 59° 24′ North, 1° 22′ East, course was set back towards Scapa.

Soon after 1330 that day, the destroyers *Foresight*, *Forester* and *Fury* of the 8th Flotilla joined the destroyer screen, and at 1709 *Royal Sovereign* again entered the Flow, having completed her first wartime sweep uneventfully. She came to starboard anchor with seven shackles in twelve fathoms of water. As always, the first task on returning from a sortie was to prepare for the next one. There was never any period of 'Phoney War' for the fleet as there was on land and in the air, or especially in Fleet Street! They were, of course, old hands at this routine, but now the commonplace and routine chores took on a new meaning and urgency, for every time they put to sea might bring the enemy under their guns.

One of the youngest men aboard the *Royal Sovereign* at this period was Marine E.C. Moore. He had only joined the ship on 28 August:

> I had just finished eleven months' recruit training, and along with many of my new squad mates and other naval personnel we were marched from the Royal Marine Barracks at Chatham on that Friday night to board a train bound for Thurso, Scotland. We were full of expectancy and pride. We transferred to a destroyer for a four-hour journey across the Pentland Firth and arrived at Kirkwall in the Orkneys. We eventually arrived on board the *Royal Sovereign* at 0200 that Sunday and found that we had to be present at 'Divisions' [Church Parade] at 0900 hours in full ceremonial dress!

After their first sweep Marine Moore recalls that they were stationed in the Flow as guard ship for a period, and were always at defence stations. On the 15th they had a visit from the Rear Admiral 2nd Battle Squadron, and three days later were visited by the captain of the light cruiser *Enterprise*. These meetings were concerned with the preliminary planning for the movement of Britain's gold bullion reserves from London to the safety of Canada and were very hush-hush. Gunnery exercises were conducted within the Flow on the 20th, but their orders now were to sail south on their mission of great urgency. This brought about their first contact with the enemy, and maybe also saved them from a sad fate.

Royal Sovereign weighed anchor half an hour before midnight on the 23rd and passed the Hoxa boom at 0002, setting a course for the Pentland Firth. Her destroyer escort was provided by the minelaying destroyers *Esk* and *Express* acting in their more conventional anti-submarine role. By 0342 Cape Wrath was abeam. Progress was steadily made; Skerryvore Light was passed at 1314. Their passage was destined to be not completely uneventful, as T.W. Pope remembers:

> It was while we were on passage to Portsmouth that we encountered a U-boat. It was the Sunday evening, about 1800 hours, while we were still off the coast of Scotland and were passing a fishing fleet on our port side. In the distance there could be seen one of these fishing boats on its own, and as we came up to her, our port side destroyer escort suddenly sounded six short blasts on her siren, went full ahead and fired her depth charge throwers. I was standing on the fo'c'sle at the time, and for a moment or two I wondered what was happening, as the penny hadn't dropped. It was not until we turned away to starboard and increased to full speed that I realised that an enemy submarine had been sighted on the far side of that fishing boat. Our other destroyer escort joined in the hunt, and between them they kept the submarine down with further depth charges until we got clear.

The destroyers were certainly effective, and although they did not sink the submarine their prompt action pre-empted any torpedoes being fired at the *Royal Sovereign* herself. By 2155 that night the Mull of Kintyre was passed. All though that night and during the 25th they made their way down the western coast of Scotland. By the early hours of the 26th the Eddystone Light was abeam, Portland Bill passed at 0505 and at 1109 they passed through the boom to enter Portsmouth harbour, securing to No. 6 buoy at 1220.

They spent the best part of a fortnight at Portsmouth preparing for the new mission. But first the *Royal Sovereign* was to undergo a refit, which was badly needed. The ship was partly de-ammunitioned on the 27th and 28th, while refuelling took place on the 29th. It had been planned for both her and the *Ramillies* to be modernised in order that they might hold their place in the battle-line until the new King George V class of battleships could commission. Back in February it had been proposed that the main-deck protection of both these vessels be increased by the addition of 4-inch and 2-inch non-cemented armour. This would give them extra strength against the plunging effect of long-range shellfire, and such an improvement had already been carried out to *Royal Oak*. To take the increased top weight this extra steel would add it was proposed that the tops of the external anti-submarine bulges be modified at the same time to give the ships the necessary additional stability to compensate.

The bridge was to have been modified also on the lines of the *Royal Oak*. Another modification of vital importance mooted at this time was the increasing of the main armament elevation to 30 degrees. This would have been a much-welcomed increase to the ranges of their big guns. Alas, shortage of funds and dockyard space, the pressing need for more modern ships to have similar work done on them and the approach of the war led to all these highly desirable improvements being gradually dropped, one by one, from April 1939 onwards. With the outbreak of war all this work was indefinitely postponed.

The arrival of Churchill back at the Admiralty saw a flurry of half-baked ideas begin to flow from London, many of which featured the Royal Sovereign-class ships. The first of these was Operation Catherine. Really little more than a rehashing of one of Admiral 'Jackie' Fisher's ideas dating from the 1914 period, this scheme was mooted again almost immediately by Churchill, and many long and tedious hours were wasted at the Admiralty as the First Sea Lord, Admiral Sir Dudley Pound, and his naval advisers tried to point out the difficulties, not to say the suicidal nature, of this obsession. In the end Churchill gave way, but with very bad grace, and he continued to return to the idea like a dog to a bone down the months until Germany's occupation of the rest of Europe made it even more impracticable.

The scheme envisaged a grand naval offensive in the enclosed waters of the Baltic Sea. The Royal Navy was to somehow force an entry to the Baltic and maintain a naval squadron there to bombard the enemy and generally harass them. How this large squadron of surface ships was to be maintained in the face of dive-bomber and submarine attacks on itself and its supply ships was unclear. A detailed plan was drawn up by Admirals Drax and Dickens, which was discussed by Churchill between 18 and 20 September, and Admiral of the Fleet Lord Cork and Orrery was brought in to lead it. He was an 'offensively minded' officer, just the sort that Churchill admired above all others, but even he had grave reservations about Catherine, describing it as 'very hazardous'. Churchill brooked no arguments, and when one of the more intelligent naval officers consulted, Captain V.H. Danckwerts, Director of Plans, dared to criticise the idea he was promptly removed from his post. None the less the idea was subsequently quietly dropped.

However, the early planning for it was built around the conversion of several of the Royal Sovereign-class battleships. On each ship two of the four twin 15-inch turrets were to be removed, and the weight thus saved was to be utilised for extra anti-torpedo bulges, extra armour protection and anti-aircraft guns. With converted merchant ships acting as 'mine-bumpers' preceding them, and flanked by two destroyer flotillas, five cruisers and an aircraft carrier, they were then to force their way into the Baltic! Of course sheer shortage of all the other types of warships ruled the whole enterprise impracticable from the start, while we have already seen that pressure on dockyard space had already led the self-same Churchill to cancel the building of two of the new Lion-class battleships and to the postponing of earlier, more practical, modernisation of the older ones.

Although Catherine was halted and this 'suicide mission' never took place, Churchill, when Premier, kept returning to his theme that the 'Royal Sovereigns' were obsolete 'coffin ships' and that his idea was the only practical one to make good use of them. He never understood the excellent work they had been doing in the Atlantic Ocean. A year later, for example, on 7 September 1940, he was urging Pound:

I should be glad if you would let me have a short *resumé* of the different occasions when I pressed, as First Lord, for the preparation of the Ramillies-class (*sic*) ships to withstand air bombardment by thick deck armour and larger bulges. If those ships had been put in hand when I repeatedly pressed for them to be, we should now have the means to attack the Italian shores . . .

Again, on 9 September: 'I am not content at all with the refusal to reconstruct the Royal Sovereign class.' And on the 14th he was back again:

I should be content if two R-class vessels were taken in hand as soon as the invasion situation has cleared and we get *King George V* in commission. Meanwhile material can be collected and preparations made. This should enable them to be ready in eighteen months from now – i.e. the summer of 1942.

But in the summer of 1942, as we shall see, it was just as well this work had *not* been done, for the ships were desperately required to shore-up the results of another of Winston's harebrained schemes in the Far East. Moreover, having been thwarted, Churchill typically never ceased to criticise and snipe at the 'Royal Sovereigns' at every opportunity.

Meanwhile the proposed fitting of extra deck armour was reintroduced, using flame-cut armour plating supported as well as possible, but even this rough and ready upgrade proved impracticable and was not proceeded with. And so while she was at Portsmouth only minor alterations were carried out on the ship. The aircraft catapult had been removed just prior the war, but the funnel was not yet 'capped' to deflect the smoke from the bridge.

One modern weapon of war that did affect the 'Tiddly Quid' in these early days was the magnetic mine. When the fleet flagship *Nelson* was incapacitated by one of these infernal devices and two cruisers were severely damaged by them, quick countermeasures had to be taken. This led to the development and fitting of degaussing cables to all ships, and the need for *Royal Sovereign* to have this equipment urgently necessitated her sailing to Devonport dockyard.

Tugs secured forward at 1731 on 6 October, and she proceeded out of Portsmouth harbour, anchoring in Spithead an hour later. At 0042 that night she sailed for Plymouth, escorted by the destroyers *Saladin* and *Scimitar*, arriving off Drake's Island at 1240 and securing to No. 9 buoy. The ship was further de-ammunitioned on 10 October, and next day tugs towed her up to the North Yard, where she entered No. 5 berth. The 4-inch ammunition was unloaded there before she went into the floating dock on the morning of 18 October. Here she remained until the 19th, having her anti-magnetic mine cabling installed, and then she returned to No. 5 basin for her further modifications, which lasted until the New Year. The only event during this period was a visit on board by His Majesty King George VI on 18 December.

It was also while the *Royal Sovereign* lay immobilised here that they received the horrendous news of the loss of their 'chummy ship', *Royal Oak*, by a daring submarine attack in the Flow on the night of 13/14 October. It was a bitter blow. Incredulity that the enemy could have been allowed to enter the main fleet anchorage with impunity was mixed with anger and sorrow at the loss of so many former shipmates and friends from her ship's company. No fewer than 833 officers and men went down with her, a stunning casualty list. This disaster, coming on top of the loss of the aircraft carrier *Courageous* and damage to the *Nelson*, led many to think that the Royal Navy was not as well prepared for the new war as the nation had been led to believe. It brought home to the crew of the *Royal Sovereign* that the war was going to be a long and hard slog, and no walkover after all. Just how long and how hard few, if any, could have possible foreseen as the old year died.

Although their ship was out of the war for a short period, some of the 'Royal Sovereigns' themselves found gainful employment, one such being E.C. Moore:

> While at Devonport HMS *Hood was* also in port, and she received orders to proceed towards Iceland at short notice.

Half her crew were on leave, so I was one of the many detailed to transfer to her, the object apparently being to try and intercept the German heavy ships that had surprised and sunk the armed merchant cruiser *Rawalpindi* or *Jervis Bay*, I cannot remember which.

Being a Royal Marine, I was assigned to 'X' 15-inch turret, which on all big ships was traditionally the Royal Marines' turret. I served aboard her for a few weeks, during which time I had my first experience of a heavily rolling ship, rough seas and sea-sickness. On one of the many occasions that I poked my head out of the back of the turret for fresh air I spotted what I now know was phosphorus, but when I asked the sergeant of the turret what it was washing all over the quarterdeck he replied, 'Fishes with headlights' (a sorry tale!).

After a while we returned to Devonport and back to the *Sovereign*, which was another bit of luck, as the *Hood* went down with nearly all hands in 1941. After Christmas leave we rejoined the ship, which was readying herself to sail north to pick up a convoy for Halifax.

On 1 January 1940, the flag of Admiral S.S. Bonham-Carter, Rear Admiral 3rd Battle Squadron, was hoisted at her masthead. Her new duties had been assigned to her as flagship of the Halifax Escort Force. She was to be based at Halifax, Nova Scotia, and from there was to provide heavy ship escort for the vital troop and supply convoys leaving Canada for European waters. Although the *Admiral Graf Spee* had been hounded to her destruction in December, other German raiders were thought to be out on the convoy routes, and the presence of a battleship was deemed essential for such valuable ships. Thus, on the morning of the 3rd, she left the basin secured alongside a buoy and commenced the long job of re-embarking her full complement of ammunition once more in readiness for sea service.

They had one more item to embark before they left British waters, and that duly arrived at the last-minute prior to their sailing, as T.W. Pope recalled to me:

January 1940 saw us on our way to Halifax with a convoy, the first of many, and with a considerable quantity of gold bullion on board. The gold arrived, just before we sailed from Plymouth, in an unmarked van, no escort of any kind, but when we unloaded in Halifax the ship and pier were surrounded by Royal Canadian Mounted Police, all carrying guns very obviously. Thus *Royal Sovereign* went to fight in the Battle of the Atlantic materially valued at considerably more sovereigns than she ever had been before or was to be thereafter!

CHAPTER FOUR

Halifax Escort Force

aving left Devonport dockyard on 6 January, *Royal Sovereign* anchored in Plymouth Sound at 1555, and not until early the following morning did she pass through the boom and again steam up-Channel back to Portsmouth. She actually arrived off the Nab Tower at 1630, but the fog was so thick that day that she was unable to enter Portsmouth harbour itself and remained off St Catherine's for a time before sailing back to Portland Bill while waiting for the weather to clear. Not until just after midday did she secure alongside Pitch House jetty. On the 9th she left harbour and anchored in Spithead at four hours' notice to steam, and there she spent the next two days in testing her degaussing equipment to see if it was working satisfactorily.

Therefore it was the afternoon of 14 January that the 'Tiddly Quid' finally left home waters for her Canadian assignment. She weighed anchor at 1145 and proceeded to sea escorted by the destroyers *Achates*, *Anthony* and *Arrow*. These three were relieved by the *Vanquisher*, *Viscount* and *Windsor* at 1640 the following day, and by 2300 the little squadron was off the Lizard. The final link with England, Bishop Rock lighthouse, was passed at 0200 next morning. Once out into the broad Atlantic she set a solitary course, her speed and her zigzagging being her only protection. With the bulk of the German submarines withdrawn to the Fatherland at this period, the danger was more imagined than real and she had no adventures.

With some £5,000,000 sterling of bullion aboard it was just as well. However, if the enemy was kind to the *Royal Sovereign* on this passage, the North Atlantic weather in winter was vicious. The winter storms were intense and the temperature plummeted. She encountered mountainous seas which, coupled with the severe icing, severely incapacitated her. So badly were her 6-inch, 4-inch and smaller guns iced up that for the last day of her passage they were unworkable, only her main turrets remaining usable. The newly installed degaussing equipment failed to stand up to its first voyage, and many of the coils burnt themselves out due to poor insulation. The great seas also carried away many of her upper deck fittings and damaged some of her ship's boats as well. There were human casualties also, severely buffeted and bruised, violently seasick or just plain exhausted. Many of her crew were fresh-faced youngsters, and this trip was a grim introduction to what was to become their normal lifestyle, 'Winter North Atlantic' being a phrase which brings back distinct memories to any old sailor who took part on the Atlantic convoy battle between 1939 and 1945. T.W. Pope certainly has vivid memories of it:

We sailors had to contend with the cold weather when on watch, there being no warm clothing, apart from balaclava helmets and your own oilskins or overcoats to keep you warm. Duffel coats were issued, but there were only a few on board at this stage of the war and we had to hand them over to our reliefs at the end of each watch.

The pattern of life aboard at this time was one of a continuous battle to keep the messdecks, and ourselves, dry. The North Atlantic in winter can be very rough, to say the least, and although the ship was a 30,000-ton battleship the seas still threw her about and did quite a bit of damage. The starboard screen door and a 3-inch steel support to the boat deck were both bent like cardboard, and the breakwater on the fo'c'sle sprang a few rivets. Water was pouring into the messdeck through the deckhead and was also finding its way down some of the air vents. The locker was also flooded and the portholes were closed with the deadlights down. This was routine when at sea, but the water still found a few places to come through and the fo'c'sle mess-deck always had water swilling around on the deck. This condition also applied to the 6-inch gun batteries. If we had gone into action I very much doubt whether the 6-inch guns would have been able to fire, as most of the time they would have been more or less submerged!

I will not even try to describe the state the heads were in, suffice it to say that the ship's company had to use the Chiefs' and they in turn had to use the Warrant Officers' facilities.

The reason for this was that the non-return valve on the ship's side was damaged by the sea, and instead of the toilets flushing outboard they were being flushed inboard! The hatches leading from the forward messdeck were always kept closed while at sea, as were the water-tight doors on the lower messdecks, so the air on the messdecks was always damp and stale. The washrooms, being below the lower messes, were kept shut and only opened at certain times for short periods.

At 0735 on 23 January two Canadian destroyers, the *Ottawa* and the *Saguenay*, joined her as a screen for the final leg of her journey, and they secured alongside in Halifax harbour at 1755.

The force which they now joined had been set up to oversee the organisation of the North American end of Britain's vital life-line by way of which her essential supplies, oil and the ever-growing outpourings of the United States and Canada war plants, safe from German molestation, could pour into the home island and sustain her population and armed forces for the great struggle ahead. No 1,000-plane bomber operation, no major invasion, no warlike operations at all could have been mounted had this tenuous link ever been severed for any length of time. It never was, but it came perilously close to it on several occasions. Nor does the smooth-running of this crucial artery ever seem to have been other than taken completely for granted by both the other services or the populace as a whole. That the United Kingdom would have fallen without those ships is certain, that this fact was understood even remotely by the vast majority at the time is doubtful, that it is understood or appreciated by those same people today is unlikely.

The first convoy had actually sailed from Halifax on 16 September 1939. This was HX1. Fast convoys (usually tankers and the like) were designated HXF, and the first of these sailed for Great Britain on the 19th of the same month. The battleships *Resolution* and *Revenge* and the cruisers *Emerald* and *Enterprise* had been based there on this duty from the earliest days, and Admiral Bonham-Carter took command with two more battleships, the *Royal Sovereign* and *Malaya*, at the beginning of 1940. This was to be the peak strength of the force, because other commitments, not least the need to reinforce the Mediterranean Fleet when Italy threatened to enter the conflict against us after the fall of France in May 1940, were soon to reduce this squadron again for a period. The substitution of AMCs for battleships proved to be no deterrent to pocket battleships. HX convoys enjoyed almost complete safety from surface molestation until the battleship cover was withdrawn. The sad fate of Convoy HX84, destroyed by the *Admiral Scheer* in November 1940, showed that only the battleships could guarantee this immunity. Slow as they were, the old battleships always had a knot or two in hand over the ships they were escorting, and the sight of a British battleship's top-hamper on the horizon made many a German raider think twice and then forget it.

The gravest danger to the escorting battleships themselves was of course from below the sea, but although the *Malaya* was hit by torpedoes during this duty no British battleship was ever lost or seriously crippled fulfilling this function. The normal routine was to place the battleship in the dead centre of the convoy; even so there were some narrow squeaks on occasions. As for the routine, T.W. Pope again:

> Our convoy duties took us from Halifax to a point 300 miles off the coast of Ireland, where we handed the convoy over to other of HM ships and took over the return convoy for Halifax. From the time of our departure until our return we spent an average of fourteen to seventeen days at sea, depending on whether it was a fast or slow convoy we were

escorting. During the whole of this period at sea we were at ocean cruising stations, and my position was the forward HA director. From here I had a very good view of the whole convoy, which covered a vast area of ocean. When we came on duty we were able to count the ships to see if any had dropped out during the night. We could also study the troops on the ship's upper decks through our telescopes, and we often wondered how the Canadian soldiers coped with the rolling and pitching of the troopships in the rough seas.

Although we were on these convoy duties continuously from January to April, we never came under attack from submarines or surface ships, and all our convoys got through without loss while in our presence.

Marine Moore also remembers these vast arrays of maritime might well:

We spent many long days at sea working out of Nova Scotia convoying ships to within a few hundred miles of England and taking others back to Halifax again. We rarely spent more than one or two days in harbour before leaving on our next convoy. The weather seemed uniformly bad the whole time.

I was fortunate in that I was corporal of the watch, and my officer of the watch was a Canadian RNVR lieutenant who used to share his impressive food parcels from home with us. He was also the entertainments officer, with special responsibility for our cinema. One day he asked me if I had seen two years before the mast. I thought he was making conversation and replied, 'No sir, not quite, only twenty months in fact.' He burst out laughing and replied, 'No you fool, the film!' Needless to say, it was a pleasure to be on watch with him.

We spent quite a few months on the Atlantic convoy run. I shall always remember the sight of the ships of the convoys spread over miles of sea and the escorting destroyers 'whooping' on their sirens as they weaved in and out of the convoy lines delivering orders or hunting submarine contacts, real or make-believe. The ocean itself was so rough at times that on many occasions the escorting destroyers, often Canadian ships, were forced to return to harbour within a couple of days, while we with our larger bulk just stuck it out. When in harbour we sometimes got asked aboard these Canadian destroyers for meals. Compared to our conditions and food it was utter luxury.

Captain Jacomb's reports on these convoys give some insight into the complexities of marshalling so many large vessels into some semblance of order. They also highlight the constant battle he had in maintaining that order throughout the voyage in spite of both the weather conditions and the merchant ships' natural dislike of disciplined column steaming.

Convoy HX18, for example, sailed on the last day of January 1940, and consisted of forty-three ships (including four neutrals who were also given protection) steaming in eight columns at an average speed of eight and a half knots. *Royal Sovereign* was positioned at the head of this phalanx between the leading ships of the fourth and fifth columns. Fog delayed the sailing of the convoy for two hours. In addition to this, a submarine sighting at the head of the swept channel through the defending mine-fields caused the convoy Commodore to increase his speed before the rearmost ships had left the channel, and thus they were unable to form up in the desired columns before darkness fell.

Chaos resulted. During the hours of darkness ten ships which had not completely formed passed the port wing of the convoy and got well ahead of the rest. The Canadian destroyer *Saguenay* had to be sent out after them the next day, and eventually brought them back into the fold, but it was a long process and took the best part of 1 February to achieve. Thus it was not until the third day that the convoy was finally herded into some semblance of the required order. This was finally achieved just before dusk, but necessitated a reduction of speed to eight knots to allow stragglers to close up.

During that night the wind freshened from the WNW and visibility was reduced. The merchant ships showed a marked tendency for the leading starboard-wing ships to crowd in on the centre of the convoy. Dimmed bow lights were switched on while the lines on this side of the convoy were straightened out by the faithful destroyers once more. By daybreak on Sunday, 4 February, the strong west-north-westerly wind was blowing sleet and snow across the convoy, reducing visibility considerably. For a short period during the day conditions eased, but only twenty-three merchantmen could be counted from *Royal Sovereign*'s fighting top before the weather closed down again. Conditions continued to deteriorate, and by the afternoon it was blowing a full-force gale and high seas were running. Visibility was never better than three cables at best, and sometimes it was difficult for even the ships leading the columns on either side of the battleship to be made out.

Under such adverse weather conditions the obvious dangers of the convoy becoming completely dispersed, or of collisions, were uppermost in everyone's mind. The ideal was for them to 'heave to' and ride out the gale, and Captain Jacomb and Commodore Fitzmaurice exchanged views on the matter. They came to the conclusion that the best bet in this case was to allow the convoy to proceed. They listed the reasons for their decision thus:

(a) Call signs for the convoy as a whole had not been issued in accordance with Paragraph 67(b) of Mercantile Convoy. Instructions Form AI appeared to indicate that the convoy distinguishing signal was to be used for this purpose, but the signal would then appear to be addressed to any other convoy that might read it.

(b) The two-letter group for 'Heave-to' would have to be used for the benefit of neutral ships, which was undesirable.

(c) It involved breaking W/T silence.

(d) It was probable that a number of ships would not have set W/T watch, as they were still with the convoy and not actually in fog, or for some other reason they might not receive the signal.

(e) The conditions of visibility.

Captain Jacomb considered that with conditions as they existed it would have been 'most dangerous' to have attempted to order forty-three ships to stop by wireless telegraphy 'in circumstances which had never been envisaged'. Moreover at the pre-sailing conference it had been definitely stated that 'no attempt would be made to heave to in the dark', and 'conditions prevailing were tantamount to darkness.'

They therefore decided to allow the convoy to proceed, with the hope that they could re-form the next day. The appalling sea conditions had reduced the general speed of the convoy to a mere three knots. Fortunately the weather did moderate during the night, although at dawn on the 5th visibility was still poor. Unfortunately only eleven ships remained in company. The Commodore was left the task of re-forming these into columns again while *Royal Sovereign* herself turned back to sweep astern and across to the south of the convoy's track. As she steamed through the murk, which was interspersed with periodic sleet squalls reducing visibility to zero, not one of the other merchant ships was sighted in this sweep, and the battleship rejoined the Commodore's little group at dusk with nothing to show for a lot of hard steaming. Although they were reluctant to break wireless silence lest the U-boats home in on them, a rendezvous signal was broadcast for the rest of the convoy for the second day ahead.

The next day was a rerun of the Monday. The westerly gale continued to howl about them, bringing heavy snowfalls from time to time. *Royal Sovereign* and her group of eleven ships managed to stay more or less together, and on the eighth day all these were still in company. This was the day of the rendezvous, and in order to help gather in the ships the battleship was taken fourteen miles out to the northward of the Commodore's group. Heavy sleet squalls persisted all day, and although during brief periods of clearer visibility one oiler was sighted on the horizon ahead, and another astern, they were quickly lost again, and no other ships appeared. On rejoining the Commodore they found that three more ships had joined him and one of the oilers sighted by *Royal Sovereign* had dropped back, bringing the convoy total to fifteen ships in all.

Another ship had picked up on them by dawn on Thursday

the 8th, while yet another was in sight astern. The suggestion that another wireless transmission be made for the noon rendezvous on the 10th was turned down by the convoy Commodore, but Captain Jacomb agreed to transmit this signal during the next night after he had parted company from the merchantmen. Another four ships meanwhile joined up during the hours of daylight to give a total of twenty, with the smoke of two others visible, one ahead and one to starboard, at dusk.

As previously arranged, the battleship parted company at midnight in position 49° 17′ North, 30° 59′ West after informing the C-in-C Western Approaches of the current state of the convoy.

While thus employed guarding the North Atlantic lifelines from surface threat, the men of the Halifax Escort Force were always aware of the hidden threat from beneath the seas. The Royal Sovereigns themselves could not help but be aware of their vulnerability in this respect; the fate of their sister, with her improved underwater protection, was a constant example. However they consoled themselves with the fact that she was a stationary target and that they, even at 18 knots, and in the midst of a large convoy, would present any U-boat commander with a much more difficult target.

As we have seen, once the convoys left the relatively narrow band of cover provided by the destroyers of the Royal Canadian Navy, and before they picked up British destroyers off the North-West Approaches, these large concentrations of valuable merchant vessels were without air or surface protection from the underwater threat. There was, in fact, a severe shortage of destroyers and slower escorts, and this situation was to be made even more acute from April 1940 onward.

The reasons for this are not hard to find. The heavy losses that the destroyer flotillas suffered at the hands of the *Luftwaffe* off Norway in April, off the Low Countries, Dunkirk and the Channel ports in May and June, and the need to hold back a large proportion of what destroyers remained for their anti-invasion role from July onward, all combined to make ocean escorting out of the question. As an indication of how desperate things were, after the fall of France the Royal Navy was left with but seventy-eight destroyers with which to carry out her world-wide commitments, and from June 1940 those commitments included reinforcing the Mediterranean Fleet.

Even prior to these disasters, the shortage of destroyers, hundreds of which had been sent to the scrapyards in the 1920s and 1930s by unthinking politicians, meant that the fast HXF convoys had to be stopped for a while. This was at a time, moreover, when more and more ships were clamouring for protection, including many neutral nations' vessels. To ease the congestion another convoy route was opened – the BHX series, which formed up at Bermuda and joined up with the Halifax ships in about 41° North 43° West. The hazards of forming up such convoys have been illustrated above, but this was made more complex by the new conditions. The closing of the Mediterranean Sea and the rerouteing of convoys via the Cape further stretched the very limited resources to breaking point.

But in March the normal FIX convoys were continuing to run. The threat from enemy capital ships had temporarily waned, for the severe casualties inflicted upon the German Navy during the Norwegian Campaign and elsewhere had kept what heavy ships they did still have firmly in dockyard hands. Not until September and October did the pocket battleship *Admiral Scheer*, the heavy cruiser *Admiral Hipper* and the two battle-cruisers *Scharnhorst* and *Gneisenau* prepare to sortie against them again. Armed merchant raiders were loose during this time, however, and they also posed a threat, although in practice they were mainly used against independently routed ships, which were easier pickings than convoys. It is a harsh fact that many of these German raiders, both regular warships and converted merchantmen, managed to sail and evade our blockade undetected. This proved to be one of the biggest sources of worry to the Admiralty, and it necessitated battleship protection to the more important convoys during this period.

On Thursday 22 February, *Royal Sovereign* took station between the centre columns of a new convoy, HX22, which comprised thirty-five ships under the command of Commodore H.G.C. Franklin RNR, embarked aboard the *Counsellor*. This convoy had sailed from Halifax, and by dusk had formed up successfully under the protection of two Canadian destroyers. These remained in company until 1800 on the 23rd.

In stark contrast to the previous episode, this convoy enjoyed mainly favourable weather conditions, except for one severe gale on the night of the Wednesday and the forenoon of the Thursday. The ships managed to maintain excellent station keeping, and there were no stragglers. A steady speed of 7.8 knots was maintained, and there were no untoward incidents. *Royal Sovereign* herself remained in company until 0800 on Saturday 2 March, when, in position 48° 10′ North, 29° 10′ West, she left them steaming steadily homewards.

After a quiet voyage back to Halifax, another large convoy was planned, but owing to the reasons outlined above this was delayed, and eventually the build-up of ships equivalent to two convoys made Convoy HX28 a large one. In all there were sixty-one merchant vessels under the command of Commodore E.D. Cochrane RN, aboard the *Empire Confidence*. This vast number of ships called for careful handling, and they were organised in nine columns, with the Commodore's vessel leading the sixth column, the Vice-Commodore the third column and the Rear Commodore the ninth. This convoy sailed from Halifax on the morning of 18 March, but because of its size it was not fully formed up before dusk that night. The ships managed to keep together during the night with the aid of bright moonlight, and completed their correct formation the following morning without any loss. The speed of the convoy was 8.27 knots, and mainly fair weather enabled this to be maintained. *Royal Sovereign* herself took station between the fourth and fifth columns, and the usual pair of Canadian destroyers accompanied them until 1800 on 19 March.

Much of the difficulty in forming up such large numbers of ships into the columns and making the required turns during their passage was due to the fact that the convoy Commodore's flagship was, naturally, a modern motor vessel. All well and good, but, not being an older-type 'steamer', she lacked a powerful siren. This seemingly minor problem was in fact quite serious, because all the signals to the ships in company from the Commodore were made by sounding her siren in previously laid down codes.

No convoy ever ploughed its way majestically across the Atlantic in a straight line. At pre-set times emergency turns were made in order to frustrate any enterprising U-boat commander who might be tracking them and lining up such juicy targets in his sights. When the *Empire Confidence* sounded her signals it was reported that these were only just audible by the leading ships of the columns adjacent to her on either side; the rest heard nothing! Luckily these turns had been timed and made clear in the orders for the convoys, so no great harm was done on this occasion. It was recommended that the Merchant Navy code of instructions be modified to include the requisite that in future the leading ships of all the columns should repeat the long 15-second blast in the case of an emergency turn. 'At present there is always a doubt among leaders of columns whether they should do so or not, and Merchant Navy code does not indicate that they should', wrote Captain Jacomb.

Thick weather was encountered by this convoy on Wednesday 20 March, and early the following day *Royal Sovereign* turned back to the rear of the convoy to check on stragglers. They spotted a couple of gaps, and eventually made out one ship lagging about four miles astern. This proved to be the *Scoresby*. She in turn reported that one of the tankers had dropped astern in the mist the previous day and had not been seen since then. This proved to be the *Lucerna*. Although *Scoresby* managed to rejoin the convoy, the tanker was never seen again during the convoy's passage. She survived, but paid the price in another convoy in August, when she was torpedoed. This was the only incident, and again the battleship turned back at 1800 on the 27th in position 50° 17′ West, 24° 20′ West. They arrived back at Halifax on 7 March, securing to No. 5 berth at 1010 that morning.

They remained there until 1408 on 18 March, when they once more put to sea to act as ocean escort for Convoy HX28 of sixty-one ships. The local escort was the destroyers *Saguenay* and *Skeena*, which remained in company until 1800 on the 19th. Their passage was again made in vile weather, but without undue incident, and the battleship left the convoy intact on the 27th, arriving back at her berth on 2 April. Another week inside and they were off once more.

Convoy HX34, which sailed from Halifax at 0912 on Wednesday 10 April, was another typical escort job for the *Royal*

Sovereign, and part and parcel of what had become her routine. This routine involved the maximum sea time, crossing and recrossing the Atlantic in all types of weather conditions. This is in strict contrast to what the pundits safe at home in their beds were writing of the battleships, which in their hackneyed view were 'always swinging round their anchors'. Such was very far from the case, but like many other such myths, this has been perpetuated by many post-war writers on naval affairs who have not bothered to check their 'facts'.

The convoy consisted of twenty-eight merchant ships, a far more manageable group this time. The convoy's Commodore was Sir Eric Fullerton RNR, embarked aboard the *Merchant Prince*, and the convoy was organised in nine columns, with the Commodore leading the fourth column, the Vice-Commodore the seventh and with *Royal Sovereign* herself forming the fifth column and taking station between the leading ships of the fourth and sixth columns. Once more the two local escort destroyers remained in company only until 1800 on 11 April.

Fog had slightly delayed their departure and had prevented the average speed of 8.8 knots being achieved. The likelihood of further fog patches brought about exercises by the convoy during periods of good visibility, in which manoeuvring by sound signal alone was practised four times. Captain Jacomb recorded that these exercises were failures: 'It is considered that in fog communication by W/T must be made use of.'

On Saturday 13 April a lone tanker, the Norwegian-registered *Ida Knudsen*, was intercepted by the *Royal Sovereign* as she attempted to steer across the track of the convoy. She was sent in to Halifax for examination.

Another factor which limited their speed of advance was the inability of some of the merchantmen to even attain this low speed. Three ships, the British *Mount Pellion* and *Toronto City*, and the Estonia freighter *Lake Halliwell*, all had difficulty in keeping station at anything more than 8.5 knots. As a result the mean average speed of the convoy was reduced to 8.2 knots.

The latter vessel had other problems during the voyage. On the afternoon of Friday 19 April, it was noticed that she had dropped a mile astern of the convoy and was frantically signalling. *Royal Sovereign* therefore dropped back through the massed ranks of the merchant ships and closed her. The Estonian signalled that she required medical advice, but when the battleship attempted to signal medical instructions to her these were ignored, and instead the freighter lowered a boat. This forced the battleship also to halt in mid-ocean, some six miles astern of the convoy. Here they were sitting ducks, providing any opportunist U-boat commander with a heaven-sent opportunity. Fortunately none availed themselves of this chance, and the patient, an Arab native from Aden, was embarked and found to have knife wounds in his right hand and forearm, the results of a quarrel aboard the merchant ship. For this one of Britain's few capital ships had been hazarded!

Meanwhile an urgent signal had come in from the Admiralty, which ordered *Royal Sovereign* to leave the convoy and proceed at her best possible speed for Gibraltar. Therefore, in position 48° 52′ North 23° 36′ West, at 0415 on Saturday the 20th, she parted company with her charges. The convoy was naturally somewhat behind schedule for the rendezvous with the British local escort coming to meet it, but it was estimated that the convoy would need to average between 7.8 and 8.8 knots to be less than the acceptable six hours late. Once the 'Tiddly Quid' was out of sight, however, things must have become somewhat lax, for a signal from the C-in-C Western Approaches was subsequently intercepted by the battleship, stating that HX34 was forty-eight hours late! And this despite the relative rare conditions of fine weather and a calm sea. Still, once again, there had thankfully been no losses. Every one of the many hundreds of merchant ships given *Royal Sovereign*'s escort had got through safely while under her care. What their subsequent fate was after she had left them approaching the submarine-infested waters around Britain itself they were never really told. As E.C. Moore reflected, 'I believe that one convoy of seventy-two ships that we left on the British side of the lake had only about thirteen to twenty survivors a couple of days later after they ran into a U-Boat pack.'

Meanwhile events in Norway and France were moving to their inevitable climax, and in the Mediterranean the vacillating Mussolini, sensing an easy victory without too much effort on the part of Italy, was bracing himself to come into the war against us. At the same time France, our main ally, was fading out. Admiral Andrew Cunningham's main Mediterranean Fleet, at Alexandria in Egypt, had been steadily denuded of ships during the previous six months. By January he had only three old 6-inch cruisers and five equally ancient Australian destroyers. But as early as 29 April, long before the storm clouds could be seen spreading towards the Mediterranean area, Sir Dudley Pound, the wise First Sea Lord, was quietly assuring Cunningham that his fleet would again be reinforced from all over the globe.

From the Indian Ocean came *Ramillies*. She had been protecting the Australian troop convoys in much the same manner as 'Tiddly Quid' had the Canadian, but with better weather conditions. Likewise the *Malaya* and *Warspite*, the latter more recently the victor of the Second Battle of Narvik, were sailed for the Med. And thus it was that, out of the blue, *Royal Sovereign* was called upon to once again take up front-line duties with the 1st Battle Squadron. 'One day we were on our way back to Halifax, having delivered yet another convoy intact to the Western Approaches, when we suddenly received orders to proceed to Alexandria', recalls Mr Moore. 'So, turning 180 degrees, we made our way out to the Mediterranean.'

The battleship made good time and was met by the destroyers *Keppel* and *Watchman*, which escorted her into Gibraltar. She lay at the Mole between the 24th and 27th, and then sailed in company with the battleship *Malaya* for Alexandria. The two battleships were escorted by the destroyers *Vendetta*, *Velox*, *Watchman* and *Waterhen* for the passage through the central Mediterranean. The two Gibraltar-force destroyers, *Velox* and *Watchman*, were relieved by the *Stuart* and *Vampire* at 1435 on the 30th, and the two battleships and four Australian destroyers arrived safely at Alexandria on 3 May. Here they found *Ramillies* in dry dock. One of the most stirring periods in 'Tiddly Quid's' long career was about to open.

The R-class battleships had been represented at the Norwegian campaign by the presence of HMS *Resolution*. Earlier, in December, she had escorted in the first Canadian troop convoy to Britain, along with the *Repulse* and the aircraft carrier *Furious*. The *Revenge* had safely escorted in the second convoy at Christmas. Until the German invasion of Norway in April, the *Resolution* had led a fairly quiet life conducting similar escort missions.

Here they had encountered at first hand the efficiency of the German *Luftwaffe* and the accuracy of their dive-bombing attacks. These were to prove far more serious than the Italian methods of high-altitude formation attacks, and the *Resolution* had shown that, although an elderly lady, she could stand up to the best that the Axis had to offer.

In May HMS *Resolution* found herself anchored in Tjeldsundet, which was some thirty miles from the vital Norwegian ore port of Narvik. Already the two famous naval battles of that name were history. The Germans were entrenched ashore there, and the British and French were preparing for a final land assault to drive them out. The naval commander, Admiral of the Fleet the Earl Cork and Orrery, and the British land commander, Major-General P.J. Macksey, failed to agree on the best method to achieve this, and much time was taken in discussion while the Germans entrenched themselves still further.

The much postponed land attacks finally got under way on 14 May 1940. Two battalions of the French Foreign Legion were landed by sea to storm Bjerkvik at the head of Herjangsfiord. The possession of this little hamlet was considered a necessary preliminary for the main assault on Narvik town itself, which was planned for 27/28 May.

In conjunction with this the *Chasseurs-Alpins* were to make a land advance down the Gratangen road, while the Norwegian 6th Brigade was to advance through the mountains on their flank. As always, the Royal Navy had the job of proceeding up the narrow fiords in the perpetual daylight, with no fighter cover from the almost continuous *Luftwaffe* attacks, in order to provide the heavy firepower to support these attacks. For the first time the Allied soldiers were to have the support of tanks, four of which had been embarked aboard the *Resolution*, together with some of the early landing craft, MLCs (Motor Landing Craft), which would carry them ashore.

However, the battleship was not properly equipped to act as a specialised Landing Ship, Assault, and not surprisingly some difficulties were encountered in hoisting these large MLCs out from her correctly. Thus it was that these craft arrived late, and the troops were already ashore by the time they reached the beaches. None the less, their cargo was eagerly awaited, and the operation went forward to a neat little victory.

There was another pause before the final main assault took place, but meantime more ominous news had been coming from the Low Countries and France. It was clear that, even once Narvik had been taken, it could never be held. The men and the ships were required more urgently further south. None the less, the attack went forward. The *Resolution* was due to act in bombardment support of this assault, but in the event was unable to do so.

It was on 16 May that the *Luftwaffe* and the *Resolution* made their closest contact with each other. Several Heinkel 111 bombers from *III/KG 26* attacked the anchorage, dropping an estimated fifty bombs. Only one of these struck any of their targets.

The 250 lb missile (though German sources state it was a 1,000 kg bomb) hit the battleship on the upper deck aft between 'X' and 'Y' turrets. It penetrated the deck and plunged down through two more upper decks to reach the middle deck before exploding. Thus the bomb did not even reach the main 4-inch armour. Two men were killed and twenty-seven others injured by this bomb. But the physical damage such a small bomb could do to a battleship proved slight. Apart from the ragged hole and small fires, which started among the officers' clothing and bedding and were easily put out, the ship's efficiency was in no way impaired. Despite this, she was sent back to Scapa Flow, and although she carried on with her duties for a whole month with the temporary shipboard 'patching up' before returning to dock for more permanent repairs to be done, she took no further part in the Narvik operation.

CHAPTER FIVE

Under Cunningham's Command

By the time Italy finally came into the war on the Axis side, on 9 June 1940, Admiral Sir Andrew Cunningham had four British and three French battleships (soon reduced to one, the *Lorraine*) as his main battle fleet. Also present was the aircraft carrier *Eagle* (with two or three operational biplane fighters but no fighter pilots, and some Swordfish torpedo-bombers embarked), three French 8-inch cruisers, nine British and one French 6-inch cruisers and twenty-eight destroyers, three of them French. Opposed to him the Italians had four old battleships (which had been completely modernised), while four brand-new battleships were under construction, the first pair of which were known to be almost ready for sea. Eight modern 8-inch cruisers, ten 6-inch cruisers and over one hundred modern destroyers and torpedo-boats, plus seventy-odd submarines, completed the picture. In addition the Italian Air Force was an unknown quantity but possessed many hundreds of long-range bombers and up-to-date fighter aircraft.

The island fortress of Malta was left virtually defenceless at this period of the war, and the only other Allied units were the main French Mediterranean Fleet at Toulon and a British local defence destroyer flotilla at Gibraltar. When France caved in we lost their main units, and so a hastily assembled scratch British squadron had to be sent out from home to form Force 'H', under the command of Admiral Sir James Somerville. This was based at the Rock, and was built around two or three capital ships, the aircraft carrier *Ark Royal*, a few cruisers and two destroyer flotillas, the 8th and the 13th.

Admiral Cunningham was full of enthusiasm and eager to test his fleet's mettle against the Italians, but in view of his lack of supporting ships and complete absence of any modern fighter aircraft of his own, he was limited in what he could achieve. What proved to be a major handicap was the disparity of speed between the Italian and British ships. All their warships were built with high-speed steaming as a priority. Even their old battleships had an eight-to-ten-knot margin over their British equivalents. This enabled them to avoid combat with the older and slower British units if they chose. And they usually chose to do so, unless possessing overwhelming numbers. There was very little that Cunningham could do to redress this disadvantage. To compensate for the Italian dominance in the air and their warships' swiftness, a few British warships arrived fitted with primitive forms of radar equipment. This, coupled with the British pre-war training in night-fighting tactics, of which the Italians had little or none, gave the British an edge if they could bring the enemy to bay.

As the war in the Mediterranean turned out, successful actions could be fought by the British surface ships, always provided the Italian ships could be damaged and slowed down. If that occurred then they could be sunk. If not, then only a frustrating series of stern chases, with little concrete results forthcoming from long-range duelling, took place. The key to damaging the fast Italian battleships and cruisers proved to be the ability of the Fleet Air Arm torpedo-bombers to hit them from the air. Gallantly flown and in only pathetic penny-packet numbers, they endeavoured to do this, but were not finally rewarded until Matapan.

None the less, Cunningham was a fighter, and offensive sweeps formed the backbone of his policy. The need to keep the garrison at Malta supplied with food, oil fuel, munitions and ultimately fighter aircraft led to a series of hard-fought convoys, which usually required the support of the whole battle fleet to fight through. This gave opportunities for fleet action when the Italian heavy ships ventured out. More normally it gave the Italian Air Force ample and prolonged target practice in which to demonstrate the inability of high-altitude bombers to hit, let alone sink, battleships.

Ever since Billy Mitchell had bombed and sunk the hulk of an obsolete German Dreadnought anchored in Chesapeake Bay in the 1920s the air lobby had been shrilly claiming it could sink whole fleets within a few hours. Between June and December 1940 the *Regia Aeronautica* proved decisively that they could not. It was *Royal Sovereign* and her compatriots who turned out to be the live targets in this debate.

Churchill, now Prime Minister, was never satisfied in his mind that Cunningham's plans were aggressive enough, and constantly bombarded him with calls for action. Numerous ideas arrived on the Admiral's desk – occupy Pantelleria, raid Rhodes, block Tripoli and so on – all of which were completely impracticable and would have been of little lasting value. Cunningham was strong enough to resist this constant needling and misguided pressure. His successors were not so resilient, and this resulted in some notable disasters. Fortunately, during the 'Tiddly Quid's' time in the Mediterranean, 'ABC', as the C-in-C was affectionately known, kept these bizarre brainstorms at arm's length and concentrated on defeating the enemy on his own terms without taking crippling losses to his own limited strength, which would have rendered Britain's position untenable.

After *Royal Sovereign*'s arrival at Alexandria on 4 May, the rest of the month was spent in preparations. On 5 May she proceeded to sea for exercises and returned the same day. During this period several new crew members joined her from other ships of the fleet to replace others who were being sent home to man new ships being commissioned. Among the newcomers was S.E. Crouch, who joined from the netlayer *Protector* just out from the UK:

The trip through the Med was like a cruise, as Italy hadn't entered the war at that time. However, you can imagine my chagrin when, on arrival at Alex we were ferried across from *Protector* in semi-darkness to the quarterdeck of the *Royal Sovereign*. My first impression was of two enormous 15-inch guns sticking out from under the awning, and I knew that now things were going to get serious.

Another newcomer was Boy Seaman Lawrence Dixon, who transferred from the depot ship *Medway*:

HMS *Medway* was tucked away in a corner of Alex harbour, and as I'd arrived by train from Port Said at night there was not much that I could see of my first ship initially. Having received my draft chit for the *Sovereign*, I was taken by surprise at the sight of such a large fleet in the outer harbour as our boat rounded a corner the next day. After climbing the ladder with my kitbag I looked at 'Y' turret and the size of the guns and thought to myself, 'I bet they are noisy!' After the usual formalities on joining ship I went to my allotted messdeck and was greeted by Boy J. Charlton. We had trained together aboard HMS *Caledonia* at Rosyth and we also came from the same home town, West Hartlepool.

My first harbour duty was gangway staff side-boy. It proved to be my first encounter with Mr Farmer, a senior commissioned gunner.

On my second forenoon watch he was officer of the watch (OOW). I didn't know who he was at the time of course. He was standing right aft near the ship's ensign and he suddenly shouted, 'Side-boy!' I immediately doubled aft, stopped in front of him and gave a smart salute to make a good impression. He looked down at me – he was a very large man – and said, 'Go and tell . . .' I waited for him to finish but he just repeated, 'Go and tell . . .' I remained still until he let out a roar of wrath and screamed again, 'Go and tell . . '

I saluted, about-turned and doubled away. I was about halfway back along the quarterdeck when he shouted, 'Side-boy! Come back here.' When I returned he asked me, 'Where the Hell are you going?' and I replied 'I'm going to tell . . .' Then he said, 'You are a bloody fool and ought to turn in your hammock with boxing gloves on.' He then asked me to inform the snotty (the midshipman) of the watch that he was wanted. This was my introduction to the peculiar ways of Mr Farmer.

After a week of this I was given a more interesting job as admiral's staff messenger, taking signals from the SDO to those entitled to receive them.

With the outbreak of war the Mediterranean Fleet stepped up a gear and the *Ramillies* was taken out of dock, her refit incomplete. Cunningham went to sea with part of the fleet on the 11th, returning on the 14th without sighting the enemy, but lost the cruiser *Calypso* to submarine attack on the 12th. A French cruiser squadron swept the Aegean without result, and two British cruisers engaged Italian minesweepers and bombarded shore batteries off Tobruk the same day.

Royal Sovereign did not participate in these operations, but further aggressive action was planned in which she had a part. On 22 June Operation BQ was set in motion. The plan was to bring out a convoy of merchant ships from Malta to Alexandria and to provide covering strength during the crucial period of its passage. This was the defensive side of the scheme. In conjunction with this, Vice-Admiral Sir John Tovey took the French battleship *Lorraine*, three British cruisers and four destroyers to sea on 20 June to carry out a bombardment of Bardia the next morning. Five further destroyers sailed to sweep along the Libyan coastline to the vicinity of Tobruk, and two French 8-inch cruisers, *Duguay Trouin* and *Suffren*, with three further British destroyers, sailed as a back-up force.

The main offensive, however, was the bold penetration of the battleships into the heart of the Mediterranean as far as Sicily. The night bombardment of Port Augusta by the heavy ships while the destroyers hunted for enemy convoys in the Straits of Messina would bring home to Mussolini what he had taken on. Such an audacious scheme should have satisfied the impatient Premier in London, as well, and shown him that courage and audacity were not lacking in the Mediterranean. The main force, Force 'C', consisting of the *Ramillies* and *Royal Sovereign*, the aircraft carrier *Eagle* and the 2nd Destroyer Flotilla. They sailed from Alexandria on 22 June, the battleships clearing the Ras-el-Tin lighthouse at 2000 that evening. They were blacked out and steering westward when, at 2153, the Admiralty ordered that the operation be deferred. On receipt of this signal from London, Admiral Cunningham had no choice but to cancel all movements, and the fleet returned to harbour, *Royal Sovereign* re-entering Alexandria at 1045 on 23 June.

The reason for the Admiralty's intervention soon became clear. France was on the brink of giving up the fight, and the attitude of the French Navy to orders from the new collaborationist government of Marshal Pétain at Vichy was unclear. On 24 June the capitulation was signed. While Vice-Admiral Godfroy's squadron remained idle, the British ships of the Mediterranean Fleet had to get on with the war.

Several important convoys were in train between Port Said and the Aegean (Operation AS1), where trade with neutral Greece and Turkey was being maintained despite the Italian forces in the Dodecanese and on Rhodes. These movements were covered by the cruisers *Caledon* and *Capetown* with four destroyers. Two further convoys were at sea, those consisting of the merchant ships from Malta divided into a fast and a slow group. The light cruisers *Liverpool* and *Gloucester* were out in a covering position.

It was to give all these forces heavy ship support that Force 'B' left Alexandria to sweep westward at 1230 on 28 June, to carry out Operation MA1. Escorting *Royal Sovereign*, *Ramillies* and *Eagle* were the destroyers *Hasty*, *Havock*, *Hero*, *Hereward*, *Hyperion*, *Janus* and *Juno*.

On the 28th the ships of the 7th Cruiser Squadron intercepted three Italians destroyers off Cape Matapan. The Italian vessels promptly fled at full speed, but not before one of them, *Espero*, was hit and sunk. This caused the postponement of the Malta convoys sailing for a few hours until things became clearer. Therefore the two British battleships found themselves marking time some fifty miles south of Gavdos Island at noon on the 29th, still steering west, and during the night course was shaped to the south of Vilkera. In the early hours of the 30th Force 'B' reversed course to the east to pass through position 33° 46′ North, 23° 10′

East, not finally sighting convoy AS1 until 1555 on 1 July, when still some 200 miles from Alexandria. The battleship force returned to harbour at 1015 on the morning of the 2nd.

The question of how to dispose of the French fleet now came to the fore once more and caused a short interval in dealing with the real enemy.

Admiral Godfroy, although on very good terms with Admiral Cunningham, became more and more withdrawn, and the consensus in his squadron among the officers and men was that the war was over and that they wished to return home to their families as soon as possible. They saw no likelihood of Great Britain's surviving for much longer and wanted no part of any further combat.

The British captains, many of whom were friends of their opposite numbers in the French ships, implored them to carry on the fight, and a few did so, volunteering to join the Free French forces who rallied round General Charles de Gaulle. The majority had little stomach left for fighting, however, and the British Government was determined that they would not be able to sail their ships to French ports where they would be available to the German and Italians at a future date. Admiral Cunningham was desperately short of 8-inch cruisers and destroyers, and had hoped to take over and man one of the former and three of the latter if the French would not fight them themselves, but even this was denied to him.

At home the War Cabinet had come out in favour of strong and abrupt action. The French ships were to be given an ultimatum and then seized by force. Naturally this caused great distress to the British officers charged with carrying out such a task. In British ports most of the French vessels were so taken over, but with some bloodshed. At the western end of the Mediterranean Admiral Somerville failed to talk the French into complying with the terms offered, and opened fire on them at Mers-el-Kebir. Great slaughter was done but some of the most important ships managed to escape unscathed. Only at Alexandria did common sense and reason prevail, thanks to Admiral Cunningham's deft and sensitive handling of the situation, for which he got little thanks from home. But even at Alexandria it looked for a time as if it might come to a fight, and the British battleships trained their guns on their French opposite numbers when it seemed likely that Godfroy's ships were going to fight their way out of the harbour. Thankfully careful negotiations reached a compromise without such dire necessity, but not before there were several tense hours on the brink.

It was HMS *Resolution* that represented the 'R's at the Mers-el-Kebir action. Force 'H' itself had been hastily set up to replace the French fleet in the Western Mediterranean, being based on Gibraltar and commanded by Vice-Admiral Sir James Somerville, recalled from the retired list to flag rank once more. The *Resolution* had been one of the original founder members of this squadron, which included the *Ark Royal, Hood* (flag), *Valiant, Arethusa* and the 8th Destroyer Flotilla. Operation Catapult, the destruction of the French fleet at Mers-el-Kebir on 3 July 1940, was their first operation.

Under the command of the French admiral Marcel-Bruno Gensoul were two of their best capital ships, the new battlecruisers *Dunkerque* (flag) and *Strasbourg*, along with two old battleships, *Bretagne* and *Provence*. Also in harbour were the seaplane carrier *Commandante Teste*, and six destroyers *Kersaint, Le Terrible, Lynx, Mogador, Tigre* and *Volta*. Guarding the harbour were powerful forts: Fort Canastelle to the north-east had three 9.2-inch guns and was backed by Fort Santon mounting four 7.5-inch guns, with Fort de Santa-Cruz to the south.

Negotiations lasted well past the deadlines authorised by the War Cabinet in London, and it was not until almost dusk (1735) that the destroyer *Foxhound*, carrying Captain Holland, the chief negotiator, left the French harbour, and she was almost immediately fired upon by French land batteries, although flying the white flag. Zig-zagging and making smoke, the little destroyer escaped being hit, but such actions illustrated eloquently enough the attitude of the French Navy.

Even so it was not until 1754 that Admiral Somerville reluctantly gave the order for the British ships to return the fire, and events were to prove that he had left decisive action far too late to be totally effective. Leaving aside the question of whether the British were right or wrong not to trust the word of Adolf Hitler that he would not take over French ships (and that gentleman had not hitherto been much concerned with breaking rather more significant and solemn obligations), if the job had to be done it should have been done correctly. But it was botched.

The French ships were moored behind the outer mole, while the British were firing over the high headland from the north, in order to prevent 'overs' falling on civilian targets ashore, none of which facilitated accuracy; and the failing light made things even more difficult to spot the fall of shot correctly. Only a few salvoes from the French ships fell near the British battle-line, however, while the 15-inch salvoes from the *Hood*, *Valiant* and *Resolution*, steaming in line ahead at seventeen knots, made a steady practice on the four French heavy ships.

The conditions of visibility over the target area were poor and made spotting the fall of shot difficult. Evening was coming on and the French ships were under a pall of their own funnel smoke as they raised steam to attempt to get under way. This and the heat haze along the harbour shoreline combined to diffuse the sharp outlines of their masts and fighting tops on which the British gunnery officers were ranging.

French fire soon slackened off, and it ceased altogether at 1804.

The British capital ships (each mounting eight 15-inch guns) fired a total of thirty-six salvoes. The battleship *Provence* had managed to get off several salvoes of her own but was the first French ship to be hit, at 1803, when she was struck aft by several 15-inch shells from the *Valiant* that wrecked her upperworks and opened her up below, forcing her crew to run her aground in shallow water at the edge of the main channel on the five-fathom line, to prevent her becoming a total loss.

Within five minutes of the British opening fire, another full salvo from *Resolution* struck the *Bretagne* aft with good effect. One penetrated to a magazine, causing a heavy internal explosion just as she too was getting under way. Heavy fires blazed up, and at 1809 a great column of smoke and steam rose up several hundred feet to merge with the general gloom over the harbour area, to which further hits added their quota of smoke and fires. The old French battleship was unable to absorb such punishment. She began to settle by the stern as fires raged and spread throughout her whole hull abaft the bridge. Within two minutes she had capsized, taking 1,012 officers and men of her crew to the bottom with her.

One 15-inch British shell hit the aircraft hangar of the battle-cruiser *Dunkerque* just as she was slipping her moorings. This penetrated down and carried away the steering-gear linkage, making her instantly unmanoeuvrable. Within another minute three more one-ton projectiles arrived to score more direct hits on the *Dunkerque* while she was still trying to get under way, which was really excellent shooting in such conditions.

This blow was serious. One shell destroyed the main generators of the battle-cruiser and she immediately lost all electrical power, which compounded her existing difficulties. Another smashed the hydraulic machinery which operated the internal watertight doors, so that they could not be moved. This hit also severed the high-pressure steam pipes in the starboard boiler room, and fires broke out here. The third missile hit one of her turrets, immobilising it and killing most of the turret crew outright. The cordite began to smoulder in the gun hoists and her imminent destruction by explosion of a magazine seemed certain.

The fires were quelled; the ship went to hand steering, and, using the two still intact boilers, she managed to get under way at very slow speed. The emergency generators came into operation and she resumed limited firing again. The *Hood* had her as her main target and dropped forty heavy shells on or very near the *Dunkerque*.

Heavily damaged and with some of her guns out of action, the *Dunkerque* could only struggle to the far end of the harbour, where, at 2000, Gensoul ordered her captain to 'sink the ship slowly by the bows on the sandy bottom off St Andre'. She finally settled with her bows pointing west in eight metres of waters by the bow and thirteen by the stern.

Another 15-inch shell arrived aboard the destroyer *Mogador*, igniting the sixteen depth charges stowed on her quarterdeck, which in turn blew her entire stern section off. Fires broke out as she began to settle by the stern, and she too was hastily towed away by a tug to be beached in the shallow water of the Bains la Reine.

Admiral Somerville was later to pay tribute to the British

gunners, stating that their salvoes 'appeared to be accurate and effective', although later he directly contradicted himself and wrote that 'the gunnery and fleet work leave a lot to be desired . . .'. This would have been hardly surprising, as the ships that constituted his force had never worked together prior to this operation and had come from wildly differing parts of the world to form it. It was also reported, 'There was difficulty of observation of fire under action conditions. It was of course accentuated in this case by the haze and the fact that the ships were not moving and the smoke remained all around them. The smoke from the big explosion obscured practically everything inside the harbour.' This smoke forced the British to use the lighthouse at the harbour entrance as their ranging and aiming pointer.

With three out of the four enemy ships put out of action in a bombardment lasting less than fifteen minutes, the standard of the British gunnery would appear to have been quite adequate! But even so the battle-cruiser *Strasbourg* remained unscathed, and when Somerville ordered a ceasefire at 1810 she took the opportunity to get under way, and with an escort of the remaining five destroyers she broke from the harbour and got clean away. Worse still, the British squadron had been badly positioned away to the west and was in the wrong place to inter-cept her. Somerville himself was forced to admit that he made a tactical error in not keeping to the north-east of Oran, so cutting off any such escape attempt. Thus one of the most powerful of the Vichy ships managed to reach Toulon, shrugging off attacks by torpedo-bombers *en route*. Here she was even closer to her German and Italian overseers. Realising his blunder, Somerville had set off with the *Hood* and *Ark Royal* in hopeless pursuit, taking with him *all* the British destroyers. This left the *Resolution* and the *Valiant* horribly exposed and highly vulnerable to submarine attack, and it is perhaps highly fortunate that this second error was not more harshly punished.

In his subsequent report Somerville gave his reasons for calling off the chase as that 'Without HMS *Resolution* and HMS *Valiant* I had no margin of strength', adding further, 'HMS *Resolution* and HMS *Valiant* were without screen.' He also stated, 'I assumed Their Lordships did not wish me to incur

serious loss especially of destroyers in these operations . . .'
Quite how the loss of two battleships to submarine attack while
without destroyer protection would have been viewed by Their
Lordships he did not say. Nor did he explain how the combination of the 42,100-ton *Hood* with her eight 15-inch guns, 31 knots,
and the *Ark Royal*, with her squadrons of torpedo- and dive-
bombers did not constitute a superior force to the *Strasbourg*
(26,500 tons, eight 13-inch guns, 29 knots). Be that as it may, the
whole British squadron returned to Gibraltar that same night
unharmed. When the next day they returned to Mers-el-Kebir to
finish off what remained of the French fleet, *Resolution* and one
destroyer were not included.

Things came to a head on Thursday 4 July. The grim news
from Mers-el-Kebir had hardened the hearts of the French, and
they were more opposed to co-operation than ever before. Early
that morning the French squadron started to raise steam, and
their guns were cleared for action. Three last-ditch alternatives
faced Cunningham. He could try to take the French ships by
force with boarding parties, as had been done in English ports.
He could sink them by gunfire and torpedo where they lay, as at
Mers-el-Kebir, or he could try one more time to persuade
Godfroy to intern or surrender his ships. Cunningham knew the
French admiral would favour scuttling his squadron first, and
such a course would not only be a waste of first-class warships
which might one day take up the struggle again, it would also
cause maximum inconvenience to his main, indeed his only,
fleet anchorage, and hazard future operations by the
Mediterranean Fleet itself.

Cunningham had already prepared for the worst. The British
battleships had been kedged round so that their main armament
broadsides would bear on the French ships and the gun
tompions had been removed. The British destroyers had torpedoes trained on the French ships ready to fire at a moment's
notice. It would have been a massacre of tragic proportions. As
Lawrence Dixon recalls:

My Action Station was in 'A' turret, in the cabinet as phone
number, but later that was changed to sight-setter on the
left-hand gun of the same turret. We stood to at Action

Stations all that night in Alexandria harbour with our 15-inch guns loaded and trained on them ready to open fire if they attempted to move out. There was movement of crew on their upper deck, but after a while they seemed to think better of it.

Inside 'X' turret Royal Marine Bill Heffernan had a similar experience:

Imagine our surprise during the early hours of that fateful morning when we were called to Action Stations in our own harbour. I found myself looking at the French battle-ships' waterline through a gunlayer's telescope, and we remained ready until they agreed to dismantle their guns.

In the end Admiral Godfroy seemed to realise that to fight would be futile. He agreed to reduce his ships' complements to thirty per cent, to discharge oil fuel so that they could not put to sea, to land vital gunnery equipment, which rendered their weapons inoperational, under the care of the French Consulate-General. By 7 July the crisis was over and the Mediterranean Fleet could take up the struggle against the Axis once again. They did not delay.

Personalities abounded in the Med Fleet at this time, and many of the leading naval officers of World War Two cut their teeth in this hard school. Everybody knew 'ABC', of course. The C-in-C was a spry and dapper little figure in immaculate 'whites', ever eager to get to sea and hunt the enemy. He would pace up and down his flagship's bridge as if by sheer mileage he could will the *Warspite* to an extra few knots to catch the Italians. An ex-destroyer man, he threw his battle fleet into combat with the same vim and vigour as he had commanded a flotilla. But the crew of the *Royal Sovereign* only had infrequent glimpses of him. More well known, of course, apart from her own new commanding officer, Captain H. Jacomb, who had relieved Captain L.V. Morgan CBE, MVO, DSC, in January, was the officer commanding 1st Battle Squadron, Rear Admiral H.D. Pridham-Wippell. Cunningham himself desribed him thus:

A friend of Dardanelles days, and an ex-destroyer officer of great experience and merit, I had the greatest faith in him and confidence in his judgment. In the difficult times through which we were to pass he never failed.[1]

A more personal lower-deck viewpoint of the great man on *Royal Sovereign*'s bridge at this time is given by Lawrence Dixon:

The Admiral smoked, and young as I was, so soon did I. We both smoked, but different quality. There was I, pay six shillings (30p) per fortnight in my Duck jumper smoking from a packet of twenty Players, and the Admiral pulled out a packet of small Woodbines and lit up. Well, even *large* Woodbines were only 4½d (1½p) for twenty, but I suppose he liked them like that!

John Charlton asked me if I would like to be a 'hammock boy'. This meant slinging two or three midshipmen's hammocks every night, then lashing them up each morning. For this we got half-a-crown (2/6d, or 12½p) per month. The boy seamen routine while in harbour was 0530 call. In Alex it was muster on the quarterdeck and jump over the side (a dive) into the dirty harbour water. Your name was ticked off as you came up the officers' ladder. We had different things for different climes of course. Our leave in Alex consisted of 3½ days per fortnight, from 1300 to 1800 with the chaplain in charge of us. We either went to a cinema or swimming at Ras-el-Tin beach.

At sea we had different states of readiness. In Alex we were usually at certain notices for steam, i.e. two hours, four hours, eight hours, etc. This factor decided what shore leave could be given, and such was the pace in the Mediterranean Fleet that I only had two runs ashore there in all the months we were based there. At sea the routine for the boys was the same as the men. Nobody had a hammock to sleep in once we left harbour. Our 'bed' was a 'corker', a piece of canvas or an oilskin laid on the messdeck and a half-inflated lifebelt as a pillow. The locker flats and bathrooms had armoured hatches and could only be opened at certain times when at sea. 'Tanky', the inevitable old stoker, would come round the messdecks and turn on fresh water with a special key to fill the little drinking-water tanks. After a little while one could shave with it and it tasted horrible!

C.E. Moore also remembers lack of sleep while in harbour, but for different reasons:

While in Alex very little sleep was had as our picket boats were constantly patrolling the anchorage on the alert for Italian frogmen. To deter them they kept dropping small charges at random intervals all night long.

Shortly after noon on 7 July the battle squadron weighed anchor and sailed for the central Mediterranean. These were the preliminary moves in what became the first major surface fleet action in the Mediterranean in World War Two, the Battle of Calabria. The background to the battle was that the much-postponed sailing of the two convoys from Malta was finally got under way, MF1 with three ships and MS1 with another four, escorted by three destroyers, *Diamond*, *Jervis* and *Vendetta*. To give protection the main British fleet was to take up a covering position to the east of Cape Passero on the afternoon of 9 July.

The cruiser squadron, with four 6-inch ships, *Neptune*, *Orion*, *Gloucester* and *Sydney*, with the destroyer *Stuart*, was out ahead, and the C-in-C went out in *Warspite* with the five destroyers *Decoy*, *Hereward*, *Hero*, *Mohawk* and *Nubian*, while the main fleet followed on. All three groups were to rendezvous and concentrate on the 9th.

With Admiral Pridham-Wippell flying his flag aboard *Royal Sovereign*, the main force, known as Force 'C', comprised the battleship *Malaya*, the carrier *Eagle* and destroyers *Dainty*, *Defender*, *Hasty*, *Hostile*, *Hyperion*, *Ilex*, *Imperial*, *Janus*, *Juno*, *Vampire* and *Voyager*.

Unbeknown to Cunningham the Italian fleet under Admiral Campioni was also at sea, covering convoys to Libya. They had two battleships, six 8-inch cruisers, twelve 6-inch cruisers and between sixteen and thirty-two destroyers at sea in the central Mediterranean.

Heavy and prolonged bombing by the Italian Air Force from its bases in the Dodecanese, Libya and Italy was an almost continuous feature of this operation. They commenced against Force 'C' at 0951 on 8 July and were practically non-stop thereafter. Some eighty bombs were aimed this first day alone, but none hit. Admiral Cunningham was not deterred, but he was worried about 'the old ships *Royal Sovereign* and *Eagle*, which were not well protected. A clutch of those eggs hitting either must have sent her to the bottom.' In fact both ships were more modern than either *Warspite* or *Malaya*, although the former had been modernised. The *Royal Sovereign*'s protection was as good as the *Malaya*'s and much superior to the *Renown*, a battle-cruiser flying the flag of Admiral Somerville in Force 'H', which was subjected to equally ferocious bombing during 1940/41. But this seems to have been overlooked by the two admirals, who were almost as guilty as the Premier in underestimating the R-class battleships' strength. Of course the true weakness of the *Royal Sovereign* and her three remaining sister ships was their lack of speed. This Achilles Heel factor the subsequent battle was to expose only too well.

After some preliminary cruiser skirmishing, the *Warspite* came up in support of the 7th Squadron, and action was joined with the two Italian heavy ships at 1548 on the 9th. The other two British battleships were at this time some sixty miles astern and hard pressed at nineteen knots to close the gap. None the less, they tried to do so and get into range. Only *Malaya*, by changing places with *Royal Sovereign*, managed to support the fleet flagship, but even her seven salvoes fell short. No doubt more would have been done by both her and *Royal Sovereign* had the Italians made a fight of it, but after *Warspite* hit the Italian flagship with one of the 15-inch shells at extreme range, all Campioni's desire to slug it out instantly vanished and he set a hurried course for Taranto harbour. Cunningham tried to follow him and get in another blow, but could not match the pace. For the 'Tiddly Quid' the fighting was over before she could even get started.

One eyewitness account of the battle was given me by Lawrence Dixon:

I was sitting on the fo'c'sle when my friend, Boy Telegraphist Harkness, came and sat next to me. He looked tense and told me that we'd had a sighting report of the Italian fleet. There were two battleships, ten cruisers and twenty destroyers up ahead and we were on our way to engage them. The flagship, *Warspite*, was somewhere up ahead and we were greatly outnumbered. Ten minutes after he told me this startling news, 'Action Stations' were sounded off by Royal Marine buglers.

My job in 'A' turret had been changed again, to range-finder/trainer. I had a periscope to keep the range-finder on the target for the range-taker to get a 'cut'. I could see the smoke of the Italian ships way out on the far horizon seemingly coming towards us, but in fact steaming as hard as they could in the opposite direction. Our 15-inch guns were all loaded and I know I felt a little scared. I was only sixteen and it seemed likely that our turret would sustain a direct hit, and other gory thoughts passed though my mind.

I then observed the *Malaya* piling on the steam and leaving us standing off our starboard bow with her 15-inch guns at full elevation and crashing away as she tried to get into the action in support of *Warspite*. I could see now that the Italian fleet was turning away at full speed and heading for Italy as fast as they could manage! Try as we might we could not catch them, and the poor old 'Tiddly Quid' nearly ruptured herself trying to keep up so we could have a crack at them ourselves. The Italian press called us the ship with the rubber guns after this action because we didn't get the chance to fire them. If they would have stopped and fought we would have shown them differently but we just were not fast enough to get into range.

The Captain of Marines aboard the *Royal Sovereign* was Captain C.L. Price RM. He relates:

I was OOQ 'X' turret, and as such felt it my privilege to poke my head out to see what was going on during the battle. We were then miles astern of everyone else but there seemed to be a lot of dirt flying about still forrard. It was frustrating on returning to Alexandria, to be told that the Italian papers' account of the engagement said 'Up lumbered another British battleship – this one had rubber guns.' We never did get close enough to the enemy to fire our 15-inch guns.

Leading Seaman Stanley Terry, who had served aboard the 'Tiddly Quid' between 1932 and 1935, got a different view of his old ship from the *Malaya* as she overhauled her:

We and the *Warspite* engaged the Italian battleships at long range, but the poor old *Royal Sovereign*, doing less than 19 knots it seemed, was left over the horizon and wasn't in the show at all. So much for all our spit and polish and so-called efficiency between the wars. She was a splendid ship in peacetime but unless the enemy came to her was useless in action due to her low speed.

T.W. Pope gives this account:

I was gunlayer on S.1 gun. Being below decks in the 6-inch battery, we could not see what was going on up top, but as the ranges were passed down and the 15-inch were ordered to load, we knew that we were to engage the enemy. We were second ship in line, *Warspite* leading, *Malaya* astern. I looked through the gunlayer's telescope and away on the starboard side were our cruisers and destroyers steaming at full speed with battle ensigns streaming out in the wind. It was quite a sight!

Although the *Warspite* and *Malaya* opened fire, and the Italian shells were dropping close to us, we did not return the fire as we were too slow and all the time dropping astern, the *Malaya* crashing past to take our place in line. One of the enemy battleships took a heavy hit and under cover of a smokesreen they all turned away and retreated. We followed for a time, but the C-in-C concluded that they were leading us into a submarine trap so discontinued the action.

It was then that the Italian bombers came over and released quite a few bombs, this being the first of many attacks. Although numerous bombs were dropped, no ship was hit, though we had near-misses. Some very minor damage to the underwater part of our hull was received, mainly rivets missing and seawater getting into our fresh-water tanks. It was because of this, and the obvious fact that we were now too slow to work with the fleet, that the decision was later made to replace us.

The following day the battle fleet patiently patrolled off the enemy's doorstep in the hope he would pop his nose out again, but this he steadfastly refused to do. Instead he sent out his air force again and again.

Mr Moore has other recollections of the air attacks that followed the battle:

My main memories are of constant bombing, three or four days at a time and from sunrise to sunset. All our HA guns were constantly in action. I also remember how on the upper decks the fire hoses were in constant use to keep the decks wet so that they blended with the sea and made us harder to sight on for the Italian bomb-aimers.

S.E. Crouch remembered that:

We saw little or nothing of the Italian fleet, but their air force gave us a few headaches with their almost daily bombing attacks, sometimes several times a day. I cannot recollect any damage being done to our own vessel by these raids, but there were a few 'close shaves'. One of the main targets seemed to be the aircraft carrier *Eagle*. I suppose her flight deck looked an easy mark for an airman, but they couldn't hit her for love nor money. However, as we were frequently in her company as her guard battleship we got splashed by some of the 'overs' from time to time, as well as our own share. I think we were fortunate in one respect, and that was that the *Luftwaffe* dive-bombers had not yet entered the Mediterranean. The Italian raids were conducted from a very high altitude, but even so some of them came too close for comfort.

Lawrence Dixon recalls vividly the Admiral Pridham-Wippell's unofficial 'Action Station' during air attacks:

> We got rid of thousands of 4-inch anti-aircraft shells during the high-level raids. Admiral Pridham-Wippell would lie on his back on the ADP (Air Defence Position) and observe the bombs leaving the aircraft and then give the appropriate course alterations.

There remained nothing for the fleet to do but escort the two convoys safely back to Egypt. Before doing so, however, opportunity was taken to refuel the *Royal Sovereign* at Malta. She was escorted there by the destroyers *Nubian*, *Mohawk* and *Janus*, and this squadron was detached from the main fleet at 2030 on the evening of 10 July, arriving in Valetta harbour early on the 11th.

The sight of a British battleship in Grand Harbour once more was something to raise the spirits of the island. Since the outbreak of hostilities they had been bombed continually by the *Regia Aeronautica*, and felt isolated. However, news of the victory at sea and proof in the menacing bulk of 'Tiddly Quid' dominating the narrow waterways once more as of old did much to raise morale.

On completion of her oiling *Royal Sovereign* sailed again and rejoined the Commander-in-Chief at 0800 on the 11th. While *Warspite* returned to Alexandria, the rest of the battle squadron and the *Eagle* covered the two convoys, which arrived without loss. The *Royal Sovereign* arrived back at Alexandria at 0820 on the 14th, having survived her ordeal by bombs and with no casualties.

Note:

[1] Cunningham, A.B. of Hyndhope, *Sailor's Odyssey*, Hutchinson, 1951

CHAPTER SIX

Long Voyages

Admiral Cunningham has recorded how he wrote to the First Sea Lord, Sir Dudley Pound, in the aftermath of the battle. The fact that neither *Royal Sovereign* nor *Malaya* crossed the target and that the enemy would not stand and fight to enable them to do so weighed heavily on him: 'I must have one more ship that can shoot at a good range', he said. He was to get his wish. Both the reconstructed *Queen Elizabeth* and *Valiant* were assigned to him, but until they arrived on station he had to soldier on with the ships he had.

Nobody could blame the engine-room staff of the *Royal Sovereign* for her inability to get into the fight. They had worked with total dedication to coax every last ounce of steam from her ancient boilers. The dense clouds of smoke that poured from her uncapped funnel left a pall over her as she steamed as if fit to bust. In fact the Italian press published an aerial photograph of her doing just that. They deliberately printed it upside down and claimed it showed her being hit by bombs and set on fire, a claim that caused considerable hilarity aboard the ship herself! The effects of that great effort soon manifested itself, and her boiler tubes clearly required complete replacement. The *Ramillies* was in a similar state and the *Malaya* was suffering condenser problems. All needed refits but none could be immediately spared.

On 30 July two forces sailed from Alexandria to carry out Operation MA9 and to create a diversion for Operation Hurry. The latter was a flying-off of Hawker Hurricane fighters for Malta's defence from the aircraft carrier *Argus*, which had come out from home via Gibraltar. In the hope of taking some of the weight from Admiral Somerville's Force 'H', which would be escorting her, Admiral Cunningham laid on this show of strength in the eastern basin. Force 'B', consisting of *Royal Sovereign* (flag), *Malaya* and *Eagle*, escorted by the destroyers *Hasty*, *Hereward*, *Hero*, *Hostile*, *Ilex*, *Imperial*, *Jervis* and *Vendetta*, sailed at 1420 that day. They carried out gunnery practice and then set course westward toward Gavdos Island, hoping to be sighted by the enemy. They planned to hold that course until after nightfall before reversing course. However, *Malaya* developed a cloud in her condenser and the force had to return to Alexandria early, arriving back in harbour at 1100 on 1 August. The friendly rivalry between the two ships ensured that *Malaya*'s difficulties did not pass unnoticed, the Royal Sovereigns themselves having been the butt of sarcastic comments about her 'sensitive innards'!

Her own problems could no longer be ignored, however, and the arrival of *Barham* and *Valiant* enabled Admiral Cunningham to dispense with her at last. She was to return to Britain for a full refit, but first she had to be patched up sufficiently to make that long voyage. *Royal Sovereign* finally sailed from Alexandria at 1515 on 11 August *en route* on the first leg of that journey. She was escorted by the destroyers *Dainty*, *Decoy* and *Defender*. She reached Port Said at 0800 on the 12th and passed through the Suez Canal southward, entering the Red Sea at 2226 on the 12th. The whole force then sailed at very slow speed down the Red Sea as far as Aden, which they reached at 1731 on the 16th, securing at No. 6 berth at 1731 that evening with every one of her boilers out of action.

She was in a bad way and unable to move on. The resources of Aden were patently insufficient to do more than patch her up and pass her along. On the 19th the C-in-C of the East Indies Station signalled the Admiralty that her sailing had been delayed because of the condition of her boilers and makeshift repairs were being carried out. Another signal followed on 23

August, when it was reported that she would arrive at Durban with only 15½ per cent fuel, and would therefore need to oil at Durban before proceeding to Capetown, It was intended to sail her from Aden when twelve boilers were ready for all-round steaming. Repairs to her boilers continued until the 28th of that month. She lay isolated in the blistering heat of midsummer in Arabia while the fitters sweated and perspired below decks, the plates of which grew too hot to walk on.

Aden is remembered with little fondness by Leading Seaman Crouch:

> What a dump that was, and while there I experienced my one and only sandstorm. This happened one evening when a liner returning with troops and wounded who were being landed after being kicked out of Italian Somaliland. As they were being disembarked at two different jetties a communications rating was required on each one to let the other know if and when more boatloads could be accepted.
>
> I was one of those 'volunteered' to go ashore on this duty. So, with my battery-operated Aldis signalling lamp, I was dumped ashore early in the evening. For some time things were more or less going smoothly but about eight or nine o'clock the wind suddenly got up and the sand began to fly. Although we were out at the end of the jetty we might just as well have been hundreds of miles inland. Things rapidly went from bad to worse, the wind rising almost to gale force and the sand with it. It was only when communications between the liner and the jetty became impossible that the operation was abandoned. We remained at Aden for several days, most of which was spent trying to remove the sand from very nook and cranny of the ship. It seemed to penetrate below decks via companionways, ventilating shafts and such.

Finally the temporary repairs to her tubes were sufficient to enable her to put to sea again, and she sailed from Aden at 1500 on the 29th. The plan was for a complete re-tubing to be carried out at Durban itself. Again she could only crawl along as she proceeded down the eastern coast of Africa through the Indian Ocean. Day after day followed as she painfully dragged herself southward. The more philosophical looked upon it as a cruise in the sun, and tried hard to recall the conditions off Halifax the year before.

Lawrence Dixon:

After leaving Aden we could only crawl down the African coast at about three knots. The port 6-inch battery casements were full of stokers who had passed out from the heat further below. The conditions were terrible for them really; we had warm drinking water from little tanks on the messdecks. The ventilation was very bad as all watertight doors had to be kept closed.

Signalman Crouch:

While passing down the Indian Ocean to Durban the 'Crossing the Line' ceremony was performed (with Father Neptune and his retinue coming aboard). But there was also a sad moment during this part of our voyaging when we had a burial at sea. It was the result of an accident below decks, and a seaman died of his injuries. The captain announced over our ship's Tannoy that, although the deceased man was unknown to most of the ship's company, he hoped that as many as possible would attend the service on the quarterdeck. He stipulated that the 'rig of the day' would not be required for any rating attending the service. So you can imagine the scene of the battleship's quarterdeck, ninety-five per cent of the crew of some six hundred or so gathered to pay their respects to a man most had never met. I think that, with a few exceptions, the only people in full uniform were the burial party, the band and of course the firing party. And, if I remember correctly, even the main engines were stopped during the ceremony, which lent an eerie atmosphere to the situation. Unfortunately I was on watch on the flag deck at the time so didn't get the chance to take any photographs of this unique occasion.

By 31 August she was in position 13° 16′ North, 52° 15′ East. By 2000 the next day she was in position 10° North, 54° East. She did not finally arrive at Durban until 1402 on 15 September. Here she entered the Graving Dock at 1540, and was secured at 1630. From the 16th to the 30th she lay here refitting. S.E. Crouch:

> We were put straight into dry dock and remained there for a long period. I've seen many small ships in dry dock, but to see a 30,000-ton battleship high and dry is something special. The hospitality of the citizens of Durban was, to say the least, magnificent, and it wasn't long before most of the crew were taken into someone's home and treated like one of the family.

Lawrence Dixon:

> When we arrived at Durban, the Bluff and the surrounding land were crowded with people to welcome us in. We were the first battleship to visit the place for twenty years. We went straight into the Graving Dock and convicts began the job of scraping the side and bottom of the ship once we had settled on the chocks.
>
> I had often heard my shipmates using the phrase 'Strangle the Baron' when I first joined *Royal Sovereign*. It actually means a person or a family who 'adopted' a matelot or two and took them home for a dinner party or a weekend break. Obviously they were talking about their time in Canada earlier, so on the way down to Durban there were high hopes that we might get the same treatment in South Africa. Indeed we did! In fact, as soon as the men went ashore they were almost mobbed by the South African people. When you got invited to somebody's place it was called 'Up Homers'. Us boy seamen were only allowed our usual three days per fortnight leave but some families from 'Up Country' requested that some young sailors spend five days with them. They were a little community of white people living near Verulam Canelands. Three of us went to a family called Baker at a sugar plantation there and we

lived like lords. We were at Durban for six weeks only, but even in that short space of time some of the crew found themselves wives. Still, how long does it take!

Similar happy memories were related by Marine Moore:

We were invited out to weekends on outlying farms by the 'Barons and Baronesses', and a good time was had by all. I was lucky in that I made friends with a family by the name of Bates and another by the name of James. Both families lived in Pinetown near Durban.

When the job was eventually completed, the *Royal Sovereign* sailed to complete the next leg of her journey home, calling at Cape Town, then Freetown and finally reaching Gibraltar, where she was again docked. E.C. Moore states that:

At Freetown in West Africa (the 'White Man's Grave') we experienced ulcerated legs through mosquito bites. The native 'bum boats' used to come alongside, and natives would dive for pennies from the dugout canoes and also sell their wares. One of these boatmen had apparently served in the US Navy at one time, and used to cause laughter by imitating Bosun Calls and calling 'Away Boat's Crew' until the fire hose was turned on him and he gave it up.

When we arrived at Gibraltar we were greeted by an air raid warning at 1150 hours. We all closed up to defence stations, only to be told not to worry, as it was only 'Persistent Percy'. This was the name given to an Italian reconnaissance plane that daily flew over at noon and never ever dropped any bombs.

Another of the 'R's had close acquaintance with Freetown, West Africa, but her memories were hardly likely to have been such carefree ones. When the French surrendered in June 1940 and the collaborationist Vichy regime took over, Charles de Gaulle had raised the flag of the Free French in London. However, he was by no means a popular man in France, nor did the French exactly flock to join him. In fact the majority were glad the war was over, and most supported the Vichy leadership, resenting any attempt to lure them back into the fighting. De Gaulle had an exaggerated idea of his own influence and importance, and expected many of the former French colonies to join his cause. In fact hardly any did, and the West Indies, French Indo-China and the North African territories of Morocco, Algeria and Tunisia spurned him and were steadfast to those of Pétain's, Laval's and Darlan's ilk.

Despite this cold shoulder, de Gaulle managed to convince some of the more important Whitehall Warriors that he only had to appear with a show of force at Dakar, in Senegal, and the populace and armed forces there would rally to him with either no or only token resistance. He could then spread his Free French base across central Africa. The idea was attractive, especially as no serious resistance was expected. Unfortunately de Gaulle was completely wrong and none of the French in Senegal wanted anything to do with him. More than that, they were prepared to shed their blood, and anybody else's, to ensure Vichy remained in charge here as elsewhere. The scene was set for tragedy, and Operation Menace duly supplied it, along with a high degree of farce.

The Free French had almost no ships and no warships, indeed had few military resources of their own, and so the British had to find a task force to both transport Gaullist warriors thither and support them with the minimum force required should it come to a showdown. Daily expecting invasion from across the Channel, friendless in the world and with the Axis at its peak of power and influence, Britain had little that could be spared, but by taking ships from Force 'H', from the Indian Ocean and from the Home Fleet, quite an impressive force was eventually assembled. It consisted of the battleships *Barham* and *Resolution*, the aircraft carrier *Ark Royal*, the 8-inch cruisers *Australia*, *Cumberland* and *Devonshire* and the destroyers *Eclipse, Echo, Escapade, Faulknor, Foresight, Forester, Fortune, Fury, Greyhound* and *Inglefield*, plus five sloops, three of them French, and lesser vessels. There were twelve troop transports carrying the British and Free French troops, but as these never even got ashore they need not concern us here.

The *Resolution* had sailed from Gibraltar with the rest of the Force 'H' part of the fleet (*Ark Royal* and the 8th Destroyer Flotilla), on 6 September 1940 along with *Barham* and her four destroyers. They rendezvoused with the troop convoy during the afternoon of the 13th, and the whole force, under the command of Admiral J.D. Cunningham, sailed down to Freetown, where final preparations were put in hand for the invasion. The destroyer *Eclipse* had to fall out due to problems with her engines, but the 6-inch cruiser *Dragon* joined the force there. It was thus not until 0500 on the morning of 23 September that the force arrived off Dakar harbour to issue its ultimatum. The British battle fleet was steering an easterly course at a steady 15 knots at this time, eleven miles further out to sea, but by 0515 they had moved to a covering position about 30,000 yards offshore from Dakar, ready to lend a hand should de Gaulle's 'stroll ashore invasion' hit any snags. In fact it did nothing else but!

The French had powerful shore batteries protecting the naval base of Dakar, dominated by the two 9.4-inch guns at Cape Manuel and two others mounted on the island of Goree, along with four 5.4-inch and two 3.5-inch guns at the same place. Two more 9.4-inch guns protected the northern side of the harbour at Bel-Air Point, while to the south there were four 5.4-inch guns on the island of La Madeleine, four 6-inch guns at Yof and two 3.7-inch guns around the bay at Rufisque.

This was bad enough, but added to these land defences was quite a considerable naval force. There was the brand-new battleship *Richelieu*, for example, with eight 15-inch guns as her main armament but with only one quadruple turret operational. Newly arrived were two 6-inch cruisers *Georges Leygues* and *Montcalm*, four destroyers *Hardi*, *L'Audacieux*, *Le Fantasque* and *Le Malin* and three submarines *Ajax*, *Bévéziers* and *Persée*. The Vichy forces also had far the best of it in the air, opposing the twenty-one Skua dive-bombers (being asked to also operate as fighters) and thirty Fairey Swordfish torpedo-bombers (the latter being biplanes!) with twenty-two modern American-built Glenn Martin bombers and two squadrons of American-built Curtiss P-40 fighter aircraft. Thus the intended reliance of the British battleships on the Fairey Swordfish aircraft to 'spot' for their big guns was negated by the fact that the highly efficient French fighter aircraft easily drove these airborne antiques away.

Equally important to how the operation turned out was the climate. When the British battleships arrived off the port they found it shrouded by 'the dark, dripping, warm wetness of the tropical fog', and the rising of the sun failed to do anything to clear it or clarify their vision of their possible targets ashore. Visibility actually fell from three to five miles down to between two and three miles, with obvious difficulties for accurate gunnery.

We can skip the preliminary negotiations, which the Vichy rejected with total disdain. Goree Island put the matter beyond doubt by firing on the parleying Free French ship while still under the white flag and wounding some of the peace mission officers. The *Richelieu* also disdained the internationally recognised truce flag, and at 0755 began firing salvoes against the Free French sloop *Sauvignon de Brazza*.

The other Vichy batteries gradually joined in, directing their shells against the British battle fleet, and Cunningham signalled to them at 1007: 'If fire is continued on my ships, I shall regretfully be compelled to return it.' The Vichy answer was to continue firing and signal back, ordering the British to remove themselves forthwith. Cunningham therefore closed to within 4,000 yards of the forts, withholding his fire until 1104. The targets of the Cape Manuel and Goree Island batteries and the almost invisible *Richelieu* behind her breakwater in the harbour were difficult to make out in the mist and fog. The smoke from the French guns did nothing to aid visibility when the action became general.

Resolution and *Barham* fired over one hundred 15-inch shells at these targets during the first bombardment, which only lasted from 1104 to 1135, but none of these was very effective. Cunningham called off the attack so quickly as he still hoped a peaceful solution might be obtained (a somewhat naive hope at this stage of the proceedings) and because he had been instructed to use minimum force, which the wholesale engagement of two battleships and three heavy cruisers clearly was not! However the fog was probably an equally important factor, as no targets could be made out for more than a few minutes at a time and the British supply of 15-inch shell was not infinite.

Be that as it may, the *Resolution* and her companions altered course away 40 degrees to the southward, and the first day's action for them was terminated. The Vichy submarine *Persée* was hit by a shell from *Barham* and finished off by depth charges, and the British *Cumberland*, *Foresight* and *Inglefield* were damaged by shellfire, the first one seriously.

This premature withdrawal was naturally hailed as a great victory ashore, and Vichy morale and confidence soared even higher, while British distaste and half-heartedness was increased proportionally. Later in the day the French warships took advantage of the fog to sortie out against the troop transports. The destroyer *L'Audacieux* was sighted by the *Australia* and the destroyers *Fury* and *Greyhound*, who dealt with her very efficiently. Eight-inch salvoes from the *Australia* at 4,000 yards' range reduced the French destroyer to a blazing wreck, blowing her bridge away and killing eighty-one of her crew. The destroyer, now just a burning hulk, drifted ashore next day and was later salvaged. But the two Vichy cruisers, accompanied by *Le Malin*, broke out cleanly. Undetected, they came dangerously close to the Free French convoy before returning to harbour without sighting anything. This was the one occasion when the mist worked in the Allies' favour, but it had been a close shave.

The bombardment was resumed again on the 24th; the two battleships and the two remaining heavy cruisers closed the coast again by 0700, and once more found fog, though far less dense than the day before. However, it was still thick enough to prevent any of the target forts being seen from the ships at 0725, and the intended long-range bombardment planned by Cunningham had to be abandoned. It had been hoped that by firing at the maximum range for the 15-inch guns of the two battleships (about 23,400 yards) at 20 degrees maximum elevation) the heaviest of the Vichy shore guns (the 9.4s) would have been unable to reply effectively and so could have been slowly eradicated by methodical bombardment. This still left the French battleship, however, and, being a modern ship with 35-degree elevation for her 15-inch turret, she could therefore always outrange the two British veterans quite comfortably by at least 10,000 yards.

The destroyer *Hardi* steamed up and down adding her own smoke screen to the natural murk as well, and neither of the British battleships was fitted with radar control for their guns at this stage of the war.

Resolution was again assigned the fort at Cape Manuel as her principal target, while sharing the *Richelieu* with *Barham* when required.

The most dangerous Vichy response came from their two remaining submarines, which made determined attempts to torpedo the battleships. The first one, *Ajax*, was fortunately detected by the destroyer *Fortune*, which forced her to the surface with accurate depth-charging and duly sank her after her crew had abandoned her.

At 0935 the Vichy batteries opened a hot fire on the British squadron, and one minute later *Resolution* and her colleagues replied in kind, taking as their initial target the *Richelieu*, which they engaged at ranges varying from 13,500 to 15,000 yards. Again both British battleships fired off about fifty rounds apiece from the main armaments without scoring a single hit on the French giant or any of the fifty-four merchant ships crowded in the harbour. The *Resolution* then shifted target to engage the guns at Cape Manuel. It proved just as elusive, and many of the 15-inch shells overshot the fort to land in the town itself, but this was unintentional.

Matters were made worse aboard *Resolution* when, at 0945, her director training gear broke down for a time. Her own spotter aircraft had been damaged earlier on, and the substitute had not worked with the ship before, and so experienced difficulty in communicating with her. Frustration followed frustration, and again a heavy expenditure of shell only achieved one near-miss on the *Richelieu*, which sent a shell splinter through her hull above the water line. Then, at 1155, Cunningham again signalled the cease-fire, and the British ships withdrew to think things over.

A resumption of the bombardment was decided upon after some discussion, and at 1300 the heavy ships began moving back to the coast. Fire was reopened at 1305, with *Resolution*

The battleship HMS *Royal Sovereign* in her prime as one of the newest and most powerful battleships anywhere in the world. She is seen with the Grand Fleet in 1918. Notice the individual elevations of each gun in 'B' turret, the numerous searchlight platforms emplaced as a lesson of the night fighting at Jutland eighteen months earlier and splinter padding around the exposed upper platforms of the bridge structure. (*Royal Marines Museum, Eastney*)

A good wartime view of HMS *Royal Sovereign* while serving with the Grand Fleet soon after her original construction. She is shown wearing her full dazzle paint scheme designed to confuse enemy range finders and with baffles on her mainmast for the same purpose. Both after 'X' and 'Y' turrets are trained in their fully forward positions. If the guns had been fired in this position the blast damage to her upperworks would have been extensive. (*Royal Marines Museum, Eastney*)

HMS *Royal Sovereign* in floating dock at Invergordon in 1918. The underwater ram bow can clearly be seen in this unique view, along with the aircraft-launching platform atop 'B' turret and other late wartime modifications. (*Royal Marines Museum, Eastney*)

The breech of the left-hand 15-inch gun of 'X' turret aboard HMS *Royal Sovereign* in 1919.
(*Royal Marines Museum, Eastney*)

One of the 6-inch Mk XII guns of the port battery of HMS *Royal Sovereign*'s casemates in 1919. (*Royal Marines Museum, Eastney*)

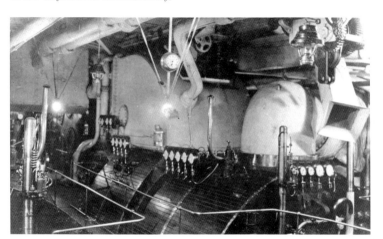

The engine room of the battleship HMS *Royal Sovereign* in 1919.
(*Royal Marines Museum, Eastney*)

View of the wardroom of HMS *Royal Sovereign* showing billiard and card tables and an armchair in front of the burnished stove. (*Royal Marines Museum, Eastney*)

HMS *Royal Sovereign* passes HMS *Victory* in Portsmouth Harbour in 1922 as the battleship leaves the dockyard where she was original built. (*Geoffrey P. Jones*)

The Jubilee Review of 1935, with HMS *Royal Sovereign* really living up to her nickname, 'Tiddley Quid', resplendent in her Mediterranean livery at the head of the line. Notice the anti-torpedo bulge, the top of which can just be made out at the ship's waterline. They were added in some ships, built in to others. They proved ineffective when the torpedoes exploded beneath the ship's keel (as in the case of the *Royal Oak*) but helped save the *Resolution* off Dakar a year later. (*The News, Portsmouth*)

The Battle Honours Board of HMS *Royal Sovereign* in 1940. (*Bill Heffernan*)

The tompion of one of the HMS *Royal Sovereign*'s 15-inch guns, featuring the ships crest, which was exactly the same as that carried by the nuclear submarine HMS *Sovereign* forty years later. (*Bill Heffernan*)

HMS *Royal Sovereign*'s Ship's Bell in 1940. (*Bill Heffernan*)

The forbidding bulk of HMS *Royal Sovereign* seen from Southsea as she glides towards the entrance to Portsmouth harbour, circa 1937. (*The News, Portsmouth*)

HMS *Royal Sovereign* dressed overall for the Coronation Review of 1937. (*F. W. Hawks*)

A squad of His Majesty's 'Jollies' musters on the quarterdeck of HMS *Royal Sovereign* in Scapa Flow in late 1939. A Royal Marine detachment was sent up from Chatham to bring her 'Bootneck' complement up to strength. (*C. L. Price*)

'Taking it Green', the North Atlantic Ocean comes in over the fo'c'sle during the spring of 1940. On one of HMS *Royal Sovereign*'s many convoy escort voyages 'A' turret is trained as far to starboard and astern as it can be to mitigate the worst effects of the weather. (*C. L. Price*)

HMS *Royal Sovereign* snowed-under at Halifax, Nova Scotia, their main base for escorting the HX convoys eastward during the early months of 1940. (*C. E. Moore*)

'Just like a Christmas Cake.' The effects of sub-zero temperatures on one of the twin 4-inch HA mountings aboard HMS *Royal Sovereign* in 1940. Such conditions could not only render weapons inoperational but added tons of top-weight to a ship, sometimes critically affecting her stability. As the war went on, counter-measures such as steam hoses, were brought into use more and more to combat such conditions, especially in the Arctic regions. Note that the seaman has no special 'warm' clothing – apart from the balaclava-helmet under his normal cap. (*C. E. Moore*)

Ice and snow amidships during the hard winter of 1940 in the North Atlantic. (*C. E. Moore*)

Looking astern aboard HMS *Royal Sovereign*, with both after turrets trained to starboard, North Atlantic 1940. No German raider, be she battle-cruiser, pocket battleship or armed merchant raider, ever dared to tangle with any British convoy with a set of these big guns in their midst. The British battleship was an effective deterrent. (*Bill Heffernan*)

The 1st Battle Squadron at sea in the Eastern Mediterranean in June 1940. In the distance is HMS *Warspite*, the fleet flagship, followed by HMS *Royal Sovereign* and then HMS *Malaya*. Photo taken from the aircraft-carrier HMS *Eagle*.
(*E. B. Mackenzie*)

Alexandria, Egypt. HMS *Royal Sovereign* joins the main Mediterranean Fleet under Admiral Andrew Cunningham. Gleaming and freshly re-painted, she now sports a funnel cap to help obviate smoke problems on her bridge. (*S. E. Crouch*)

Faithful companions; the carrier HMS *Eagle* seen astern of HMS *Royal Sovereign*. 'Tiddley Quid' was *Eagle*'s constant shadow as they swept the Eastern Mediterranean seaways in 1940. She often got soaked by the 'overs' from sticks of bombs aimed at the carrier, which always missed and landed instead close to her companion. (*C. E. Moore*)

'A Close Shave'. This 1,000-lb bomb was a bit too close for comfort and gave them a good shaking up. Of the 500 or so bombs aimed at the Mediterranean Fleet on this trip, only one hit any ship of the force, and she, the light cruiser HMS *Gloucester*, was still able to maintain her place in the line. Nobody aboard HMS *Royal Sovereign* was ever so much as scratched by any of this sustained bombing. (*S. E. Crouch*)

A stick of bombs falls astern of HMS *Royal Sovereign* and well clear of HMS *Eagle*. (*S. E. Crouch*)

The 'Tiddley Quid' loosens off a broadside from her eight 15-inch guns. Note the concussion from all guns firing abeam sends shock waves across the sea and kicks the 32,000-ton warship to port. (*C. E. Moore*)

Bombs, bombs and bombs. Another stick of Italian nastiness makes large holes in the Mediterranean Sea in July 1940.
(*S. E. Crouch*)

A forest of bombs. Several aeronautical salvoes are laid in an elongated 'stick' across the battle-fleet but, as seen here from the deck of HMS *Royal Sovereign*, HMS *Malaya* comes steadily through unharmed. (*Lawrence Dixon*)

Seen again from HMS *Eagle*, HMS *Royal Sovereign* turns away sharply to avoid yet another salvo of heavy bombs. July 1940. (*E. B. Mackenzie*)

'Crossing the Line'. On the long, slow voyage south from Aden to Durban in late 1940 to repair her worn-out engines, the wallowing battleship barely made movement through the scorching waters of the Indian Ocean. The traditional ducking ceremony must have been extremely welcome to all novice matelots.
(*S. E. Crouch*)

Father Neptune's 'Barbers' go about their deadly work while the Captain and his officers look from a safe distance. Indian Ocean 1940.
(*S. E. Crouch*)

Heading north up the West African coast with another convoy. A temporary swimming pool is erected in the lee of 'A' turret while 'Bunts' airs his signal flags on the guardrails.
(*S. E. Crouch*)

Taking the air off South Africa, a party poses in the lee of one of the 4-inch HA guns. Note the Carley floats stacked around the ship's upperworks. Warships were grossly overcrowded during the war and only a small percentage of their numbers could hope to survive sinking. (*Bill Heffernan*)

The seas get rougher again, and, while heading north for Halifax once more, two of the ship's gangways are carried away in storms. (*Bill Heffernan*)

taking on the Goree Island battery at a range of 16,000 yards this time. Return fire from the Vichy gunners was accurate and hot, *Resolution* herself being straddled by 5.4-inch shells more than once without being struck, but *Barham* was hit four times, fortunately without serious effect. Still, another 400 15-inch shells had been fired off in the general direction of Africa without denting Vichy resolve one iota. By 1326 the battleships again steamed dismally away, leaving the Vichy defenders to celebrate another fine little victory.

After more talks between de Gaulle and the British commanders, yet another attempt was decided upon for 25 September, and this time the omens looked good, for the weather was bright and clear with maximum visibility. Now at last *Resolution* gunners could do themselves justice and repeat their Mers-el-Kebir accuracy. By 0600, therefore, the heavy ships were once more steaming towards the coast to take up their bombarding positions. *Resolution* had again been allocated the Goree Island battery as her target. Even before the British ships had come round to their bombardment course the French battleship was dropping 15-inch shells close by from a range of 23,000 yards.

At 0901 the signal was made for a 70-degree turn together, and as *Resolution* began to comply with this, the Vichy submarine *Bévéziers*, which had been stalking them undetected by the British destroyer escorts, struck hard. She fired a full salvo of four torpedoes at a range of 2,700 yards. Two of these passed right under the *Resolution*, A third was not seen, but the fourth almost proved fatal.

It was a direct hit, the torpedo striking home on her port side amidships while she was still turning under full helm at nineteen knots. The detonation sent up a huge column of water. This blow caused severe flooding immediately in her port boiler rooms, and she instantly took on a 12½ degree list. This rendered her main armament inoperational, as the turrets jammed up and would not train. This list was slowly reduced by transferring oil fuel to her starboard tanks. The port 6-inch battery was damaged by the sheer weight of water that came inboard with the explosion.

Small electrical fires broke out in several adjoining compartments, which were soon extinguished. However, leaking oil fuel in a forward boiler room which ignited caused a much more serious fire, which was not discovered until an hour after the torpedo had hit her. As this boiler room flooded, this fire extinguished itself. The resulting loss of power reduced her speed to a mere 12 knots under cover of a smokesreen. The Vichy submarine got clean away after this audacious attack. It was a bitter blow, and there was no question of *Resolution*'s resuming the action – the damage was too great.

In fact this one torpedo hit decided the fate of Dakar and the whole of Operation Menace, for soon afterwards the decision to abandon the whole farcical enterprise was taken, and the British decided to cut their losses and leave French West Africa to stew in its own juice. Many at the time blamed the normally accepted dictum that ships could never take on forts on equal terms, but this was a hasty conclusion, which did not take account of the special weather conditions that met the British battleships at Dakar. None the less, the failure was complete and humiliating, and a valuable convoy escort battleship was put out of the war for a whole year because of it.

Meanwhile, aboard the *Resolution* such considerations were academic; self-preservation was all that counted. Damage-control parties were fighting to save their ship. After four and a half hours the main machinery forced lubrication failed and the ship was immobilised. Dedicated work had only managed to reduce her list to 11 degrees during the night of the 26th/27th, but some of the fires were still raging below. Fire fighting in the sticky tropical heat in an old ship not equipped with proper ventilation was a horror story in itself, but gradually compartments were sealed off and quenched. There still remained the fact that she was badly crippled and a sitting duck for any further French, German or Italian submarine that might be lured to the scene by such a tempting target.

Next day, at 0945, the *Barham* passed a tow into the *Resolution*, and in this undignified manner she returned at an agonising six knots to Freetown, with her upper decks only a few feet above the waterline. Fortunately the weather held and so did her bulkheads below. They eventually struggled into harbour at 0600 on 29 September, by which time the primitive fresh-water supply of the old battleship was at its last gasp. This was to prove another portent for their future deployment further east in later years.

Divers went down and found a hole in her side big enough to drive a double-decker bus through. Her double bottom had been destroyed over a thirty-foot length, and her anti-torpedo bulge had been wrecked along a fifty-foot area. She was eventually patched up temporarily and sailed for a proper docking at Gibraltar.

It was not until February 1941 that *Resolution* finally returned home to the UK for more repairs. At this time it was proposed that advantage be taken to fit her with extra deck armour and an improved anti-torpedo bulge, but this idea was finally rejected by the Board. Similar plans to increase the elevation of the main armament to 30 degrees for 'A' and 'B' turrets only were, strangely, not carried out, either. However, later it was decided to fit her with extra 2-inch deck armour over her main magazines only. In addition two of her forward 6-inch guns were to be removed to increase stability and seaworthiness. It was decided to combine this with a full refit, and accordingly she sailed for the US Navy Yard at Philadelphia. Not for a further five months did *Resolution* resume her part in the Navy's war, by which time much had happened.

On arrival at the Rock in November, the Royal Sovereigns found Admiral Somerville and Force 'H' in the middle of a whole series of operations that involved the passing of convoys and reinforcements right through the Mediterranean and to Malta, Operation Collar.

Admiral Cunningham's fleet had just carried out the successful Taranto and Straits of Otranto attacks, but the Italians still had three battleships left fit for service, and most of their cruiser strength was intact. Somerville had for the only capital ship on his strength the battle-cruiser *Renown* with which to face them. The *Ramillies* would be coming west from Malta to join Force 'H' for the voyage home, but until they could concentrate each force was vulnerable to interception by a superior Italian squadron. Somerville was reputedly an 'air minded' admiral, and he had the *Ark Royal* in company, but even he recognised the value of having as many extra 15-inch guns on his side as possible, and he signalled home to the Admiralty asking if *Royal Sovereign* could be added to his force. The Admiralty agreed that, 'if he considered it necessary', she could be.

Unfortunately her docking prevented this, and so the resulting Battle of Spartivento was fought by her sister and the *Renown* without 'Tiddly Quid' being able to add her weight of metal. It was a rerun of Calabria, with *Renown* chasing the Italians on her own like *Warspite* had, and *Ramillies* straining along as long-stop and trying to get in on the act with some hopeful long-range salvoes. The crew of *Royal Sovereign* turned out on her upper deck to cheer the victorious squadron back to port, while the Royal Marine band played 'Run, Rabbit, Run'.

Prior to putting the operation in train, Admiral Somerville had informed the Admiralty that:

> I consider the inclusion of *Royal Sovereign* (undergoing repairs in Gibraltar) in my force was desirable in view of a possible Italian concentration in the Western Mediterranean that I estimated could reach a total of three battleships, five to seven 8-inch cruisers; several 6-inch cruisers and other light forces.
>
> The Admiralty reply indicated that some doubt was entertained concerning the necessity for this reinforcement, but approval was eventually given for the inclusion of *Royal Sovereign* in Force 'B' if I considered this essential.
>
> The Commander-in-Chief, Mediterranean, was frankly sceptical and considered I was unduly pessimistic. In his opinion, the probability of an Italian concentration in the Western Mediterranean was more remote now than at any time since Operation Hats (30 August to 5 September).
>
> Since the defects in *Royal Sovereign* could not be completed in time she was unable to take part in the operation.

During Operation Collar, HMS *Ramillies*, the 8-inch cruiser *Berwick*, the 6-inch cruiser *Newcastle*, the anti-aircraft cruiser *Coventry* and their escorting destroyers *Defender*, *Greyhound*, *Griffin* and *Hereward*, were known as Force 'D'. They were to rendezvous with Somerville's ships at approximate noon on 27 November, at a point south of Sardinia in the western basin. When all the various British groups had assembled they were to proceed in company to a position west of Skerki Bank, which they hoped to reach at dusk, in order to present the strongest possible force to deter the Italian Navy from attacking the merchant convoy. After nightfall the *Coventry* and the five Force 'D' destroyers were to return to Cunningham's half of the Mediterranean, with the convoy proceeding through the Narrows to join him next day. Meanwhile *Ramillies*, *Berwick* and *Newcastle* were to return to Gibraltar with Force 'H' on their way back to the UK to refIt The condenser trouble of the battleship had been temporarily cured, but she needed a proper refit, the *Berwick* was not capable of more than 27 knots according to her captain, owing to the removal of some rows of turbine blades and to the higher water temperature in the Mediterranean affecting her vacuum, while *Newcastle*'s boilers had developed defects and could not be considered entirely reliable.

Such was the plan. But, contrary to all expectations at the Admiralty and by Cunningham, the Italian Fleet did manage to sail two of its battleships with accompanying light forces and interposed themselves south of Sardinia in readiness to attack. Most of Admiral Somerville's dire warnings thus came to pass, and it gave *Ramillies* a fleeting chance to take up the challenge that *Royal Sovereign* had been presented with at Calabria three months earlier.

The *Ramillies* and her companions sailed from Alexandria on 24 November and proceeded toward the central Mediterranean in company with Force 'C', the battleships *Barham* and *Malaya*, carrier *Eagle* and destroyers, with the main fleet (Force 'A') under Cunningham (battleships *Warspite* and *Valiant*, carrier *Illustrious*, the 6-inch cruisers *Ajax*, *Orion* and *Sydney* with more destroyers) the next day. At the same time a convoy sailed for Malta covered by the 8-inch cruiser *York* and 6-inch cruisers *Gloucester* and *Glasgow*. The secrecy of the whole operation was jeopardised as early as the 25th, when an Italian aircraft overflew Force 'D' and made a sighting report. The Italians had in place the submarines *Dessie* and *Tembien* south of Malta to intercept, but they failed to sight the *Ramillies* group. The 10th Italian Destroyer Squadron (comprising the *Alcione*, *Sagittario*, *Sirio* and *Vega*) was also at sea in the Narrows on the night of the 26th/27th and they did sight the British squadron at 0033 on the 27th. However, only one of these ships contented itself with firing a hasty salvo of torpedoes at extreme range before prudently withdrawing, and none of these missiles passed anywhere near the British ships.

However, the enemy now knew approximately where *Ramillies* and her escorts were, for the *Sirio* had signalled back to her base at Trapani at 0055 that she had attacked 'seven un-identified units'. It was not until seven hours later that the *Sirio*'s captain bothered to amplify this report. Then, at 0840, he signalled a longer report, again vague in detail. The Italian high command in Rome had to wait until 1000 before this worthy finally gave the information that his targets might well have included a *Piuttosto Grandi* (a battleship). This report, when it finally reached the Italian commander at sea (the same Admiral Campioni who had led them at Calabria) was to have the im-mediate effect of tempering his hitherto bold policy, and from then on chances of a decisive engagement were largely lost, as the Italians decided to return to harbour.

The *Ramillies* group was not further molested, however, even though four further Italian submarines, *Alagi*, *Aradam*, *Axum* and *Diaspro*, were in waiting positions south of Sardinia.

Early on 21 November came the crucial point of the convoy, where the rendezvous of the various forces was to be made and the convoy would be at its most vulnerable point, approaching the Narrows from the west, when the heavy ships of Somerville would have to turn back and those of Cunningham would still be beyond intervention range to the south of Malta. *Ramillies* and the rest of Force 'D' had passed through the Narrows under cover of darkness and were steering north-west toward the Skerki Bank. The Chief-of-Staff, Mediterranean, back at Alexandria signalled Somerville at 0330 hours that morning the news that Force 'D' *might* well have been detected by the enemy, which indicates that the *Sirio*'s signals had been intercepted.

By 0800 then Force 'D' was well on course to join *Renown*'s group, being north-east of Galita Island heading west, but still retaining radio silence, so that Somerville had no firm word of their exact whereabouts. Thus it was when, at 0852, Somerville received the first sighting report from one of *Ark Royal*'s Swordfish aircraft of the presence of the Italian fleet. Initially there was some doubt in case she was actually sighting Force

'D', and this uncertainty was not fully resolved for some time. But in case of the worst Somerville prepared his ships for action, sending his oldest ships to guard the convoy and take it away south to safety, instructing the carrier to prepare a torpedo striking force, and steering at his best speed with *Renown*, *Manchester*, *Sheffield* and *Southampton* to join forces with Force 'D' before taking on Campioni's ships.

A signal was dispatched to *Ramillies* at 1035, giving *Renown*'s position, course and speed, in order to facilitate this rendezvous without undue delay. At 1058 an RAF Sunderland from Malta gave Force 'H' the welcome news that *Ramillies* and her consorts were some thirty-four miles away on a bearing of 070 degrees and closing fast. This reassured Somerville that the meeting of the British capital ships would be effected in good time, and at the same time sighting reports were coming in of the Italian fleet thrown into confusion by the violent changes of course ordered after the presence of Force 'H' and Force 'D' had reached them. Somerville's dispatch on the battle read:

> An observer witnessing this alteration of course reported that the Eastern group of cruisers appeared to be thrown into a state of confusion. The leading ship turned 180 degrees while the two following ships turned only 90 degrees. Collisions appeared to have been narrowly averted, and at one point all three ships appeared to be stopped with their bows nearly touching each other.

From a westerly course indicated from the initial sightings, by 1115 the Italian fleet was in full retreat eastwards. The convoy was now safe, but Somerville decided to continue his deployment, close the enemy in an attempt to cut them off and force a battle if he could catch them, and thus make certain that there would be no possible future threat to his charges. The British deployment therefore continued with a view to battle, the Italian deployment to retreat.

At 1128 the welcome sight of the *Ramillies* was seen from the fighting-top of the *Renown*, bearing 073 degrees at a distance of twenty-four miles. As the first Swordfish striking force passed overhead on its way to try and slow down the flying enemy,

Somerville signalled *Ramillies* to steer 045 degrees, to 'cut the corner' and not to lose ground on the faster *Renown* (which, being a battle-cruiser, was making a good 28 knots, with some in reserve, as against *Ramillies*'s best of 20.7 knots.

By 1140 the five British cruisers were forming a line ahead of the *Renown*, with the five destroyers of the 8th Flotilla (*Faulknor*, *Firedrake*, *Forester*, *Fury* and *Encounter*) being joined by four from Force 'D' (*Defender*, *Greyhound*, *Griffin* and *Hereward*) to form a striking force two miles astern of the cruisers. They eventually took up a position five miles and 040 degrees from *Renown*, ready to counter-attack any attempt by the Italian destroyers against the two British capital ships, but such an attack seemed to be the last thing on their opponents' minds.

The gallant old *Ramillies* was now straining every fibre and pushing her ancient boilers to unheard-of limits to keep up with the *Renown* and present a common face to the enemy, and turning onto a parallel course some ten miles fine of Somerville's flagship's starboard bow. An eyewitness desribed how her 15-inch guns were at full elevation and her battle ensign was flying stiff as a poker in the breeze as she pounded her way north towards the distant smoke that marked her reluctant foe.

The enemy was passing rapidly from left to right on the distant horizon, and it was clear that they were intent on escape. Flak bursts peppered the sky as the Swordfish went in, but hopes that they might score hits and slow the Italians down a bit were to be dashed, for their only success was against one destroyer. The Italian ships commenced the engagement by opening fire at 1220 against the *Manchester* in the van, and four minutes later *Renown* replied at the extreme range of 26,500 yards with her six 15-inch guns. Two minutes later *Ramillies* tried her hand, loosing off two salvoes at the maximum elevation of her main armament to test the range. Her salvoes fell short, and thereafter she continued to drop back out of the action, following in the wake of the *Renown* to give support if required. Their only hope now was that the Italians would be crippled or accept battle. Neither was to be realised, and when a second torpedo-bomber striking force was as unsuccessful as the first the action was clearly to be another unfruitful one.

None the less, the *Ramillies* was still full of the will to win and kept up her futile pursuit of the now invisible enemy. Even *Renown* could not catch the Italians now, a fact recognised by Somerville at about 1320. He wrote:

> There was no sign that any of the enemy ships and especially his battleships had suffered damage, nor was there reasonable prospect of inflicting damage by gunfire in view of their superior speed. Unless the speed of the enemy battleships was reduced very materially he could enter Cagliari before I could bring him to action with *Renown* and *Ramillies*.

For this decision he was to be cruelly treated by Winston Churchill, but there is no doubt that his decision was here the correct one. And so *Ramillies* had the same frustrating experience as *Royal Sovereign*. However, her eagerness to engage the enemy, no matter what the odds, reflected the same indomitable spirit as that of her sister. She was cheered to the echo by the *Royal Sovereign*'s crew when she finally reached Gibraltar with the rest of the squadron.

While the *Royal Sovereign* and *Ramillies* had been kept fully occupied outfacing the Italian Navy in the Mediterranean, one of their sisters was doing equally excellent work against the other Axis partner. HMS *Revenge* (Captain E.R. Archer) had been based at Portsmouth during the summer and autumn of 1940 as the Channel Guard battleship. This duty involved frequent excursions out into the North Atlantic to meet incoming convoys on the Halifax route, in fact covering the opposite end of the same vital route that *Royal Sovereign* had been policing earlier in the year. With the fall of France her position now became very much in the front line of things, with the enemy less than thirty miles away across a now totally hostile English Channel. Frequent attempts were made by the *Luftwaffe* during the Battle of Britain to immobilise this powerful threat to their invasion plans, but she was never hit in any of the bombing raids directed against Portsmouth harbour. A particularly heavy dive-bombing attack was directed at the naval base on 24 August, but, although the destroyer *Acheron* was hit and badly damaged alongside the north-west wall, the *Revenge*, close by, escaped any damage whatsoever.

The assembling of the German invasion barges and tugs in the harbours of Belgium and the northern French ports caused much concern in London throughout the autumn, as the enemy's Operation Sealion was expected to take place almost nightly. British destroyer flotillas patrolled every night with cruiser support in order to intercept any invasion force, and the other way in which the Royal Navy acted aggressively was by bombardments of those ports from the sea. Initially the monitor *Erebus* was used, but she was so slow that it was decided to carry out a battleship bombardment with the *Revenge*. It was felt that a contribution from her eight 15-inch guns to the discomfiture of invasion shipping assembled at Cherbourg would cause a great deal of damage. In addition, such a weight of heavy metal might dampen the German army's enthusiasm a bit if it was driven home to them that they would have to face such missiles at sea should they ever venture forth towards the English coast. The sheer power of a 15-inch broadside was something that German Army personnel were not familiar with; the *Revenge* planned to rectify that omission from their experience without further delay.

Captain Archer himself paid tribute to his officers and men for the way they threw themselves into this period of careful planning and dedicated training. The need to work the guns' crews up to a peak of efficiency, as there had been so few real opportunities to carry out gunnery practice since the outbreak of the war, was one of the most vital tasks, and Lieutenant-Commander W.F.H.C. Rutherford, the battleship's gunnery officer, received a special pat on the back for his efforts in this respect. Captain Archer commended 'his zeal and patient training of personnel over a period of many months in bombardment procedure. If any success has attended this operation, in so far as bombardment by *Revenge* is concerned, I feel it is largely due to his effort.'

The absolute essential was, of course, pinpoint accuracy in navigation to enable the battleship to cross the target and deliver the goods correctly. The precise navigation to the firing position, which affected the optimum range and fuse setting, etc., had to take into account not only the vagaries of night navigation in coastal waters dominated by the enemy, with all the hazards such an enterprise might entail, but also the disturbing factors of tides, currents and wind, coupled with the speed of the bombarding squadron itself. In all this the contribution of another young officer was paramount; this was Lieutenant-Commander G.E. Bingham-Powell. As Captain Archer later commented, this officer 'kept to an exact programme, and maintained a very accurate reckoning under difficult circumstances in a strong tideway; more especially as this officer is only lent to *Revenge* in lieu of an officer sick in hospital, and this was the first time he had been to sea in the ship.'

Thus Operation Medium was most carefully planned. The incursion of such a large and powerful warship into the enemy's own coastal waters was an audacious concept, and one which required meticulous attention to detail. It is a measure of how the Royal Navy was eager to get a grip on the situation that the bombardment of Cherbourg proved to be a model of excellence, both in preparation and in execution. It is also, perhaps, a measure of British self-deprecation that this highly successful operation is hardly mentioned in any history of the war, whereas the many failures are dwelt on at considerable length in book after book.

HMS *Revenge* sailed from Plymouth at 0200 hours on Thursday 10 October with an escort of seven destroyers from the 5th Flotilla, led by Captain (D) Lord Louis Mountbatten, embarked aboard the *Javelin*, and with *Jackal*, *Jaguar*, *Jupiter*, *Kashmir*, *Kelvin* and *Kipling* in company. Embarked aboard three of the destroyers were representatives from the British United Press Agency, the *Manchester Guardian* and the *Daily Mirror*. A departure reference was taken from Portland, off which place they affected a rendezvous with six MGBs at 0035 on the 11th. A secondary force, comprising the light cruisers *Enterprise* and *Newcastle* from Plymouth, patrolled to the western end of the Channel.

There was an air raid in progress against Portland harbour at the time, which meant that the light on Portland Bill was out, but even so, good visibility ensured that an accurate navigation 'fix' was attained. On the way across the Channel it was seen that the RAF was repaying the *Luftwaffe*'s visit in kind, and heavy German AA fire was seen over the French coast ahead.

In order to flush out any patrolling E-boats, the MGBs were unleashed at 0230 to carry out a sweep ahead and to the west of the main force. Their instructions were to keep well clear of the *Revenge* on completion of this, and to take station well astern of her once the bombardment was completed. This was necessary for their own safety, as the 6-inch battery of the battleship and the combined 4.7-inch armaments of the destroyers would be on the alert for enemy small craft and inclined to shoot first and ask questions later! None of these craft were seen again by the British force after this until they returned to harbour. No enemy surface forces were sighted by any of the British squadrons this night.

Their dead reckoning was again checked by a further 'fix' on Cap de la Hague, which was illuminated by flare-dropping aircraft. An hour later the *Revenge* was steering a course of 096 degrees at a speed of 18 knots on a bearing selected for the commencement of the bombardment in the centre of the dock-yard area. At 0333 precisely the battleship and the destroyers all opened fire, using chart range, gyro bearings and bombardment levels. The RAF had started a fire by their attacks, but this was inaccurate and not close enough to the actual target to be of any use for the warships to spot by, and the warships therefore relied exclusively on their own calculations. The enemy initially refrained from sweeping the sea with his coastal searchlights, probably under the mistaken impression that the one-ton missiles, arriving on the target in earth-shaking salvoes of four, were bombs.

The *Revenge* was thus allowed a satisfying eighteen minutes of undisturbed practice with all four 15-inch turrets firing into the inferno at a range of 15,700 yards, spreading for line and laddering for range in accordance with the prearranged plan, which was designed to cover the whole target area. In that short time the *Revenge* pumped out 120 of her big 15-inch shells. The type of shell fired by the battleship on this operation was known as CPC (common pointed cap). Obviously it was not the type of shell normally used against enemy battleships; which required armour-piercing qualities with high penetration power. The CPC type of shell had a low penetration factor coupled with a high bursting charge, and was designed for use against lightly armoured or unarmoured targets like the German destroyers known to be in port that night, as well as the barges and tugs. It was because the *main* object was to sink these flimsy enemy barges, with the need to inflict damage on stores and personnel ashore a secondary factor, that these shells were used instead of the normal shore bombardment type of HE (high explosive) shells. In the event, the Director of Training and Staff Duties Division at the Admiralty was to note, 'The 15-inch CPC shell appear to have been satisfactory and it is impossible to estimate whether these shells were less effective than HE would have been.'

This was all highly satisfying. As Captain Archer himself was to comment:

There can be little doubt that surprise and mystification was effected, proof of this being the intensification and wild character of the AA barrage as the salvoes fell. 'Flaming onions' and multi-coloured tracers were fired in all and every direction, while the searchlights gave a display worthy of a Tattoo – the whole combining to make a veritable 'Brock's Benefit', a sight worth seeing.

The fire started by the RAF outside the target area was soon to die down, but it was replaced by a 'bigger and better' fire some distance to the westward of it as the result of the naval bombardment. This second fire was reported to be burning strongly and spreading rapidly, with dense volumes of smoke being observed and flames leaping up hundreds of feet into the air. This blaze was still clearly visible from forty miles out at sea. By the light of it several full 15-inch salvoes were observed by eye from the battleship's fighting-top to fall smack dead centre in the target area.

After the initial stunned silence, the Germans gradually came back, and realising that they were being smashed up by something more significant than Blenheims and Wellingtons, started scouring the dark sea. But not until the *Revenge* had ceased firing and was commencing her stately and satisfied withdrawal did the enemy coastal batteries start to return her fire. One of these comprised the heaviest of guns, thought to be 13.5-inch. It was sited to the east of the town, and shelled the British force for thirty minutes as they withdrew on a course of 008 degrees. Many of the German salvoes fell close to both *Revenge* and the destroyers, but there were no hits. The German guns continued to hold the range up to about 36,000 yards out, and then started to fall short. Such accuracy was indicative that the enemy was using radar-assisted guns along this coast. This led to a wry comment from the C-in-C Western Approaches at Plymouth, whose own defences against invasion were rather more Spartan and primitive than those installed in a few short weeks on the other side of the water by the victorious German army:

> It would appear that the enemy batteries employed RD/F (radio direction finding, that strange British euphemism for radar) for range-finding and, to my knowledge, this is far in advance of anything installed at present in the fixed defences of this port. Although RD/F equipment has recently been fitted for the detection of enemy aircraft, I understand that this type is not suitable for ranging with the accuracy required for gunnery purposes, and I would therefore recommend that development on these lines should be given a high order of priority.

So much for the notorious state of Britain's unpreparedness after ten months of war. Meanwhile, back at the scene of the action, Captain Archer observed:

> Avoiding action was taken, course being altered as the flashes were observed – destroyers acting independently. The speed of retirement was 21½ knots, *Revenge*, despite her years, steamed very steadily at this speed. No casualties or damage were sustained by any ship.

The *Revenge* and the 5th Flotilla arrived safely back at Spithead at 0800 that morning after a job well done. Coupled with *Royal Sovereign*'s efforts at the Battle of Calabria and *Ramillies*'s brave and bold face at the Battle of Spartivento, *Revenge*'s contribution set the seal on the general feeling that there was still lots of life in the old dogs yet.

Aboard the *Royal Sovereign* the 'buzz' was that they were now going home at long last. Lawrence Dixon:

> We never knew were we were going on leaving any harbour until our sealed orders were opened at a certain distance out to sea. We stood on deck as we left Gibraltar, hoping to turn to starboard for the Bay of Biscay and home. It was not to be. We went straight out into the Atlantic and headed for Halifax once more.

They joined the escort of convoy SC16 on 16th December, guarding it until New Year's Eve. Signalman Crouch:

> We spent Christmas Day at sea. You can imagine how we felt after enjoying the warm climate of the Med and South Atlantic to end up at a place like Halifax in the middle of winter. The only consolation was that it was a dry crispness and not the damp cold we experience in this country. Shortly after New Year's Day 1941, we started a very tedious job of convoying, which was to last for many months. Our job was the protection of slow convoys, or should I say added protection, as each convoy had an armed merchant cruiser in attendance. We spent two or three days with each convoy staying with them for almost two-thirds of the way across the North Atlantic, after which we returned to Halifax on our own.
>
> Although we had reports of submarines in our vicinity from time to time, not one ship was lost while they were in our charge. The losses used to occur when the ships got closer to the UK.

One of the few known submarine attacks made against the *Royal Sovereign* passed completely unknown to her crew. It had happened while she was passing at slow speed down the Red Sea on the night of 13/14 August. The Italian submarine *Ferraris* claimed to have attacked her with torpedoes, but none hit, indeed none was even seen! In the wide Atlantic the chances of a U-boat getting her in its sights were far more remote.

It was indeed back to the grim Atlantic Ocean for the ship's company of the *Royal Sovereign*, pounding their familiar patch of grey sea for the next six months. The weather had not forgotten them in their absence and was waiting for them on their return. Marine Moore told me:

> Living conditions at times were extremely tough. On the convoy runs in the Atlantic we would come off duty just a little short of frost-bitten. It was painful to wash and it had to be done in cold water. Condensation on the ship's hull was caused by the ship always flooding. The deck mopping-up parties were constantly having to bail out the water that always seemed to seep in and create continuous water, which slopped about underfoot all the while. Rationing was strict. It was nothing for five or six men to have to share one bucket of water.

Lawrence Dixon remembers:

> All guns and fittings used to ice up. It used to get worse, and at times you couldn't get your fingers between the guardrails. We would take a convoy halfway or more across and turn them over to the Western Approaches command. Sometimes we would have approaching almost one hundred merchantmen around us and we would be the only warship to guard them all. Sometimes our course took us up near to Greenland, where it was too rough for the U-boats to operate. We would often be delayed by the weather; sometimes it took seventeen days round trips with just three days in harbour before we were off again. I once spent nine months aboard before stepping ashore, but that was later on.

Thus it was that between 15 and 26 January 1941 they escorted Convoy HX103, between 17 and 23 February it was the turn of Convoy TC9, and then on 15/16 March Convoy HX113 felt their presence, before changing over to Convoy HX114 for 16/17 March and Convoy HX116 between 23 and 31 March. The next month was much the same: they protected Convoy HX120 and Convoy SC28 between 12 and 20 April, and Convoy HX122 from the latter date until 9 May.

After two or three convoys we were sent down to Norfolk, Virginia, for a refit Some of the local bigwigs invited some of us boys to church and a tea party one night. Of course they had their wives and families with them. I had this bright idea. I asked the Chaplain if we could come to this church on Sunday morning instead of going to church on board. He asked the parson in charge of the party and he said yes. There were British cannonballs sticking out of the church tower and walls, left there from a bombardment during the 1812 war. We had a very pleasant six weeks there and the boys went away to a holiday camp. It was then back to Halifax and the convoys again.

Some of the waves we encountered up there were eighty feet high. Not surprisingly the ship leaked and there was water everywhere. We would be at Defence Stations on convoys: that is, half the ship's company would be closed up. We took turns on the headphones while the turret crew relaxed. We would scrape the ice from the *insides* of the turrets and the seawater would freeze solid as it came inboard. To relieve the monotony we would have a quiz from the officer in the TS and the phone number would shout out the questions.

On one convoy we got so frozen up that we had to go down to Bermuda to thaw out; we were really top-heavy – at least that's what they told us!! We'd been in Bermuda a couple of days and I was over the ship's side on a stage painting when the captain of the fo'c'sle suddenly shouted, 'Everybody inboard at the rush.' I climbed up the rope and pulled the stage in, and observed we were working cable. Apparently a signal had been received that the *Scharnhorst* and *Gneisenau* were out and attacking a convoy. We were to proceed at full speed to assist. After two days I was on the upper deck. It was about 1600 and very grey and dull when 'Action Stations' sounded.

I ran to 'A' turret, where I was centre sight-setter now. The turret crew arrived very quickly and we were ordered to load, enemy bearing Green 45. I don't mind telling you I was really scared because of our speed against two of their modern jobs. 'Enemy closing' came over the headphones, so all I was waiting for was the 'Open Fire' Ting-Ting and a watery grave. To our amazement and relief the next order was, 'Relax – open interceptors.' Radio silence had nearly got us sunk. The 'enemy' turned out to be the battleship *Rodney*. She recognised our outline and flashed her signal lamp. It was hard for us to recognise her head-on, it was like looking at a block of flats. Her 16-inch guns would have put paid to us if she had let fly first and asked questions later! She thought at first that we were one of the raiders, as she was also out looking for them.

Rodney's account of this episode read as follows:

In March 1941 the ship was covering two large convoys when raider activity developed about 250 miles to the south-eastward. The ship was in company with the west-erly of the two convoys. The easterly was in danger if the enemy turned north, but was so far ahead as to make it difficult to reach in time if attacked. The ship cruised at a high degree of readiness all night, and next day we received distress signals which indicated that the enemy was sinking independently routed, outward-bound merchantmen to the eastward. Foreseeing that the easterly convoy was now in more danger than the westerly one, we went ahead to support its escort, the armed merchant cruiser *Laconia*.

A distress signal from SS *Demeterton* was received at the same time as the upperworks of a large unidentified warship was sighted closing from the north-east. Half the hands were at tea, and were closed up at the double with the rest. The stranger was recognised just in time as the *Royal Sovereign*, short of fuel and proceeding to Halifax. She was able to remain with the westerly convoy.

The German Navy's potential for causing havoc on the Atlantic shipping lanes had been remote during the period of the *Royal Sovereign*'s last stint in these waters. But at the beginning of 1941 and through the first half of that year, the threat became a grim reality and battleship protection was never more vital. At the start of the year the enemy had the 8-inch cruiser *Admiral Hipper* almost ready for sea at Brest in France, while the battle-cruisers mentioned above were nearing readiness at Kiel. As well as these three heavyweights, the 8-inch cruiser *Prinz Eugen* was nearing completion, as was the 40,000-ton battleship *Bismarck*. Once these great vessels got out among the convoys, who could foresee the damage they could do? The pocket battleship *Admiral Scheer* was already loose.

It was clear that the only thing that worried these raiders was the presence of British battleships. Faced with the sight of the top hamper of even a solitary and slow British heavy ship looming over the horizon, and the Germans without exception backed off. Such was the case when the *Scheer* was told to hunt for Troop Convoy WS5A in January. She looked for an easier target, with weaker or no escorts.

Nor was Admiral Lütjens, with his two powerful battle-cruisers, any less nervous. Having sunk a group of five unescorted merchant ships earlier; he approached Convoy HX106 on 8 February. But when that morning he caught one glimpse of the *Ramillies* it was enough to make him back off very rapidly. He then approached Convoy SL67, only to find to his dismay that it was protected by the *Malaya*; again he rapidly steered away without attempting to engage her. But back on the Halifax route, this squadron fell in with another two groups of unescorted merchantmen, and it quickly sent sixteen of them to the bottom before returning to Brest.

Likewise, *Admiral Hipper* was roughly handled by the cruisers escorting a troop convoy, but had easier pickings when she fell in with nineteen unescorted ships north-west of the Azores on 12 February and sank seven of them. In all she destroyed sixteen merchant ships. That the AMCs were no deterrent was proved by the fate of the *Jervis Bay*, which, although gallantly handled, stood no chance against a proper warship.

Ex-Leading Stoker 'Buck' Taylor joined the ship's company at Halifax:

> I was part of a group sent over to Halifax to take delivery of one of the old 'Town' ex-American 'four-stacker' destroyers, HMS *Buxton*. While there I took part in a football match and suffered a rupture and had an operation. I

was transferred to the 'Tiddly Quid' for my passage home, but this took eight months because she was involved on Atlantic convoys and always turned back before we reached Blighty!

It wasn't that bad, as it turned out, because we later went to Bermuda to do a 15-inch shoot. I remember that every-thing had to be made secure and that after the big bangs the messdecks seemed inches deep in cockroaches. We also had a refit at Norfolk, Virginia, which proved very pleasant. I had a girlfriend there who used to call for me at the ship's berth in her Cadillac! She also got me civilian clothes so that I could relax on the nearby beaches, twenty-five miles of golden sands. I seemed to be the only Pompey rating on board at this time. After the refit we went back on the Atlantic convoys again, from Halifax to the Western Approaches, before we finally finished up at Greenock.

Royal Sovereign was refitting at the time of the *Bismarck* action, and so missed being part of the net which closed on her and sent her to a well-deserved grave to avenge the *Hood*. Most of the modifications related to her close-range and anti-aircraft weapons, fire-control and radar equipment. While at the Norfolk Navy Yard in June, ten single 20 mm Oerlikon cannon were fitted, two of them on the quarterdeck, but she lost her two quadruple 0.5-inch multiple machine-guns. She retained the eight 4-inch Mk XVI HA/LA guns in four twin mountings and her sixteen 2-pdr pom-poms in quadruple Mk V mountings, so could field a pretty formidable barrage when called upon. Not until August 1941 did she sail for the Clyde to give long overdue leave.

Following a refit, *Ramillies*, commanded by Captain A.D. Read, once more resumed for Atlantic convoy escort duties in 1941. During the *Bismarck* episode on 24 May 1941, she was the Ocean Escort for Convoy HX127 in mid-Atlantic. Like several other ships, when the *Hood* was blown up *Ramillies* was ordered to leave her convoy and close and intercept the German giant from the westward. She had been steaming at the usual convoy speed of 8 knots when this dramatic signal came in, and im-mediately Captain Read signalled down for 18 knots, but even this took a considerable time to attain. As Russell Grenfell was to note in the process:

> She unavoidably emitted volumes of black funnel smoke. Captain Read felt very awkward about this, since he had made a number of reproving signals during the previous days to various merchant ships of the convoy for doing the same thing, and he felt that the Masters must now be enjoying themselves. In half an hour, he had left the convoy behind and was steering north-north-west to get to the westward of the *Bismarck*.[1]

Taking his 27-year-old vessel to meet the brand-new German monster that had just destroyed the pride of the British Navy within a few minutes was the sort of courage that the British public takes for granted of the Royal Navy. As Grenfell recorded, the *Bismarck* was, as he knew from the *Norfolk*'s and *Suffolk*'s reports, coming almost straight towards him. In his opinion, she was making for the South Atlantic; and if so, he ought easily to be able to reach an intercepting position. But even if he could, Captain Read doubted, in view of *Bismarck*'s much higher speed, whether the *Ramillies* would be able to bring her to action if she was disinclined to fight. He might, however, be able to head her off for a short period, which might possibly allow some of the other hunting forces to gain ground.

His confidence and bravery were enormous. Back at the Admiralty there were rather colder feet. Later on the same day a signal reached *Ramillies*'s bridge ordering her not to become fully engaged with the *Bismarck* unless the latter were in action with other British forces. This was a lunatic signal (Churchill again, probably), for if she sighted the *Bismarck* as she had been specifically told to do, how could a 20-knot ship avoid action with a 32-knot ship if the latter deliberately sought it?

Her sister ship *Revenge* was at Halifax on the 24th, and she too was ordered to raise steam with all dispatch and proceed to sea in order to take over protection of HX127, now that *Ramillies* had left it unguarded. She would also be on hand should the German battleship backtrack again to return to Germany 'northabout'.

During the terrible period on 25 May when all contact with

the enemy ship was lost, each British battleship's captain had to make his own guesses and decisions. By 1800 that day *Ramillies* was some 400 miles south of the last reported position of the *Bismarck*, and with Captain Read still firm in his belief that she was heading for the South Atlantic for a secret refuelling rendezvous with supply tankers, he estimated she would pass to the west of his existing position on a south-south-easterly course, and so he steered a north-westerly course to get to the west of her and comply with his last orders from the Admiralty. At 1047 the C-in-C Home Fleet signalled that he estimated the enemy's probable position as between 57° North and 33° West, and ordered all ships to alter their hunting patterns to conform to that estimate. This left *Ramillies* some 400 miles astern of the *Bismarck*, with clearly no hope of finding her. Captain Read was still far from convinced that the German battleship was heading for the North Sea, but none the less complied until another signal from the Admiralty directed him to abandon his part in the chase. He was told instead to locate the unescorted liner *Britannic* and then to escort her safely to Halifax. This intervention from London meant that *Ramillies* was no longer available when the true position of the *Bismarck* was discovered, not the first case of distant control being counter-productive.

Major I.F. Wray RM joined the *Royal Sovereign* in September 1941 as junior subaltern under the OCRM Lieutenant-Colonel C.L. Price:

She was my first ship and I loved her. I still have the 50′ to 1″ [1:600] waterline model of her, which I made in 1943/4, so I can't really forget her. During World War Two she convoyed over a million tons of shipping and never even had a convoy attacked. During my time on board in the middle of a large convoy she 'zigged' instead of 'zagged', missing the liner *Capetown Castle* by what looked to me like feet rather than yards. The fact was that the officer of the watch had written zigzag down inside out! Later in the war, her steering jammed and she avoided the Canadian Pacific line *Empress of Australia* by a similar margin.

Some ships are happy and some not, no matter who is 'driving'. In my first year on board, the commander was an officer of the old school. [He] was relieved by Commander Peter Skelton. At about the same time, the captain, R.H. Portal (brother of the air marshal), who had become ill, was relieved by a splendid extrovert, Captain D.N.C. Tufnell. He introduced himself to the ship's company at a 'clear lower deck' by saying that he knew the commander well as he was an old drinking pal!

The ship was putting on a ship's company concert party, run by the signals officer, W.F. Paterson. The rehearsal was a disaster and the buzz had gone round the ship. We sharpened it up and asked Commander Skelton to introduce it. He did. He told a very funny Welsh story and then gave the best recital of the story of the piccolo player I've ever heard. The ship's company was still laughing, no matter what the 'turns' were up to! A fine man, an understanding man and a first-class leader. He had much to do with making the ship a truly happy one. A man whom I consider to have been privileged to serve under.

As I'm sure you know, the ship's company were divided into three 'Divisions' – Fo'c'sle, Top and Quarterdeck. The Royal Marines lived on a messdeck immediately forrard of the officers' cabins, which were on the main deck under the quarterdeck. Tradition is a marvellous thing. The reason that they were there – the most uncomfortable part, right above the four propellers – is of course that in ships of HMS *Victory* vintage, right aft was the most spacious and comfortable part of the vessel. It really was a potty arrangement. When Action Stations sounded, seamen would come hurrying aft to man 'Y' turret, while the likes of gunnery control officers, such as I, fought their way against the stream to get to their stations in the bridge structure!

The Royal Marines detachment was about 120 NCOs and Marines. Its duties, for action, were to man the port battery of 6-inch guns, one 15-inch mounting (always by tradition 'X' turret – the superimposed after one) and a 4-inch twin mounting. They also provided guards and sentries and wardroom attendants – serving in the wardroom and looking after the officers. (Royal Marines Officers' personal servants were known as MOAs (Marine Officers' Attendants), not Batmen!)

The detachment had three officers – a captain and two lieutenants. There is an old and hoary conundrum: Who does the least work in a ship – the chaplain or the Captain of Marines? The answer is that whereas both of them do nothing, the Captain of Marines has two subalterns to help him.

As junior subaltern, my duties were primarily gunnery – in those days all regular RM officers were trained as fire-control officers. To start with I had the port battery and later was 6-inch control officer and, for cruising or defence stations, 15-inch control. Then of course there were duties such as seeing that the parts of the ship which were the responsibility of the Marines to keep clean and tidy *were* clean and tidy. The most interesting job was that of officer of the watch in harbour – a job one shared with seaman officers. As such, you were responsible for running the ship's routine, including, if the ship was not alongside, which she usually wasn't, running the ship's boat routine.

Captain's rounds were a weekly routine, having with it the solemnity of a religious service. The point of it was to let the captain see that his ship was clean, smart and all the rest of it. (Some captains wore white gloves to pass their hands on the tops of fan trunking to see if they'd been dusted.) The ritual started with a Royal Marines bugler leading the conga, headed by the captain, the commander and, in descending order of seniority, heads of departments. Thing was, the route this procession was to take was a secret until the captain told the bugler. Result: as one went traipsing round, figures – usually clad in underpants – were to be seen hurrying furtively round corners carrying buckets of gash. Messrs Gieves once produced a wonderful cartoon – silhouette figures, with the captain turning round to blame the commander and so on, finishing with the unfortunate ship's cat.

When I joined her, she was in Greenock fitting the new-fangled radar. (One day, I was OOW when the dockyard mateys were rushing aft to catch the 'puffer' taking them ashore after work. I had just ordered the bugler to sound off – it was 'Sunset'. The mateys were still coming aft, so in my best parade-ground manner I shouted, 'Stand still, face aft and take your hats off.' They did – instantly. Three days later I was sent for by the captain. He had had a complaint that I had held the mateys up. After I had been ticked off by the captain he then said, in effect, well done but for goodness sake don't do that again!).

Leading Wren Jean Patterson was then on the staff of FOIC Northern Patrol at HMS *Fortitude* at Largs, and she recalled her visit to 'Tiddly Quid' at this period:

From Largs I went to Greenock and felt really among the big ships. HMS *Royal Sovereign* was a visitor and Harry Grant-Dalton from Lympstone days was the RM officer. He invited me to tea and I was piped aboard – a most wonderful thrill. I had tea in his cabin with a beautiful iced cake topped by the letters WRNS; the cook apparently had been in Lympstone when I was there – I was very touched.

I shall always remember the glorious sound of every ship in the Clyde welcoming in the New Year: from the smallest to the largest battleship their sirens blew.

A further nine 20 mm Oerlikons were added to the ship's close-range armament at Greenock in September, and two quadruple 2-pounder pom-poms were fitted atop 'B' and 'X' superimposed turrets early the following year. Radar arrived late for the *Royal Sovereign*, but in her Greenock refit she embarked five sets: Types 284 (a massive 26 ft wide gunnery set), 273 (short-wave surface warning set) and 279 (a barrage predictor enhanced air-warning set) and two Types 285 (lightweight Yagi arrays for long-range AA fire). No doubt this equipment would have proved itself in battle, although some doubts must be expressed concerning the value of the surface gunnery sets in the light of the following anecdote from Major Wray:

> Gunnery exercises were *very* serious occasions, the gunnery officer, Lieutenant-Commander Roddie Casement (yes, he was a relative) being in a high state of twitch. I recall him being put down by our senior subaltern, who had the uncanny knack of being able to judge distance across water. After a shoot during which the Marines' port battery had scored a very high proportion of hits on the towed target, the gunnery officer congratulated him. He asked whether he had used rangefinder range or radar. Gunnery officer not amused to learn that the control officer had used 'estimated range'!

Extra personnel to man all these new close-range weapons and radar sets increased the accommodation problems in what was an already grossly overcrowded ship, but this had to be borne.

In view of their future deployment, something ought to have been done about the fresh-water storage problems also. After all, they had the example of their experiences in the Mediterranean, Red Sea and Indian Ocean to warn them what they were in for. But this problem was not faced up to, with dire results in the immediate future. Nor was her old machinery replaced with a brand-new set of more modern equipment. This would have resulted in a longer refit, it is true, but would have paid dividends, for the expense of the extra firepower was wasted if she still lacked the necessary speed to bring it to bear on a potential target! But, again, nothing on these lines was done. A funnel cap was fitted in line with her sisters *Resolution* and *Revenge*. That was all!

Note:

[1] Grenfell, Russell, *The Bismarck Episode*, Faber & Faber, 1951

CHAPTER SEVEN

Tropical Climes

A s early as August 1941, the Admiralty had wished to build up a strong deterrent fleet in the Indian Ocean, based on the Ceylon (Sri Lanka) ports of Colombo and Trincomalee. This proposed Eastern Fleet was to comprise the battleships *Nelson*, *Rodney*, *Royal Sovereign*, *Ramillies*, *Revenge* and *Resolution*, the battle-cruiser *Renown*, the aircraft carriers *Ark Royal*, *Hermes* and *Indomitable*, plus cruisers and destroyers. The plan was for the four R-class battleships to be used in their convoy-escort role in the Indian Ocean until called upon to reinforce, as a powerful battle-line, the faster striking force of the remaining heavy ships, should they come up against superior numbers of the enemy.

Churchill overrode this. He was obsessed with the fact that the R class were 'coffin ships'. What was needed, he insisted, was a small, fast squadron. He wanted to send the new battleship *Duke of York*, the *Renown*, and the *Indomitable*, termed Force 'Z'. He finally wore down the more sensible ideas of Admiral Pound and his naval advisers, and so the *Prince of Wales* and *Repulse* were sent out, the first-choice ships not being available. The running aground of the *Indomitable* while entering harbour at Kingston, Jamaica, on 3 November ruled her out for several weeks, and she did not join them. Meanwhile the *Royal Sovereign* and *Revenge* at least were after all sent out to the Indian Ocean as convoy escorts.

Admiral Sir Tom Phillips, in command of Force 'Z' when it reached Singapore at the beginning of December, began to feel that the Premier's idea had left him dangerously exposed and outnumbered. He sent a signal to London asking that *Revenge* and *Royal Sovereign*, by this time in the Indian Ocean, join him as soon as possible, 20 December. He also requested that *Ramillies* and *Resolution* also reinforce him from the UK without delay, as well as *Warspite*. Clearly Tom Phillips firmly believed that strength was more of a deterrent than speed. Quite why Churchill should feel that the Japanese would be more scared of the battle-cruiser *Repulse*, which was as old as the R-class battle-ships, carried fewer guns and far less armour protection, than of the four battleships is unclear. Her extra ten knots speed would not allow her to stand up to enemy broadsides any better than the battle-cruisers at Jutland or the *Hood* had under the salvoes of the *Bismarck* scant months before. But he was adamant.

Royal Sovereign herself, escorted by the destroyers *Dulverton* and *Southwold*, joined Troop Convoy WS12Z off the Clyde on 16 November as their Ocean Escort, reaching Durban on the 18th and sailing again on 24 December.

Major Wray describes *Royal Sovereign*'s own voyage south to the Tropics with the news from the Far East getting grimmer and grimmer with every mile that passed. There was no doubt that the old 'Tiddly Quid' was going to where things were likely to be very warm, in every sense, and with every prospect that they would very soon get much warmer still!

> On leaving Greenock, we picked up a large convoy of size-able (10–15,000 tonners) ships bound for Durban. My interest had been ship recognition and spotting, since I was about ten years old. The junior Royal Marine officer was not thanked by the ship's first lieutenant for pointing out that the screening diagram with the ships' names inserted was wrong! That ship shown in the port column, for example, was in fact that ship in the starboard column. Not popular because this upstart young officer's claim was checked and found out to be right!

Lawrence Dixon remembers the voyage back south, covering the same miles that they had traversed in the reverse direction the year before, this way:

> We left the Clyde and picked up a troop convoy of eleven large ships off Milford Haven. As my sea station was now on the flag deck I got to see and know a lot of what was going on. We also had a radar cabinet built there now, and it was comical at times. The specially trained operators had joined with the sets, of course, and every now and then one of them would come out to check visually if what his hazy blips had told him was an escorting warship on the screen really was by looking at the real thing! We just used our eyes with no complications!

On our way south we called in at Freetown again, and the same guy we had seen diving from his dugout on our way out to Canada was still there doing the same trick. He wore a black top hat and shouted for 'Liverpool pennies'. When a coin was flipped over the side he dived for it and never failed to retrieve it.

On our way down we got the news of Pearl Harbor. Our next port of call was Cape Town and then Durban once more. By this time things were looking decidedly dodgy out East. Hong Kong had gone, and soon after leaving Durban came the dreadful news of the *Prince of Wales* and *Repulse* getting sunk, and then Singapore fell. The troops we were escorting had to divert elsewhere as they were too late to help. Perhaps they were lucky! They mainly went to the Middle East via Suez.

Stan Amesbury was one of those who first joined the ship at Greenock. His Action Stations were the port 6-inch battery and 'X' turret. He too remembers that she was known as 'The Lucky Ship':

> After leaving the United Kingdom we had to proceed via the south of Ireland, as a German U-boat 'Wolf Pack' had been reported across our route. On the way to Durban there were the first signs of prickly heat, and we had the 'Crossing the Line' ritual. We also me the giant 'Cape

rollers', waves from between 50 and 100 feet high. The ship's steering failed briefly during this period and there were some anxious moments. Three crew from our various escorts were lost overboard in these conditions. Later we saw our first whales and flying fish.

Major Wray:

In Durban, that most hospitable city to ships coming out from the UK, the buzz was that we were to join the *Prince of Wales* and the *Repulse* at Singapore (more 'lucky ship' – they were sunk while, I think, we were still at Durban). We went to Mombasa and had the doubtful privilege of being the only capital ship between Japan and the Suez Canal. Then the rest of what Admiral Somerville called his 'Old Ladies' came to join us, forming the 3rd Battle Squadron under Admiral Sir Algernon Willis. The only carrier initially was the little *Hermes*, not much younger than ourselves. Later on, *Warspite* and some modern carriers and cruisers came out to join us.

They sailed from Durban on Christmas Eve 1941, calling at the Seychelles, Zanzibar and the Maldive Islands, delivering mail and provisions for the islanders as they did so. It was 2 January when *Royal Sovereign* arrived at the Seychelles, refuelled and sailed again next morning, arriving at Mombasa on the 6th where she remained for ten days. Their stay was enlivened by some amusing episodes as a largely HO (Hostilities Only) crew tried to come to grips with full naval custom:

Somebody in their infinite wisdom decided that to spread the quarterdeck awning would make a useful evolution to help transform our green crew into sailors! This had not been done since before the war. The drill was to rig tall stanchions round the perimeter of the quarterdeck and connect them from one side to the other with wires. Then, running from right aft to a tripod on top of 'X' turret was what one might call the master wire. Then the awning, rolled up like a forty-plus-foot sausage, was positioned on the master wire. One side was then hauled outboard, the starboard side.

All very well, except that the management had forgotten that a pair of Oerlikon guns now stood on top of the long-disused catapult platform. Result, the awning got snarled up in this – and so did the commander, who was then unable to shout at anybody because he disappeared from view completely, wrapped in the awning. He eventually surfaced, almost black in the face from lack of both temper and oxygen. The drill continued and the port half of the awning was rigged without further snag.

Then came the business of overhauling the wings of the awning, which were to go either side of 'Y' turret. To do this, the ropes attached to the wings were rove through a block forward of its final destination and overhauled above the wires fixed to the stanchions. Unfortunately, many of the sailors had never done this evolution before. They didn't run aft fast enough. Result, the awning wings drooped to the deck. Further result, sailors running aft met the awning coming forward and went down like ninepins.

From my vantage point on the port ladder platform, safely out of danger, it is a wonder that my fellow subaltern and I didn't fall overboard through laughing so much. To crown the forenoon's work, the OA (Ordnance Artificer) of 'X' turret – not being in the picture about the drama being enacted on the quarterdeck, decided to train the turret. This had the spectacular effect of so bending the tripod on top of it as to cause the whole awning to sag. I loved it all.

A similar episode took place during one of their hasty departures to face to foe. The ship's boats had to be hoisted by the main derrick onto the boat deck. Major Wray recounts what happened next:

Unfortunately, somebody had forgotten to take the housing strop off the derrick. The ship had a pole (as apart from tripod) mainmast, and halfway up it had a large radar hut housing a Type 273. When the order was given, 'Up topping lift', nothing happened. The derrick stayed housed.

All the lights went out in the ship. This was not exceptional, as the motors to work the derrick tool needed a very heavy current. All of a sudden, the motors won. The strop sheered and the derrick sprang up. What had been happening, of course, was that the mast was being bent forward – until the strop broke, resuming its normal upright position 'boing-boing'. And the result of that was that the radar officer (a Canadian, Bob Battles, later a captain) scampered down the mast as white as his overalls!

Also while at Mombasa there was a march-past before the Duke of Gloucester. This was to take place on board the flagship, *Resolution*, the Flag Officer being Sir Algernon Willis. Each ship was to send a representative party, including Royal Marines. Major Wray takes up the tale:

Being the junior subaltern in *Royal Sovereign*, no prize for guessing who was detailed to take the representative team from her. To march past, the groups marched round the quarterdeck from the waist along the port side to the saluting base – i.e. right aft. The officer in charge peeled off as this conga line marched round, and reported to the Duke (in my case to say 'Royal Marines HMS *Royal Sovereign*, sir, please', to be met by nothing but a somewhat glazed stare and no response whatsoever!) The conga line then continued round to the starboard side and back to the waist of the ship.

On 17 January they sailed from Mombasa, and two days later they effected a rendezvous with Convoy DM2 (part of WS14), consisting of twenty merchant ships, in position 85° North, 42° 32′ East. Part of the convoy was destined for Malaya and Singapore, and these vessels were detached and proceeded as Convoy DM2, escorted by the *Royal Sovereign* only until she was relieved by the armed merchant cruiser *Ranchi* in 01° 10′ South, 73° 10′ East. The battleship then returned to Addu Atoll, where she arrived on 26 January.

On 1 February *Royal Sovereign* became part of the 3rd Battle Squadron, Eastern Fleet. She, with the netlayer *Guardian*, was

The battleship HMS *Ramillies* seen from HMS *Eagle*'s flight deck as she sails from Aden for Australia in February 1940. The light cruiser behind her is HMAS *Sydney*. She was to lead the take-over of Madagascar from the Vichy-French preventing an expected Japanese occupation. (*E.B. Mackenzie*)

The Eastern Fleet on the eve of battle in the Indian Ocean, a battle which, fortunately, never took place, April 1942. The battleship HMS *Warspite* leads the aircraft carrier HMS *Formidable* and battleships HMS *Resolution* and HMS *Royal Sovereign* in line ahead. (*Imperial War Museum, London*)

Awaiting the Nagumo Task Force. The Eastern Fleet battleships HMS *Resolution* and HMS *Royal Sovereign* in line abreast at dusk in the Indian Ocean, April 1942. (*Imperial War Museum, London*)

'Tiddley' once more! Completely refitted and re-furbished to American standards, and with a new 'dazzle' paint scheme, HMS *Royal Sovereign* leaves the Nay Yard at Philadelphia on 14 September 1943. (*Admiral Peter Skelton, CB*)

A fine birds-eye view of HMS *Royal Sovereign* in 1943, showing to good advantage the layout of her a armament and especially the many extra light AA mountings that now festoon her upper decks. Her armour protection had been much enhanced also at this time, but is, of course, an 'invisible' improvement. (*Admiral Peter Skelton, CB*)

Captain Peter Skelton, who took over command of HMS *Royal Sovereign* when she went into Philadelphia Dockyard for a major refit in 1943. (*Admiral Peter Skelton, CB*)

HMS *Ramillies* during the bombardment of German-manned French forts during the South France landings of 1944. (*Imperial War Museum*)

The Royal Marine Guard of Honour formed up on the quarterdeck ready to receive the Soviet Ambassador and his party at the official 'hand-over' ceremony in 1944. Despite their premature arrival, Lieutenant Wray got his men into position in the nick of time. (*Major I. F. Wray, MBE, RM*)

The Soviet Ambassador, M. Gusev ('that nonentity') jumps the gun and wanders off down the line of Royal Marines before Lieutenant Wray can bring them to the 'Salute', a fact which added insult to injury to the whole hand-over affair. The unique Captain A.T.G. Peachey, RN ('Cuffs and Collars') is in the background. (*Major I. F. Wray, MBE, RN*)

The Hammer and Sickle and Red Star of the Soviet Northern Fleet flies at the mainmast head of what is now the Soviet battleship *Arkhangelsk* at Rosyth on the morning of 30 May 1944. Major Wray recollected that he – 'had the main armament raised to as near a V-sign as I could as an expression of my and the ship's views on the matter.'
(*Major I. F. Wray, MBE, RN*)

The Russian Admiral A. Levchenko and his son aboard the escort-carrier HMS *Fencer* en route to join HMS *Royal Sovereign* at Rosyth prior to her loan to the Soviet Union in 1944.
(*Imperial War Museum, London*)

En route to Murmansk, the *Arkhangelsk* with the Royal Navy escort-carriers HMS *Striker* and HMS *Vindex* astern. (*Navsoutce.narod.ru*)

Seen from *Arkhangelsk*, the destroyer *Derzkij*, one of the ex-US four-stackers also transferred to the Soviet Navy. (*Navsoutce.narod.ru*)

Admiral Golovko on the bridge of *Arkhangelsk*. (*Navsoutce.narod.ru*)

Arkhangelsk firing a 15-inch salvo. (*Navsoutce.narod.ru*)

Home again at last. The *Arkhangelsk* passes under the Forth Bridge on 4 February 1949, her return journey back to Rosyth after five year in the Soviet Fleet. (*Charles Parker*)

Home again. February 1949. Taken from the deck of the LST/Radar Training Ship HMS *Boxer*, the *Arkhangelsk* lies at anchor in the Firth of Forth once more, with the Soviet passenger ship nearby ready to embark her crew for their return home. In the distance can be seen the light fleet carrier HMS *Theseus*. (*Des Whitby*)

detached from escorting Convoy JS1, and in order to provide the two warships with an anti-submarine escort, the minesweepers *Lismore* and *Bathurst* were allocated. However, engine defects in the *Bathurst* reduced the speed of the squadron to a mere 7 knots, and so *Royal Sovereign*, for once in her life the fastest warship in the squadron, pushed on alone and unescorted at 17 knots.

Stan Amesbury recalls:

> The first time we went to 'Action Stations' in the Eastern Fleet was while we were *en route* to Ceylon. The 'enemy' turned out to be a collection of ocean-going dhows, travelling with engines and sails set but no riding lights! It was in these waters that we saw a giant manta ray. It came out of the water vertically, like a Vulcan bomber – then just flopped down into the sea. Later we saw a large whale-like creature – it seemed as long as a submarine – which was later identified as a whale shark. Big as it was, it was harmless, but it could tip up small craft.

They duly arrived at Trincomalee at 1827 on 8 February, and there she refuelled from the oiler *Appleleaf.*

She remained alone at Trincomalee until 27 February, but the following day she sailed escorted by the Australian destroyers *Nizam* and *Vampire*, with the Australian AMC *Manoora*, to meet and escort Convoy JS3 which had sailed from Colombo for Australia. They finally sighted these vessels at 1415 on 1 March and proceeded in company until 1803 on the 3rd. After leaving them, they returned to Trincomalee, the *Royal Sovereign* refuelling the two destroyers *en route* during the afternoon of the 5th.

The German, Japanese and United States fleets were all many years in advance of the Royal Navy in the successful application of this technique of refuelling at sea. They had built special high-speed oilers to accompany their fleets, and utilised the alongside fuelling equipment, which made the job easy and fast. For years the Navy plugged along with small, slow tankers and the laborious job of astern refuelling. By 1942 it was attempting to make up for all those wasted inter-war years but was still a novice at the new method, as Major Wray vividly remembers:

The drill was that the two ships, steaming at about 10 knots, came close, set wires and then rigged an oiling hose. In our case, the oiling hose was rigged from the main derrick, a cumbersome affair that could lift twenty tons and was used for hoisting inboard the ship's boats. In retrospect, and having read K.C. Barnaby's excellent book *Some Ship Disasters and their Causes*, it is clear that the 'canal effect' was not then understood. *Vampire* was on our port side held by two springs and bow and stern wires. She started to get her stern in too close. She started to straighten up.

Now I realise she should have put on starboard helm and allowed the pressure of water between the ships to straighten her up. Instead, she put on port helm. As a result, all the wires in succession went 'twing, twang, twong' and the ships were held together by the oiling hose only. Of course it immediately parted. The oil filled her officers' heads and the first lieutenant's cabin, the scuttles having been left open – and, for good measure, blacked out her pendant number D 69. The flap that resulted can be imagined!

They finally arrived back at Trincomalee on the 7th, and the battleship oiled from the tanker *Plumleaf*. While here they almost lost one of their antique picket boats. Major Wray:

The ship had two venerable picket boats – brass-topped funnel and all. The only really reliable ship's boat was the pinnace, fitted with a Thornycroft petrol engine and Kitchen rudder. One day, in Trincomalee, the picket boat's stoker came to me on watch and said he thought the picket boat was sinking. Suppressing the strong desire to say good riddance, I called out the duty watch and worked the port derrick to put slings on the boat, thus stopping it blowing up.

Another memory of Trincomalee harbour life concerned another venerable tradition. Major Wray:

With one exception, only officers in command of HM ships and all foreign officers may be piped aboard HM ships –

with one exception. That is the officer of the guard. When a foreign ship enters a British harbour (in this case Trincomalee), the senior ship present sends the captain's representative to her to give the ship all the guff about the port, etc. This was always the job of the OOW (officer of the watch) off watch. This fell to me on one occasion. Mind you, with me in my best tropical uniform, white helmet and sword, my gangway staff could hardly pipe me over the side for laughing. But it was rather grand – into the picket boat, flying the affirmative flag – meaning that other ships as I passed had to pipe the 'Still' and 'Carry On'. And then to the foreign warship. In this case she was the USS *Marblehead* that had taken a pasting from the Japs in the Java Sea and could only steer on an erratic magnetic compass and on her main engines, the rudder being useless.

Entering harbour, a signal had been made to her that tugs would meet her. Back came a marvellous rumbustious signal saying, in effect, Hell! I've brought this ship all this way by myself and I'm darned well going to bring her into harbour myself. And he did! A super man – Captain Robinson, USN. I met him three years later when he, by then an admiral, was in charge of the US Navy team at Bremen.

In February they escorted Australian troop convoy SU1 at Colombo along with the heavy cruiser *Cornwall* and destroyers *Express*, *Nizam* and *Vampire* and escorted them toward Freemantle.

On 11 March they put to sea at 0710, and three hours later commenced sleeve target firing to give their AA gunners much-needed target practice. During the afternoon they carried out a full 15-inch sub-calibre firing. On conclusion of these exercises she sailed for Colombo escorted by the destroyers *Express* and *Tenedos*. They remained at Colombo until the 22nd, receiving a visit from the C-in-C Eastern Fleet, Admiral Sir James Somerville, on the 22nd. Next day they sailed from Colombo at 0724, escorted by the destroyers *Arrow* and *Foxhound*, the former being relieved by the *Norman* on the afternoon of the 23rd, to rendezvous with the *Ramillies* which had sailed from Trincomalee the day before, escorted by the destroyers *Griffin* and *Isaac Sweers* (Dutch). The two sisters met at 1632 on the 23rd, and course was set for Addu Atoll.

There were diversions, of course, even when away from harbour, as Major Wray remembers:

When the ship was at sea on Saturdays, we used to run a live programme on the ship's SRE, which we called *On Board Tonight* after the then weekly radio programme *In Town Tonight*. The chaplain was the 'talent spotter', and with a lot of Hostilities Only ratings aboard a wide range of previous jobs came to light, and this was great fun. It went out without any rehearsal, except that I and my oppo – Lieutenant Bill Patterson – knew the jobs of the chaps we interviewed. My best was a man who had been a tram driver and then, because he played some instrument, joined the Royal Marines Band Service. He said on being asked why, 'Well you see, I felt I was getting into a bit of a groove!', and I know he wasn't trying to be funny. The most embarrassing was a former London taxi driver. When I asked the idiot question, 'I suppose in your four-teen years of driving, you must have driven some very interesting people?' he replied, 'Yus. I once drove the Dook of Kent from one night-club to annuver – and blimey, was he plastered!' I can't remember how I got out of that one.

On Sunday at sea we used to do an *Epilogue* programme, organised by the chaplain. There were a few officers who sang well, and, broadcast from the chapel, the programme was basically a sort of shortened Evensong, prayer or two, canticle and a short lesson. We never let it be known who did this – it was a fairly well-kept secret, I'm glad to say much appreciated by the ship's company.

On arrival off the base on the following morning, the two battleships carried out further gunnery exercises, finally entering the anchorage on the afternoon of the 25th and oiling from the *Appleleaf.*

On the 26th there was a full-scale council of war between

Vice-Admiral 3rd Battle Squadron and his ships' captains, following which the whole squadron sailed for further exercises. The fleet at this time comprised the *Resolution* (Flag V/A 3rd BS), *Ramillies*, *Royal Sovereign*, the aircraft carrier *Indomitable* and destroyers *Decoy*, *Fortune*, *Foxhound*, *Griffin*, *Isaac Sweers*, *Napier*, *Norman* and *Nizam*. Full-calibre shoots of the 15-inch and 6-inch guns were carried out on the 28th against a high-speed battle target towed by the *Guardian*. On conclusion of this, the fleet returned to Addu Atoll on the 28th.

After a hasty refuelling the whole squadron sailed once more, this time with the addition of the battleship *Revenge* and the destroyer *Fortune*, and with the destroyer *Scout* replacing the *Griffin*. They were to effect a rendezvous with the rest of the Eastern Fleet under the C-in-C, who was embarked aboard *Warspite* south of Ceylon, and this meeting was made at 1600 on 31 March. The fleet was then split in Forces 'A' and 'B', effectively a fast and a slow squadron. Force 'B' comprised the four R-class battleships, the aircraft carrier *Hermes*, cruisers *Caledon*, *Dragon* and *Heemskerk* (Dutch), escorted by the destroyers *Arrow*, *Decoy*, *Fortune*, *Griffin*, *Isaac Sweers* (Dutch), *Nizam* (Australian), *Norman* (Australian), *Scout* and *Vampire* (Australian).

Both forces cruised to the south of Ceylon for three days and two nights in an area which it was hoped was outside the enemy's probable daylight search area and in striking distance at night for the enemy's probable flying-off position. By dusk on 2 April there were no further indications of a Japanese attack, and the fleet headed back to Addu Atoll to refuel. Force 'C', the aircraft carrier *Hermes* and destroyer *Vampire*, was detached to Trincomalee, and the rest of the force arrived at the atoll at 1500 on the 4th to find Force 'A' already arrived.

Soon after they had dropped anchor, Somerville received a contact report from a Catalina flying boat that she had sighted a large Japanese force steering north-west about 360 miles on a bearing 155 degrees Dondra Head, the southern tip of Ceylon. This proved that the original information had been correct. Seldom has an admiral been caught so flat footed and with his pants down as Somerville was at that moment: his force split and at anchor, without fuel, a sitting duck unable to prevent the enemy from doing exactly what it had been predicted he would be doing!

The force involved was of course the powerful Nagumo Force, which consisted of five fleet carriers packed with modern fighters, dive-bombers and torpedo-bombers, four battleships, three cruisers and eleven destroyers. They had sailed from their forward base in the Celebes on 28 March and had refuelled from their oilers south of Java before sortieing into the Indian Ocean. The Japanese admiral Nagumo, whose same ships had smashed the American fleet at Pearl Harbor and wrecked Darwin harbour, had no knowledge of Addu Atoll, but he knew about Colombo and Trincomalee all right. Strong air striking forces were dispatched to both places. Had the fleet remained concentrated they would have found both places empty, but Somerville's dispersal plans provided targets for both striking forces, and in a short and efficient manner the Japanese dive-bombers dispatched in turn, and without any loss to themselves, the aircraft carrier *Hermes*, 8-inch cruisers *Cornwall* and *Dorsetshire*, the destroyers *Tenedos* and *Vampire*, the corvette *Hollyhock* and several tankers.

The first Japanese air strike hit Colombo at 0800 on 5 April, just half an hour before Force 'B' had completed its refuelling and sailed to join Force 'A' (*Warspite*, aircraft carriers *Formidable* and *Indomitable*, cruisers *Emerald* and *Enterprise* and destroyers *Napier*, *Nestor*, *Norman*, *Paladin* and *Panther*). Admiral Somerville had finally decided that the old lessons of concentration of one's forces was still the best way to fight. Scattering squadrons all over the Indian Ocean where they could not support each other and could be picked off piecemeal was shown to be worse than useless. The four R-class battleships might be scorned as 'The Old Ladies' or the 'coffin ships', but facing imminent attack by the Nagumo force their powerful 15-inch and 6-inch batteries would be welcome protection against the four Japanese battleships, while the myriad of heavy and light anti-aircraft guns would be of immense value in putting a protecting barrage over Somerville's two vulnerable remaining aircraft carriers. He could not afford to see the *Formidable* and *Indomitable* dive-bombed and sunk the same way as *Hermes*, or be smashed up like the *Illustrious* had been in the

Mediterranean by German dive-bombers. The rendezvous was made at 0630 on the 6th.

From sighting reports of the enemy squadron Somerville estimated that Nagumo would either attack Addu Atoll by air or await the return of the Eastern Fleet to that anchorage and then make a surprise attack. The C-in-C decided his only, albeit slim, chance was to keep well clear of his base until daylight on the 7th, and hope to achieve surprise by approaching the committed enemy from an unexpected direction. Accordingly the Eastern Fleet passed through the Veinandu Channel on the 7th and approached Addu Atoll from a westerly direction, arriving in the forenoon of the 8th. *Royal Sovereign* herself anchored at 1200 and commenced a hasty refuelling from the tanker *British Genius*. Her name reflected a quality sadly lacking at this period of the war. Nagumo, still unaware of this secret Royal Navy base, had turned south after hitting Colombo harbour in readiness for his strike on Trincomalee. This took place on the 9th. The Japanese fleet then withdrew from the Indian Ocean, for ever.

Meanwhile, back at the atoll, the *Royal Sovereign* continued her patient wait for the call to arms. Below decks they sweated and waited. Lawrence Dixon again:

Those ships of ours were built for the North Sea battles of World War One. They were never meant to be in those hot climates. Most of us suffered from sweat rash and prickly heat. In those days we couldn't take our top gear off if there was the chance of action, due to the possibility of flash burns. Once down on the messdecks we could get down to our vests. On the upper decks we had to wear pith helmets to protect our heads from the sun. RPO Brown used to prowl the upper decks on the lookout for anybody appearing there without one. I poked my head out of a door once without a helmet on. All I heard was, 'Get your —— head back in, you silly bastard. Do you want to catch sunstroke . . .' He kept on mumbling to himself about the silly bastards they had in the RN these days.

Considering what the Japanese were hoping to do to us

at any moment I don't think sunstroke was high on our list of worries! When we got news of how they had sunk the POW and *Repulse*, then they sank the *Hermes* and then they wiped out the *Dorsetshire* and *Cornwall* all so quickly, I thought to myself, this is it this time, we are no match for those Jap bastards! I was sweating blood. I think most of us were more scared of the sharks if we had to go over the side than being blown to bits by bombs or gunfire. It was certainly the sharks that I was scared most of, and we later had survivors from the two cruisers aboard and what they told us convinced us we were right!

CPO Brown was really quite a character. When we used to fall in for liberty men to go ashore he used to lecture us and tell us we were British ambassadors. We would look very smart in our white suits, but whom we were impressing ashore there I never found out! And to see some of them coming back again, you would think that they had fallen over in a farmyard. Some would swim back and others were sick all over their own suits from cheap warm beer. Many years later I did the RPO's duty, and one bar owner told me, 'When the Yanks come ashore they think they own the place. When the British come ashore they don't give a —— who owns it!'

Lieutenant-Colonel C.L. Price RN:

Life at Addu Atoll was tedious, that I do remember. The water shortage meant a lack of washing facilities, and I remember when we had a tropical rainstorm that everyone not on watch rushed naked to the upper deck with a cake of soap.

It was difficult to find anything for the men to do outside the ship while at Addu Atoll, as there were no sporting facilities ashore. I did organise a small exercise for the Royal Marines one early morning: we landed on the island of Wilingili and had a 'battle' with a company of Rajputs. So there must have been a garrison of sorts. It turned out that Wilingili was only inhabited by those unfortunate

Arabs who suffered from elephantiasis, but I don't think any of us became infected.

On a sadder note, we had to bury a very promising young marine. He had contacted a virulent form of malaria while in a holiday camp near Mombasa. I think his name was Underwood. Anyway, the land at Addu Atoll was too shallow, or rather, low lying, to dig a grave, and it would have been a major operation to get the ship to sea with submarine protection, so we had to leave harbour in the pinnace. We had the best arrangements that we could make, with the padre, a firing-party and a midshipman to steer the boat. It was a solemn occasion and we felt we had done our best in difficult circumstances.

On a lighter note, the clothing of RM detachments in those days depended on regular visits to RM clothing depots, which were situated only at the home ports and Malta. The consequence was that our clothes got a little bit shabby. When we were in Bombay later, or rather, lying about two miles offshore, I went ashore and found an Army clothing depot, and for the trifling cost of a taxi and about seven signatures, I acquired 150 lightweight shirts and shorts. I had said that my men were large, but I had not realised that they were a lot wider than the average sepoy, so I'm afraid they fitted snugly but they did not fit well!

T.W. Pope agrees that life aboard an old battleship in the tropics was no sinecure:

The conditions on board were the opposite to what they had been in Halifax. There we were cold, but out east the messdecks were very hot. The ship was not really fitted out for these conditions, water was a problem, we were only allowed so much per day. Unfortunately while we were at the Maldive Islands one of our Marines died of malaria, and as we were anchored inside the reef he was taken in the ship's launch. The side was piped as he was lowered into the boat, out to sea for burial. We did have another death on board: this was when we first came from Aden to Durban when a torpedoman accidentally fell against a high-power board and was electrocuted. He was buried at sea from the quarterdeck one evening, sewn in his hammock. The ship did not heave to, but as he was committed to the deep, the ship's engines were stopped.

Once the immediate danger to India was over, the Admiralty made the decision to station the R-class battleships at Kilindini, East Africa, to protect the vital convoy and reinforcement route to the Middle East and Persian Gulf from any German or Japanese raiders. Force 'B', now consisting of the four battleships, the cruiser *Caledon* and destroyers *Arrow, Fortune, Griffin, Hotspur,* and *Isaac Sweers,* accordingly sailed from Addu Atoll for Kilindini at 0230 on the 9th. Carrying out further exercises on the way, they arrived at that port on the 14th. Their arrival was made in a spectacular manner designed to show that they were by no means cowed by their recent experiences, and nor did they consider themselves retreating from the Japanese. After all, they had not yet sighted them! Tom Pope:

> We entered Kilindini harbour, and as an evolution the battleships came along the jetty, one behind the other, at the same time, and, on signal, secured and put out booms and ladders with a simultaneous flourish. A sight never to be seen anywhere again.

They then began refuelling, but due to the absence of proper fleet oilers the battleships fuelled alongside in turn. They then commenced a period of maintenance and remedying defects, and remained at Kilindini until the 28th. There was an inspection visit of the *Royal Sovereign*'s ship's company on the morning of the 27th, and two days later she sailed to carry out a sub-calibre shoot; a battle practice target was again towed by the *Guardian,* in company with *Resolution.* Night encounter exercises followed, and on completion the force shaped course to rendezvous with the C-in-C Eastern Fleet once more for Operation Ironclad.

This was the assault and occupation of the Vichy French base of Diego Suarez in Madagascar to prevent the Japanese seizing it and outflanking the British position in the Middle East and India. The battle fleet interposed itself between the island and any attempt by the Japanese fleet to intervene. The occupation proceeded without a hitch, the *Ramillies* contributing to the bombardment force. As there was no enemy counter-moves *Royal Sovereign*, escorted by *Arrow* and *Isaac Sweers*, returned to Kilindini for convoy duty, carrying out another sub-calibre practice shoot on the way.

The part that HMS *Ramillies* played in the occupation of Madagascar, and the price she ultimately paid for the success of that operation, is deserving of record. The operation was first revealed to outsiders when Churchill informed General Smuts of South Africa, 'We have decided to storm and occupy Diego Suarez.' This decision was welcomed in South Africa, whose citizens were beginning to feel horribly exposed now that nothing but Somerville's few ships stood between them and the rampaging Japanese Navy. But the origins of Operation Ironclad went back much further than this.

Major-General R.G. Sturges RM, who was appointed to command the land forces (as Military Force Commander) for the operation, first heard of it on 23 December 1941, and work on the plans began at once, with Sturges co-operating with Rear-Admiral T.B. Drew on the naval side. Although it was alleged that planning was made difficult by lack of knowledge about the objective and its approaches, Royal Navy ships had frequently used Diego Suarez harbour. For example, the aircraft carrier *Eagle* had called there in 1940, and many of the crew had taken photographs of the place (some of which the author now has in his own collection). Perhaps the right people were not asked at the time, but, whatever the reason, aerial photography was called for and a large-scale dress rehearsal was insisted upon by Sturges. The final go-ahead was given on 18 March 1942. It was made clear to the commanders that the conquest of the whole of the huge island of Madagascar was neither desired nor planned for; getting a grip on the strategic harbour and base at its northern tip, thus denying its use to the Japanese, was all that mattered. Latter-day apologist historians have wrung their hands and stated that the Vichy would never have allowed the Japanese to get such a toehold, but one only has to remember the granting of such rights by the French to the Japanese in Indo-China in 1941, which gave Japanese naval aircraft the range that enabled them to sink the *Prince of Wales* and *Repulse*, and also harbours from which to mount their invasion convoys against Malaya and Thailand. Thus it can be readily realised just how much weight can be attached to *that* line of argument.

All concerned on the British side were extremely anxious to get it right this time, for in the words of General Smuts, 'We cannot afford another Dakar.' Indeed, the jinx of velvet-glove methods when dealing with the Vichy had made a fiasco of most of the previous operations against them, from Dakar to Syria. To greatly simplify matters, de Gaulle and his enthusiastic but erratic Free French were kept out of it, and things ran far more smoothly because of that decision. However, the price that the *Resolution* had paid at Dakar was unfortunately to be paid again at Diego Suarez. The jinx continued to hold.

Vice-Admiral Neville Syfret, a South African, and at that time in command of Force 'H' at Gibraltar, was placed in command of the naval side of the operation with the title of Combined Commander. If he appeared outwardly dry and aloof, his planning was meticulous, and due tribute is paid to it by Captain Roskill in the Official History. He termed the co-ordination of the far-flung forces and their assembling at the critical point 'a classic example of a maritime concentration'.

The main assault troops, three infantry brigade groups and a Commando, were sent out the 9,000 miles from the UK in the ships of Convoy WS17, initially to Durban. The soldiers' supplies and motor transport followed in the slow Convoys OS22 and OS23 on 13 and 23 March. The bulk of the naval force was to be provided by Force 'H'; those utilised became Force 'F' for this operation, but had to be much reinforced by warships from elsewhere. Force 'F' itself, *Malaya*, the light cruiser *Hermione* and destroyers, sailed from Gibraltar on 1 April and reached Freetown on the 6th. Here they were joined by the aircraft carrier *Illustrious*, the 8-inch cruiser *Devonshire* and four more destroyers. This combined squadron arrived at Cape Town on 19 April, and all save the *Malaya* sailed from there to Durban, which they reached on the 22nd. The battleship was used to provide heavy escort for the slow convoys as they made their way down and round the Cape before she returned to Gibraltar once more, but her place for the actual landing was taken by the *Ramillies*, then based at Kilindini. She arrived at Durban at the end of April, and Vice-Admiral Syfret hoisted his flag in her to oversee the landings.

All was now ready. The invasion force was split into three groups. The slow Convoy 'Y', which consisted of two special landing-ships, six supply transports, a fleet tanker and a hospital ship, sailed from Durban on 25 April escorted by the *Devonshire*, three destroyers and various sloops and mine-sweepers. The assault troops sailed in fast Convoy 'Z' three days later in five attack transports and three troop transports, with Syfret's main covering force in close attendance. These were joined on 3 May by further reinforcements from the Eastern Fleet, the carrier *Indomitable* and two destroyers. By the evening of the 4th the two convoys had met some ninety-five miles west of Cape Amber, the northernmost tip of the island. The plans called for the minesweepers to lead in the invasion ships and for the troops to seize Ambararata Bay and Courier Bay on the western side of the narrow neck of land that backed onto the Andrakaka Peninsula. It was here that stood the town and base of Diego Suarez, fronting the natural harbour of Diego Suarez Bay itself. It was felt that the narrow entrance to the bay from the east, the Oronjia Pass, would be too difficult to force, even with the element of surprise. Such a western approach by large ocean liners through a maze of reefs the French considered 'impassable and impractical', but it was achieved without a hitch, and the enemy was thereby completely confounded. Led in by the destroyer *Laforey*, which found and buoyed the channel, the whole vast force reached the attack position with the loss to mining of just one ship, the corvette *Auricula*.

By 0430 on the morning of the 5th the assault troops were storming ashore unopposed. Fleet Air Arm aircraft from the two carriers neutralised the enemy airfield and attacked warships in the harbour at first light. The Vichy sloop *Bougainville* and the submarine *Bévéziers* were both sunk. The destruction of the latter was particularly satisfying as it fittingly avenged the *Resolution*'s damage suffered at this vessel's hands off Dakar. The *Ramillies* operated with the two carriers, the *Hermione* and a screen of seven destroyers off the north-west point of the island. The troops quickly pushed inland, but the Vichy defenders gave their usual response to leaflets urging them to surrender without bloodshed by vowing that they would 'defend to the last'.

Even so, the British were again reluctant to take the gloves off until they came up against a fortified defensive line across the neck of the Antsirane peninsula. This formidable line had not been discovered by photo-reconnaissance, and it initially stopped them cold. Until the peninsula could be cleared, the Vichy gun batteries dominating the Oronjia Pass from the southern headlands prevented the entry of the task group into Diego Suarez Bay itself. This clearly was the crisis.

Sturges boarded the *Ramillies* in order to resolve the apparent deadlock, and the old battleship came to the rescue in two highly varied ways, which served to show her versatility – a surprise assault party and a naval bombardment. In the former case a daring plan was hatched which involved landing a storming party in the rear of the Vichy defences. 'So serious was the position ashore that Sturges considered that this bold stroke was essential and would be justified even if the destroyer was lost, as seemed likely.'[1]

Fifty of *Ramillies*'s Royal Marines, under the command of Captain M. Price RM, transferred to the destroyer *Anthony*. At 0345 she set course for the pass, and by skill, luck and brilliant seamanship managed to slip by the Vichy batteries despite very rough weather conditions. Too late the sleepy gunners spotted the destroyer and opened fire on her: the *Anthony* was through, with her own 4.7-inch guns giving a spirited reply. She was not hit, and by a very skilful manoeuvre she made a 'sternboard' approach to the quay. Her captain held his ship there for enough time for the Royal Marines to leap ashore. Captain Price immediately stormed the artillery general's house and occupied the naval depot, taking the surrender of the Commandant there. In the harbour the Vichy sloop *D'Entrecasteaux*, which had been busy laying down a barrage against the British advance ashore, was bombed by the Fleet Air Arm, damaged and beached.

While this spirited action was taking place and causing such a good diversion, the main assault was continued by the British troops inland with further attacks from the west, and by 0300 Diego Suarez town was in their hands.

HMS *Ramillies* now led the main fleet toward the pass, while the corvette *Genista* assisted the Fleet Air Arm in the prompt sinking of the Vichy submarine *Le Hero*, while she was attempting a torpedo attack on the troop transports in the anchorage. Yet a third Vichy submarine attempted to torpedo the *Indomitable*, and she was quickly pounced on by the destroyers *Active* and *Panther*, who dealt with her in double-quick time. Off the pass Syfret's main strength formed in line ahead (*Ramillies*, *Devonshire* and *Hermione*, with an escort of four destroyers) and prepared to bombard the Vichy gun batteries. Since no word had been received of the successes ashore, the first 15-inch salvoes crashed out from the battleship at 1040 on the 7th, the 8-inch guns of the *Devonshire* and the little 5.25-inch weapons of the *Hermione* joining in like two corgis yapping away behind the baying of a Great Dane! As Sturges' biographer was to write:

> There were also considerable French forces manning the batteries on the Orangea Peninsula, dominating the entrance to the harbour. Not having expected so rapid and complete a collapse of resistance, Sturges had already arranged for a naval bombardment of the Orangea positions. Thus the *Ramillies* opened fire with her 15-inch guns while negotiations for surrender were in progress. For a few uncomfortable minutes Sturges feared that the war was going to start all over again, but a signal got through rapidly and the *Ramillies* ceased fire. Though trying at the time, it is probable that the short bombardment did real good by assisting the French to make up their minds.[2]

Several salvoes had been duly delivered against the batteries when, at 1050, the news of the victory ashore was finally received and the cease-fire was ordered. The minesweepers then arrived and commenced sweeping a safe channel into the bay. By 1630 it was reported clear, and *Ramillies* led the victorious fleet in, with the transports and troopships following. It had been a neat and clean little operation with all the major objectives taken within sixty hours of the initial landing and at very light cost in men and materials. But unfortunately this was not to be the end of the story.

Although the bulk of the warships and transports soon left to disperse back to the former jobs, *Ramillies* herself remained at Diego Suarez to oversee the transition to British control and the final setting-up of the base. Unfortunately most of the destroyers and anti-submarine sloops had departed, and thus defence against underwater attack was weak. In fact for *Ramillies* Diego Suarez Bay had become the tropical equivalent to Scapa Flow, and she was to pay in a similar manner to *Royal Oak* for this temporary lack of resources.

The British authorities were forewarned that trouble was brewing when, at 1030 on 29 May, an enemy seaplane was observed making a spy sortie over the harbour. It could only have come from a Japanese warship; no carriers or cruiser forces were known to be in this part of the Indian Ocean. Nor was the presence of a large submarine suspected. In fact the Japanese *I-10* was lying offshore. She not only carried her own folding-wing reconnaissance plane but was accompanied by sister submarines *I-16* and *I-20*, both of which were equipped as mother ships for midget submarines.

They were part of the Japanese 8th Submarine Squadron under Rear Admiral Ishizaki. At the end of April the *I-10*, *I-16*, *I-18*, *I-20* and *I-30* had sailed into the Indian Ocean via Penang, and their aircraft carried out reconnaissance missions all along the East African coast. The *I-10*'s aircraft had reported sighting one 'Queen Elizabeth-type battleship' at Diego Suarez along with a cruiser and other ships. Therefore at midnight on the 30th both *I-16* and *I-20* launched their midgets from a position about ten miles from the pass. The *I-18*, which should have joined in this attack, failed to launch her midget submarine due to engine breakdowns.

The British had no conception of such a bold stroke, and yet again Japanese innovations had caught them off guard. The successes of such craft when used by the Italians at Gibraltar and Alexandria earlier in the war (when they had severely damaged both the battleships *Queen Elizabeth* and *Valiant*) and by the Japanese at Pearl Harbor (where several such midgets had been sunk) should have provided some indication of what was afoot. The British and Germans were not to employ such craft until much later in the war, but once more the Japanese were both ahead in such matters and proved themselves skilled at carrying out such attacks.

As it was, some preliminary precautions *were* taken. *Ramillies* weighed anchor and steamed at slow speed round the bay. When nothing further happened this sensible precaution was abandoned and she anchored again in the inner bay. The two midget crews were thus rewarded with stationary targets when they made their audacious penetration. Between 2000 and 2100 on the evening of 30 May the silence of the bay was broken by two large explosions. One of them was from the tanker *British Loyalty* (6,993 tons), which was sunk outright. The other was from *Ramillies*, which had been badly hurt.

The torpedo fired by the midget hit her port side, just forward of 'A' turret. The bulge at this point took the full force of the explosion, and a hole thirty feet in diameter was punched through it. The ship's outer bottom was ruptured by the explosion for a length of twenty feet and a depth of sixteen feet. Extensive internal damage resulted right up from the inner bottom to the lower deck, the shock of the detonation rippling through her old hull and causing extensive flooding. The water quickly entered both forward 15-inch magazines and shell rooms, and the forward 4-inch magazines, knocking out half her armament. The High Angle control position was also affected, and the flooding extended up to main deck level. The whole forward part of the ship from 'B' turret onward was put out of action as electric circuits failed, telephone lines went dead and power terminated. Fortunately the main engines and boilers were unaffected by the blast.

The midget from the *I-20* has been subsequently credited for the success of both these attacks. Although their respective parent submarines waited for their return at the recovery point and diligently searched for them until 2 June, neither of these brave little craft returned. After the attack the crews of both midgets had apparently landed, been detected by the Army and, after a brief fight, all been killed outright.

Ramillies was crippled by this bold attack, and it took until 3 June for her to be patched up by the local dockyard and her own artificers sufficient for her to sail at slow speed for Durban dockyard. She arrived at Durban on the 9th, and here she was given more extensive repairs in the dry dock, but even so it obviously required greater resources than were available to fully mend her wounds. This took a long while, for it was not until September that she crawled home to the UK for a full repair and refit. Even then the poor old *Ramillies* was out of action as a result of this hit for a further eleven months. On recommissioning in May 1943, she had a shake-down and then sailed for the Cape once more. Not until September 1943 did she finally rejoin the Eastern Fleet. Here she remained only until January 1944, when she sailed for the last time for home waters. But her fighting days were far from over. She was to come back from this knock and inflict quite considerable damage on the other Axis partner by way of compensation.

The *Royal Sovereign*, meanwhile, recommenced her convoy escort duties after Diego Suarez, sailing on 8 May 1942 with the same two destroyers and the AMC *Corfu* to meet Convoy WS17, which was being protected by the *Revenge*. They met the convoy in position 4° 02′ South, 40° 55′ East at 1510, and they and *Corfu* took over the Bombay and Aden sections of this group, *Royal Sovereign* proceeding with the former and arriving at the Indian port at 1320 on 16 May. They returned to Kilindini on the 30th in company with the *Emerald*, *Enterprise* and destroyer *Anthony*.

Then came the time when they said farewell to the Indian Ocean for ever. Lawrence Dixon remembers:

One day we were sent south to Tanganyika [now part of Tanzania] to Dar-es-Salaam to await a Walrus amphibian which was bringing an officer from home with draft chits for many of the crew. A lot of the newer members of the ship's company left at this time to transfer to other ships staying out East, while the original members were to go home with the ship. We sailed down to Durban once, to be greeted again by the famous 'White Lady' whose singing greeted every ship into the harbour. Our escort included the destroyer *Duncan* and one other, and we refuelled on the way from the tanker *Black Ranger*. After a spell at Durban we left for Cape Town, called in at St Helena and dropped off an officer's steward who was a native of that island. Then on to Freetown again. We had a new captain at this time whose hobby was wood carving. He never seemed to bother me for anything, no messages to run or the like. Maybe he didn't know he had a messenger!

Notes:

[1] Edwards, Kenneth, *Men of Action*, Collins, 1943
[2] *Men of Action*

CHAPTER EIGHT

American Interlude

The crew of the 'Tiddly Quid' expected that they were now on their way home, and spirits rose accordingly. Lawrence Dixon told me:

> The excitement was growing about our destination; most of us thought it could only be the UK. After all, we had survivors from *Prince of Wales*, *Cornwall* and *Dorsetshire* aboard. When we left Freetown and got far enough out to sea to open sealed orders, the commander spoke over the ship's Tannoy and said, 'The film showing tonight at the ship's cinema is appropriate to our destination.' It turned out to be *The Philadelphia Story*!

After the narrowness with which a major fleet action had been avoided against the Japanese Fleet, and with heavy losses of more modern capital ships elsewhere (the Royal Navy had lost the *Barham*, *Hood*, *Prince of Wales* and *Repulse* sunk, and the *Queen Elizabeth* and *Valiant* damaged, all between May and December 1941), it was clear that the old R class might well still have to stand in the battle-line. Churchill's early war decisions were now coming home to roost, for the delay to the new *Anson* and *Howe* and the cancellation of the larger *Lion*, *Temeraire*, *Conqueror* and *Thunderer* had left the Royal Navy in 1942 with but nine capital ships with which to face the battleships of Germany, Italy *and* Japan!

There was no longer much talk of 'coffin ships' – quite the contrary – but to face up to the modernised ships of the Axis powers the *Royal Sovereign* and her sisters clearly needed that extra protection proposed for them in 1939 and still not fitted. British dockyards were unable to supply this, but the huge resources of America could. They were already building a whole brand-new battle fleet of fifteen new battleships from the keel up, but readily accommodated some of Britain's veterans as well, so vast were these yards and so advanced their mechanisation.

It was therefore decided to fit the *Royal Sovereign*, *Resolution* and *Ramillies* with an extra 2-inch thick skin of 'rough-and-ready' extra non-cemented armour plate. This was to be flame-cut and emplaced over the ship's magazine spaces to protect them from long-range plunging fire. This additional armour weighed some 340 tons, and to compensate for this the after conning tower was to be removed completely. Another weight-saving measure was the removal of the ship's cruising turbines, which were never used anyway.

In addition, the accommodation problems caused by the myriad of extra light anti-aircraft weapons and the various radar and other technological innovations, and the crews to work them, had to be resolved. The overcrowding of the messdecks in these ships had been highlighted during their sojourn in the Indian Ocean. It was decided to completely remove the two forward 6-inch guns from both secondary batteries. This gave three immediate advantages: it enabled this notoriously leaky area to be sealed and made watertight, vastly improving conditions below decks; it reduced the crew totals by the complements of four 6-inch guns and their magazine supply parties and stowages; finally it gave vital extra space high up in the ship for messdecks and sleeping accommodation.

The tropical episode had, of course, highlighted other faults, not least the lack of fresh water. A new distillation plant was therefore to be installed. To withstand the effect of modern shell-fire and torpedoes, which the damage to all the British battleships listed above had highlighted, additional watertight integrity was another factor adopted. Extra sub-dividing of the inner hull was to be carried out by the blanking-off of side scuttles, making ventilation shafts and trunks less vulnerable, and the addition of improved access trunking. A whole new internal system of damage control to register and rectify listing following battle damage and flooding was to be built in with a centralised damage-control centre which had direct communication to all parts of the ship. Many of the *Prince of Wales*'s guns had been made inoperable, not by direct damage but owing to her listing after taking on board water from torpedo hits. Equally importantly, her engines had been affected, leaving her a sitting duck to be easily picked off by subsequent attacks which she could not manoeuvre to avoid. As part of the modification of the battle fleet, the *Royal Sovereign* was to have her main engine lubrication system so modernised that it would continue to function normally, even with a 15-degree list. At the same time internal fire-fighting systems were overhauled and extended to localise damage from shell hits.

Further additions to the close-range anti-aircraft armament included a further batch of fourteen single 20 mm Oerlikon cannon, along with sixteen twin mountings of the same weapon. This gave her close-range barrage an extra forty-six barrels. As well as more guns, the ship was fitted with a fighter-direction office so that she could act as a control ship and vector out fighter cover towards incoming bomber waves.

The elevation of her main armament was not increased to 30 degrees even now. But some improvement was made by the installation of blind-firing equipment for the 15-inch guns. Extra searchlights were also added, so clearly night engagements were considered the R-class ships' best bet in battle. The Admiralty was probably thinking on the lines of the battleship-versus-battleship slugging matches between the American and Japanese squadrons being fought off Guadalcanal at this time. In such actions the longer range of the Japanese battleship and heavy cruiser guns would be nullified by the radar and special equipment of the 'Rs' 15-inch weapons. To help in this the ship's main armament and magazines were to be adapted to take the new modified 15-inch shells, which had improved flight and penetration attributes and supercharges.

The venue for all this work was to be the great Philadelphia Navy Yard on the historic Delaware river, and it was to that harbour that she steered. The first leg of the journey across was relatively uneventful. The only incident of note is the recorded fact that when the ship's navigator of the time, Lieutenant-Commander Resigh, ascended the bridge one morning as the ship was approaching the Azores he was heard to make the memorable statement, 'My God – who put them there?'

However, when, after their diversion to St Helena, they set course north-westward to Bermuda, and from there, with two damaged destroyers and an empty tanker, they sailed on the final leg of their voyage to the United States, there was rather more incident.

On the way to the States they spent some time at action stations, for it was revealed that a German submarine was shadowing them. U-boat tactics at the time were for one boat to keep contact with a target and home the rest of the wolf pack onto it, but it was later found that their shadower was a lone 'Milch Cow', or supply boat, which had picked them up by a chance sighting. Major Wray remembers:

> In crossing the Atlantic for her major refit in October 1942, a German submarine surfaced less than 200 yards away on the port side. I and my gunnery watch opposite number were on watch at the time. This was at night and the submarine was so close that none of our guns could bear. The submarine, of course, was too close to fire a torpedo without damaging herself. In company with us was the oil tanker *Bulkoil* that had a gun fitted aft and which could have fired. *Royal Sovereign*'s new captain, Captain D.N.C. Tufnell, made a signal to her saying, in effect, why didn't you open fire? He got a marvellous Merchant Navy reply from her master that that worthy thought that was what his Royal Navy escort was for!

In the event she was unable to get in a shot during the whole three-day voyage, and vanished when the US Navy sent out destroyers and patrol aircraft to meet *Royal Sovereign* and escort her back to the Delaware. Lawrence Dixon:

I was glad to have the opportunity to steam up the Delaware. We had a good welcome, bands playing and the crowds waving. Tradition plays strange tricks in people's minds and there was a friendly rivalry between us and the Yanks fighting a common enemy. I was on the jetty once when a rookie American sailor asked me if the Sov was one of Britain's larger destroyers. I replied, 'No, she's only what we call a frigate!' I was sorry to have made fun of him afterwards, and told him so.

Talk about 'Strangling the Baron' now! We couldn't step off the streetcars without getting mobbed. Fights would occasionally break out, people saying, 'I got him first', 'He's ours', 'He's mine', etc.

Once inside the Navy Yard, the ship was de-ammunitioned at once, then she was docked alongside the berth where the 45,000-ton battleship *New Jersey* was under construction. Half as big again as the 'Tiddly Quid', with nine 16-inch guns and an enormous range of AA weapons, she dwarfed the British veteran. But the two Allied battleships soon became firm friends, and, as usual, American hospitality was lavish and unstinted.

The USS *New Jersey* was being constructed in a large dry dock a little way from us. It was amazing the number of British sailors you saw driving streetcars back to the Navy Yard. We couldn't go ashore very often on our pay, that's why we would find a Baron, or a Baron would find us. Half the ship's company had to live ashore, in the Lorraine Hotel, no less.

I went to a few parties at the Belvue Stratford given by the Variety Club. Work continued getting the ship refitted all the time, but most of us were very tired during the day. It was the late nights, etc. The American dockyard workmen found it hard to believe the lack of facilities for crew comfort on our ships. No cold-water drinking fountains, hammocks and *not* comfortable bunks and, incredible as it was, *no* ice cream on Limey warships! Ours was still the old-fashioned messing arrangement, whereby each mess collected and cooked its own meals instead of having a stainless steel canteen like the Yanks and Canadians. Each mess peeled its own spuds and took them to the galley in a spud net. The Royal Marine butcher cut joints of meat according to the size of each mess, then the leading hand carved it out as equally as possible. If you had the forenoon watch you might not get anything at all. The meals were placed in hot cupboards with each mess's number on the door. Some greedy men would take the meat or roast spuds and eat them on the spot, and then collect their own meals.

By now I was definitely interested in female company, and I was fortunate to meet one who lived way out on South 52nd Street. I would catch the elevated railway to South 50th Street and walk to 52nd. The house had a large cellar, and although it was full of junk I could see it was used for entertainment. My girlfriend told me they had parties now and again and the young man next door came and played the piano for them. He lived with his mother and he was devoted to her. His name was Valentino, and in later years I recognised him as Liberace. I wrote a letter to him as he was dying, and mentioned our meeting all those years ago.

The ship's company was being sent home in batches, so there was a scramble every time the lists went up. When my turn came it was January 1943. I was happy and sad at the same time. We entrained with our gear and went to Grand Central Station, New York City. While we were having our lunch in the dining-room, an immaculate British petty officer arrived and said, 'Hurry up, lads, you're going over on the *Queen Mary*, three days to cross.' We hurried up all right, but it wasn't the *Queen Mary* or anything like her! Fooled yet again! Our old crate took twenty-one days to stagger over the ocean to Greenock, and we 'veterans' had to nursemaid the American soldiers and sailors during the very rough weather on the way over. *Royal Sovereign* had been my whole life for three years, but I never ever saw her again.

Others stayed on. One such was Marine Moore:

Fortunately I managed to wangle to stay as 'rear party', to take Care and Maintenance. The reason my request was granted was because I had a sister whom I had never met, living with her family in a little town called Jeanette, Pennsylvania (near Pittsburgh). Our first week at Philly coincided with the US Thanksgiving Day and we had the Royal Marines' privilege of marching through the city with band playing and bayonets fixed. We also gave a drill display to the US Marine Corps.

Major Wray:

The ship was in Philadelphia for ten months, having arrived on Trafalgar Day 1942. The hospitality shown to the ship's company was marvellous. On Thanksgiving Day 1942, there were enough invitations for three ships' companies and two wardrooms. I was the link man with shore-side voluntary organisations who channelled the invitations for the wardroom, and the chaplain, the Rev. John Stow, did the same for the ratings. He was a wonderful man, who became vicar of Hertford after the war and, alas, died some years ago. One of my gunnery crew ratings, Able Seaman Nicholson, asked me once, 'Where does the chaplain mess?' I said, at the tender age of 21, 'Where do you think – by himself, like the Master-at-Arms.' Nicholson said, 'Come on, sir.' I said, 'He messes in the wardroom.' Of course naval chaplains have no rank as such, and can wear plain clothes, which John Stow did. Nicholson said, 'Is he an officer?' and I replied, 'He's a chaplain', and a finer recommendation for a chaplain could not be possible than Nicholson's question.

While in Philadelphia, we took part in a combined services parade on America's Flag Day. There were, at the time, ourselves, a Greek ship and a former Vichy-French ship in the dockyard. There was also the cruiser HMS *Argonaut*, which had had her bows and stern blown off by two torpedoes, yet made the Atlantic on her two outer screws. These ships combined with us for the parade, and because I was the junior Royal Marine officer, I got lumbered with taking the detachment! The march entailed five miles at the Slope, *not* very funny, except that instead of marching to the forming-up point we all went there by tram. Of course the parade was in reverse order of seniority – Greeks and French in front; the combined Royal Marine detachment, behind the Royal Navy one, was immediately ahead of the United States Marine Corps, the senior US Service. In retrospect, great fun!

At a children's party given by the whole ship, I was Mickey Mouse (because, I suppose, of having nice big marching boots!) My bottom was sore by the end of the party from being repeatedly pinched by horrible children asking if I was real! (The outfit and mask were admittedly very good!)

As time wore on in dockyard hands, my detachment, naturally, began to get very stale. All we had by way of regular duties was watch keeping as security sentries and serving in the wardroom. We had not done any military training for a long time. So some was organised, only to find that it was against United States law for any foreign troops to land under arms! So we turned it into a holiday – at one of Roosevelt's CCC camps near Reading, Pennsylvania.

We were lucky (again!) to have actually survived the refit at all. One day, when I was officer of the day, one of the stoker sentries came to me and said he thought that the ship was sinking! Now the ship had three enormous boiler rooms. Owing to the refit the watertight doors were left open, so there was a space some one hundred feet wide and getting on for two hundred feet long open below the water-line. The sentry said that he had stepped off a grating into four feet of water. I ordered the engineers' submersible pumps into action, and reported at once to the duty lieutenant-commander. (He, recalled from the Retired List, took full advantage of duty-free privileges.) He said something like, 'Ah, Marines, get out the collision mat.' (Yes, we actually did have one.) Knowing that it couldn't possibly either be rigged with all the power lines, etc., holding us to the pier or be the slightest use anyway, we 'went through the motions'. But it took the pumps twenty-four hours to pump us out. Apparently – and it was not thought to be sabotage – a dockyard matey had left an underwater valve open which he was refitting, presumably when the hooter went for knocking off. (I did say she was a lucky ship.)

Another strange fact was that during the refit opportunity was taken to replace the two ancient steam picket boats by two motor boats with two 250 hp Thornycroft diesel engines. But they sent these all the way across the Atlantic instead of waiting for the battleship to return home and then taking them on board.

For the period of her long refit, almost a year, the *Royal Sovereign* was given a works number, 'HMS 40', in order to keep her identity and location secret while she was out of the war. About two-thirds of her ship's company were returned to the UK while she was paid off, many as crews of newly built landing-ships and craft destined to play a prominent role at Salerno, Anzio and Normandy as the Allies slowly began to resume the offensive. Major Wray:

> During the period while the ship was refitting at Philadelphia, the Royal Marine detachment was reduced to WRAs and security sentries, a detachment of about fifty officers and men. The Captain of Marines and the senior subaltern returned to the UK and other things, and I was left as OCRM. The Detachment Sergeant Major (an honorary title) was Colour Sergeant E.W. Parker, with whom I remained in touch until his death. He was a wonderful man. He taught me my job as OCRM, and having done so never traded on it. I miss his friendship greatly. He was a mine – not a mere mine, but a goldmine – of good sense, experience and a marvellous sense of humour.

The Americans now got on with the job in hand in their usual fast manner. Major Wray recalls how their ways of working were rather different from the slow, leisurely and demarcation-dictated rigidity of British shipbuilders:

> The way the Navy Yard did the job was fascinating. They cut all the compartment partitions, cabins, etc., and cut off

two inches. After the armour had been fitted, through large holes cut in the upper deck, they simply welded them back in place. While this was going on I asked one Negro dock-yard matey, who was busy cutting a hole in our beautiful teak quarterdeck, how he was going to put it all back again. He replied, 'Ah don' know – that's Shop 63 – Ah just cut the holes.' They also fitted two General Motors 500 hp auxiliary diesels, having dismembered our venerable Merles Bickerton and Day museum pieces – huge they were, and you could see the connecting rods!

Lawrence Dixon remembers chipping away at twenty or more years of accumulated paintwork:

I was now working 'part of ship' and we had orders to chip as much paint as possible from the ship, inside and out. We got supplied with 'windy hammers' and really went to town, magazines, handling rooms, messdecks, officers' heads. We had to put the paint in buckets and then it was weighed on the jetty. I forget the total weight we got off her, but it was tremendous.

Marine Officer Wray also remembers this operation, and its subsequent effect:

The Navy Yard decided that our lead paint was an un-acceptable fire risk. They chipped it all off. They measured seven tons of paint off the upperworks alone. They replaced the paint with zinc-oxide-based material. Result, returning to the UK in bad weather, water spurted into my cabin, not through the scuttle itself but through the rivets which held it. The paint had been so useful! No wonder; she was getting old. On one occasion, one of the engi-neering officers inspecting the double bottom dropped his spanner and it went through, on account of rust!

Another Royal Marine, Stan Amesbury, has memories of how the 'Tiddly Quid' was used as a grandstand when the *New Jersey* was launched:

With the huge surge of water when the *Jersey* went into the sea, *Royal Sovereign* soon parted company with the pier. Power, water and mooring lines all broke, and gangways disappeared into the dock. They had to hastily send for a tug to push us back again!

Her Acting Captain (now Admiral) Peter Skelton CB *is* remembered by a former shipmate as 'a super commander and then captain – when you think what a ghastly job of keeping control of a ship's company in refit in Philadelphia must have been'. He told me of the final preparations for her voyage home:

When we completed our refit we went to Chesapeake Bay to work up. I told my sailors that we were cutting off our connections with Philadelphia. However, while at Chesapeake Bay, I received two requests. One sailor asked permission to visit Philadelphia as his wife was going to have a baby and he wanted to make arrangements. The other request was from a sailor who thought his wife was going to have a baby and heard that she was not. He therefore wanted urgent permission to return to Philadelphia to make sure she did have one!

Towards the end of my term in Philadelphia I was asked to take the Ambassador, his wife and secretaries home in my ship. I said it was quite impossible, but I had heard that there were a lot of schoolboys who had been evacuated to America who now wanted to return to the UK. I said I would take twenty-four. The Earl of March was chosen as the 'Prefect'. He did a good job. I heard of one young man who behaved stupidly and dangerously, climbing into the sea boat in bad weather. I thought of the ideal punishment for that young man. I sent him to the Sick Bay and told the doctor he must not leave his bed until we arrived in the UK. He would never want castor oil again!

Marine Stan Amesbury recalls her departure from the States thus:

The time came for us to leave. At this time a lot of mess-decks were empty and stripped down, but a steaming party

was sent over from the UK to bring us back home. We were
to go to Norfolk, Virginia, for stores, crossing Chesapeake
Bay. We had a fire in the boiler room during this journey,
which did not help matters.

At Norfolk our special stores came aboard. large packing
cases that would fill every available space. Much later we
were told all these cases contained mines. On the boat deck
were torpedoes in long cases, all stacked up. Our next
surprise followed, children aged between ten and sixteen
years old came aboard complete with their toys, bikes and
suitcases. They had been evacuated to the States and now,
it being safer, were returning home once more. They were
accommodated in the warrant officers' quarters right above
the propeller shafts, sleeping in hammocks.

The next guests to arrive were a group of American news
reporters in service uniform bound for Europe. We resem-
bled a floating bomb for the homeward voyage. All told,
our group consisted of us with our new 'cargo' plus our
own new ammunition, and our escort for the leg up to
Newfoundland was two new frigates and a submarine. We
were to proceed to Newfoundland, and the sea was very
rough as we headed north. It got very cold. Suddenly we
were changing course and the frigates were dropping
depth charges and firing anti-submarine mortars while we
sounded off 'Action Stations': we had run into another wolf
pack. But thankfully we arrived at Argentina, Newfoundland, safe again.

Also aboard at the time was an English statistician ('who
was *very* seasick') and a fairly big wheel from *Time* or *Life* magazines. They almost never even got to sea at all, as Major Wray
recalls:

After her refit, on finally leaving, she narrowly missed
colliding with an ammunition jetty down river. This was
because the port steering wheel was out of order and the
engineers had told the bridge to steer on the starboard
wheel. But, in error, the quartermaster was closed up on the
port wheel. When the tugs cast off there was, of course, no

response to the captain's helm orders. The engineers, not getting any helm orders, assumed that the ship was still under control of the tugs. Peter Skelton's wife told me a few years ago that he still has nightmares, if not kittens, at the thought of what would have happened to the ship, and to him (he was at the time only an acting captain!), had the ship connected with the ammunition jetty!

Captain Skelton himself remembers:

On our voyage from Newfoundland to Greenock we had four destroyers to escort us, and we were chased by submarines that kept submerging during daylight hours and tried to get ahead of us in the dark. We were lucky to get to the Clyde unscathed.

Stan Amesbury:

The final leg home took us well into Arctic waters. The seas were wild and we took a heavy beating. The children were very seasick by this time and probably wanted to die. At one point the ship started to ice up, and chipping parties were out de-icing the guns and superstructure. At last, however, we arrived off Greenock. The children had now revived and were roaming about the ship. They were the first to leave, escorted to their homes by the Royal Marines, NCOs and petty officers. Then the American reporters left. Our deadly cargo of mines and torpedoes was discharged at Rosyth dockyard.

He recollects that for the next few months they became a sort of depot ship, or base, for Royal Marine assault boats:

Our empty messdecks were soon filled with their Royal Marine crews. We expected to be part of the impending European invasion, but somebody must have changed their mind. The Marines and the boats left us and soon after we were told what the fate of the proud old ship was to be.

Major Wray describes the months following their return home as the 'doldrums':

When we came back to Greenock, and then to Rosyth, no one seemed to want us. Talk of the Invasion was in the air: were we to be one of the bombardment ships?

Their sister ship *Ramillies* was in fact so utilised, as were both *Malaya* and *Warspite*, but despite her recent expensive refit, 'Tiddly Quid' was passed over. Her crew was never told why, but examination of Admiralty documents reveals the reason the gallant old lady was left on the shelf, despite her girlish enthusiasm. The report, from Captain Pizey, DOD(H) at the Admiralty, and dated 25 January 1944, gave comprehensive details of *Royal Sovereign's* condition at that time:

Ship is in the Basin at Rosyth Dockyard at 48 hours' notice for steam in an emergency, but advisable to allow a week. Stores are on board but no ammunition. 14 days will be required to ammunition ship with full ship's company.

A defect list contained no major items except for the following gunnery problems:

Cordite and shell cage guides badly worn and requires renewal in all turrets. The gear at present works but its life may not be long. This would be a very big job and the US authorities would not undertake it during the ship's recent refit in America. 'Y' turret, walking pipes. Roller guide rail distorted and requires realigning. As far as can at present be estimated would take up to one month.

This is what ruled out any chance of the ship taking part in a shore bombardment role like some of her sisters. He also listed the radar equipment carried by the *Royal Sovereign* thus: 'W.A. Type 79. W.S. Type 273 QR. G.S. Type 284 M (three sets). G.A. 2/Type 285 M (three sets). G.C. 2/Type 282 . Interrogators. Types 242 and 243 (Mk.III)'[1] His report concluded: 'Work on reducing the ship to four months notice has been suspended until a decision is reached as to future employment.'

Meanwhile those left aboard could only fume in frustration. Major Wray:

> It was thought that she would soon be brought up to war complement again. Instead, her complement was reduced further, and she remained throughout the winter a forlorn landmark, virtually in 'Care and Maintenance'. Captain Skelton left the ship and was replaced by Captain Sidney Hopkins, who clearly did not know what had hit him! He was of that curious generation who, having left the Navy after World War One as a lieutenant, was promoted on the Retired List. The last ship he had served in was a destroyer. With some trepidation he had to take the ship to sea for trials. I did not go, as I had just come out of hospital having had a hernia. My temporary medical category precluded me going to sea. However, the ship returned safely to Rosyth. Then we knew – we were to be handed over to the Russian Navy on loan, and the operation was classified 'Secret'.

Notes:

[1] Recently this official Admiralty Report, held at the National Archives at Kew, London, was recommended to be burnt by an Internet contributor merely because he disagreed with it!

CHAPTER NINE

The Regal Rouble!

The origins of how the Royal Navy came even to contemplate the loan of one of her battleships, albeit an old one, to the Soviet Union, go back to the time of the German invasion of Russia in June 1941. Prior to that date Nazi Germany and Soviet Russia had been allies, having signed a non-aggression treaty in August 1939, with hidden clauses that allowed the two Dictators of Left and Right to carve up Poland between them. It also gave Stalin a free hand to rape and absorb the Baltic States of Latvia, Lithuania and Estonia. Despite the mental block of Communists both in Russia and elsewhere since, Stalin kept firmly to his side of this contemptible deal and loyally backed up Hitler's subsequent campaigns in Europe, calling Britain and France's resistance merely 'Capitalist warmongering'.

However, when Hitler finally decided it was time to settle accounts with the nation and system which he had all along regarded as the real and main enemy, and invaded the Soviet Union, black became white and white black for politicians of all shades! For the left wing, what was yesterday a good friend and ally became the bloodstained Fascist hyena and aggressor. In Britain those who had been opposed to the war suddenly demanded all possible aid to Russia, including the 'Second Front Now' campaign designed to take the heat off Moscow.

Churchill, who had castigated the Bolsheviks from 1917 to 1941, now stated that 'if Hitler had invaded Hell I would make a pact with the Devil', and did so. He went further, squandering our limited and precious resources like Hurricane fighter aircraft and tanks and sending them, at enormous cost in lives and expense, to Murmansk to supply the Russian armies. Such items, which would have saved the British Empire in the Far East, were instead lavished on Stalin, who, far from expressing thanks or gratitude at the cost in lives this commitment made on the Royal and Merchant Navies, merely growled for more and more of them.

When Italy surrendered in 1943, the Soviets claimed that they, as loyal allies, should be awarded a share of the surrendered Italian fleet. Quite what the Soviet Navy had contributed to the defeat of the Italian Navy is unclear, Cunningham and Somerville had not so much as one Russian seaman to aid them in their numerous battles. Nor had the Americans assisted very much in vanquishing this particular Axis partner at sea, but none the less this Russian *diktat* was promptly acceded to by President Roosevelt. By doing so unilaterally, and not consulting the British, who *had* defeated the Italian Navy, one would have thought that it would then have been up to the Americans to make good the demand. Not so, the Royal Navy it was that had to pay most of the price. In January 1944 Churchill bowed to this *fait accompli* and agreed to the issue of a telegram over the joint signatures of both the British Premier and the American President, offering Marshal Stalin what he asked for.

Naturally, the Soviets wanted the very best Italian battleship available for their own navy, but Britain held out, and eventually the *Giulio Cesare* was allocated to them. She was even older than the *Royal Sovereign*, having been originally launched in 1911, but unlike the British veteran the Italian ship had been extensively rebuilt between 1933 and 1937, when her speed had been increased to 28 knots and extra armour protection fitted. The difficulty in handing her over to the Russians was that she was in poor condition and needed refitting at a time when there were more important matters to attend to. Even if she had been fit to sail at once to the Black Sea, as requested, it would not have been possible, since it was Germany that occupied and controlled Greece and the Aegean from 1943 to 1945, and thus effectively barred her passage. Stalin would listen to no excuses, however, and demanded that a battleship be made available without delay. Churchill then offered the loan of a British capital ship until such time as the *Cesare* could be handed over, and this was agreed to, the Russians asking for a King George V-class vessel. The Royal Navy, after surveying the fleet's requirements, decided that *Royal Sovereign*, having just been refitted but not yet being in full battle order, fitted the bill nicely.

Plans therefore began to be put in hand to effect the transfer, and arrangements had to be made to bring a Soviet crew back in a returning Murmansk convoy and train them to handle their new acquisition sufficiently to steam her back home again. A new British captain was appointed to oversee this transfer smoothly – Captain A.T.G.C. Peachey. He was one of the wartime naval 'characters', larger than life in every sense, about whom the wardrooms and messdecks wove legends and tales galore.

Robin McGarel Groves was a Royal Marine officer who subsequently served under Captain Peachey, and he gave me this entertaining and illuminating portrait. Describing him as 'a somewhat unusual officer', McGarel Groves told me:

Captain Alan Thomas George Cumberland Peachey might well have come straight out of the pages of *Fabulous Admirals*. He was tallish, dark and saturnine. He wore his cap well pulled down over his eyes and had 'Bugger's grips' (sideburns) well down both cheeks. He had a sardonic and sarcastic manner. He had been a signals officer and friend of Lord Mountbatten. He could be most charming when he wanted to, and at Captain's Defaulters and dealing with welfare cases he showed a very human side. He was a clear quick thinker with the knack of expressing his thoughts, and frequently pulled no punches.

Before *Royal Sovereign* he had been captain of the *Delhi*, an old D-class cruiser rearmed with modern American 5-inch dual-purpose guns. In the Mediterranean the *Delhi* had had a pretty hectic life until torpedoes blew off her bow and her stern. Like Nelson, Alan Peachey was a chronic victim of seasickness. I can remember him huddled in the captain's chair on the bridge as I kept watch, a bucket close at hand and another in reserve nearby in charge of the captain's messenger.

I can remember one occasion when coming off to Spithead in the captain's motorboat, the boat impaled itself on a buoy, causing passengers and crew to seek safety on the buoy when the boat sank. They tried shouting for help and burning little bits of paper to no avail. Eventually Lieutenant 'Digger' Taylor RANVR started a popular version of that well-known Australian ditty, 'The Road to Gunda Gai'. The captain joined in enthusiastically, accompanied by the boat's crew and the other officers aboard. This soon did the trick, and they were rescued and brought back to the ship. The captain did, however, appoint a new captain's coxswain.

This was the man that the Russians had to deal with during the handover of the *Royal Sovereign*, and, awkward and difficult as they were throughout, I have an idea that they got as good as they gave!

Major Wray comments:

Captain Peachey was selected for the turnover. He was known to many as 'Collars and Cuffs', for he wore deep collars and visibly starched cuffs, together with a large pocket handkerchief in his breast pocket. He was always faultlessly dressed. It seemed to me that, if he made a nonsense of the turnover, Their Lordships could write him off – and if a success simply thank him. My theory is reinforced by the fact that Captain Peachey was later appointed Commodore Palestine during the very messy and unpleasant period at the end of the Protectorate. But for a better man to serve under, you would have to go a very long way. At the outset of the turnover, and before any Russians came on board, he called all the officers and (I think separately) ratings together and said, in effect, 'Be correct in all your dealings and I will back you all the way.

Step out of line and I'll chop you!' *That* is the kind of CO I've always appreciated – a strict but fair man and a first-class leader.

There was, of course, a great deal of work to be done by all departments – gunnery, engine room, supply, medical, you name it. Except Royal Marines, as the Russians did not have any. The dockyard was also kept extremely busy one way and another, such things as getting the tallies on valves, etc., translated into Russian and engraved.

The whole operation of loaning the ship to the Russians was classified as 'Secret'. This was not the desire of the British Government of the day, quite the reverse, but that was how Marshal Stalin and his cohorts wanted it and so that is how it was. The story behind this hush-hush decision is told in correspondence between the Prime Minister and the Foreign and Home Offices early in 1944.

Churchill raised the question of the hospitality to be given to the Soviet crew and the publicity that might result for the loan of warships to the Soviet Navy at a meeting of the War Cabinet on 17 April 1944. His thoughts on the matter were amplified in a Memo prepared by the Head of M(I) on 22 April, addressed to Churchill himself, with copies to the Foreign Secretary, Anthony Eden MC, MP, and the Chancellor of the Exchequer. Several points are made on both facets. On the hospitality side of the coin it was noted that:

> The presence of such a considerable body of Soviet nationals in this country will give us a great opportunity of furthering Anglo-Soviet relations and particularly of creating goodwill in the Soviet Navy. Although the Royal Navy have received very poor treatment from the Soviet in North Russia, the fault has lain with the Soviet civil bureaucracy rather than with their Navy and, in any case, we must, I consider, now take the wider view.

He went on to note that up to then Britain had fully victualled and stored the ships that the Russians were to take over (as well as the *Royal Sovereign*, six British ex-US destroyers and four

British submarines were also to be made available at the same time, together with an American cruiser), and that the Treasury had agreed that no charges were to be made to the Soviets. But it was proposed that any further victuals and stores supplied would be subject to financial adjustments with the Soviet Government. However, it was proposed that 'in view of the special circumstances, the Soviet crews should be treated as our guests during the time while they are taking over, and that no charges should be made'. It was added that the entertainment of the Soviet crews during their stay in the UK would inevitably involve the Royal Navy in some expense, and that no provision had been made for this. 'I propose that any reasonable expenditure in this connection should be met from public funds . . .'

To offset these costs, which for upward of 2,300 officers and men would be considerable, there was the publicity angle, but: 'As you point out, we shall have to obtain Soviet approval to publicity.' Before this was broached with the Soviet Mission in Britain, the question of the ceremonial transfer of the ships had to be thrashed out. In this connection it was noted:

> Upon their arrival, the Soviet crews will go straight on board, when they will at once heavily outnumber the British turnover parties. The transfer might therefore be said to take place immediately. Nevertheless, it will be quite possible to arrange a special ceremonial, if such is desired and the Soviets agree. All the Soviet ships will, by about the middle of May, be concentrated at Rosyth, where *Royal Sovereign* already lies. The ships could wear both the Soviet and British Ensigns until a ceremonial changing of the Flag had taken place at Rosyth. The details would have to be further considered but you may think that an impressive little ceremonial would tend to create the right effect.

It was also stated that as the transfer of the ships in question was only on loan, 'It may be inappropriate to make too much of the ceremony. Nevertheless, a ceremony presided over, on the British side, by myself, the First Sea Lord or Commander-in-Chief, Rosyth, might serve the purpose.'

There was also the question of a formal document of transfer.

Many other Royal Navy ships had been loaned to Allied navies during the war. Most of the European Governments in Exile had settled in London, and those officers and men who had fled the German occupation had wished to carry on the struggle in modern warships working as part of the British fleet. Thus Polish, Free-French, Norwegian, Greek and similar navies had been loaned modern British ships, usually something far smaller than a battleship of course, mainly cruisers, destroyers, submarines and corvettes. The same principle had applied to all these loans in that such a transfer document, setting out the details of the loan, had hitherto always been applied to keep things formal and above board. But this case was to be regarded as something different from this norm:

> We are acting on the assumption that such a document is inappropriate to the present case, and that the basis of the transfer must be simply the offer made in the message you and the President delivered jointly in your telegram of 23 January. On the other hand, we feel that there might be some advantage in drawing attention to the fact that the ships are being lent upon the terms of your offer.

It was therefore suggested that once a decision had been made on the actual handing-over date, Admiral Cunningham should write to Admiral Kharlamov, head of the Soviet Mission, to confirm the arrangements for the transfer and to make reference to the joint message. The Foreign Office was consulted and was in general agreement. The thorny question of jurisdiction of aliens while in the United Kingdom was also brought up. It was revealed that the FO had also been consulted on the question of applying the Allied Forces Act, which appertained to jurisdiction over American and other Allied troops based in Britain, to the Soviet personnel, 'But the question of jurisdiction is linked with our struggle to obtain jurisdiction over our own men in North Russia for all minor offences. The opportunity is being taken to use the presence of the Soviet personnel in the UK as a lever to obtain this jurisdiction.'

Similar reservations were expressed in an attached signal addressed to the First Lord of the Admiralty, A.V. Alexander,

the First Sea Lord, Admiral Sir Andrew Cunningham, the Vice-
and Assistant Chiefs of Naval Staff and the Secretary to the
Admiralty. After a similar outline preamble, it explained in
greater detail why the Royal Navy should treat the Russians far
better than the Russians had hitherto treated their Royal Navy
allies:

> The Royal Navy have suffered serious discomforts and
> discourtesies from the Soviet Authorities in North Russia.
> Although, therefore, it goes somewhat against the grain to
> advocate the granting of special favours to the Soviets, I
> consider that we must make a very special effort to impress
> favourably the Soviet officers and men coming to this
> country to take over *Royal Sovereign* and the other warships.
> I suppose never before will such a considerable body of
> Soviet nationals have been in direct contact with the British,
> and it is very desirable that they should return to Russia
> favourably impressed.

It added, as further bait: 'The party visiting us may include men
who will reach high rank in the Soviet Navy, and the Soviet
Navy may after the war become a more important factor in
Soviet affairs. We must surely, therefore, merely for reasons of
self-interest, do what we can to create goodwill.' Prophetic
words indeed, but who could have foreseen just how the hitherto unremarkable Soviet Navy, through a combination of their
post-war leaders' determination and our own leaders' lack of
interest, foresight and will, would have so completely eclipsed
the Royal Navy in those post-war decades?

The net result was a 'Top Secret' signal to the Commander-in-
Chief, Rosyth, Admiral Archer, in which he was instructed that:

> HMG's policy in connection with impending transfer of
> British warships to the Soviet Navy is that every possible
> effort should be made
>
> (a) to fit out the ships to the satisfaction of the Russians,
>
> (b) to impress favourably the Soviet personnel with the
>   British war effort and the British way of life.

These ideals were easily promulgated, but, as Admiral Archer, Captain Peachey and their supporting officers and men were to find to their cost, *not* so easy to carry out! If the previous Russian reactions to British and American aid had not given them numerous clues as to how the Soviet authorities would react to the above suggestions, then the British Government was soon to receive a quite clear and unambiguous response!

It was routine for the men of the warships and convoys to North Russia, having fought their way through dive- and torpedo-bombers, U-boat packs and the threat of the active intervention by the *Tirpitz* or other German heavy ships, to find the precious supplies they had transported on the last convoy still to be lying on the quayside. It was equally routine to watch with wry amusement how each tank, fighter plane or truck offloaded was quickly and efficiently relieved of each and every mark that might indicate its origin. Ambulances lovingly inscribed 'A present from the people of Coventry' would have such messages of solidarity against a common foe rapidly covered with camouflage paint and prominent Red Stars. Marshal Stalin feared only one thing more than Hitler's legions, and that was that his countrymen might discover that the Soviet Union was beholden in any way at all to the Capitalist warmongers of the West!

Despite this, on 13 May 1944 Anthony Eden wrote a long letter to the Soviet Ambassador, M. Feodor Tarasovitch Gousev. In it Eden stated that HM Government 'had under consideration the question of publicity in connection with the forthcoming transfer on loan . . . of a number of warships in accordance with the decision of the Prime Minister communicated to Marshal Stalin.'

He went on to spell out HMG's feelings on the matter:

M. Molotov has been informed by His Majesty's Ambassador in Moscow that we are much looking forward to receiving the Russian sailors who are to take over the ships in this country and that the Prime Minister has given directions that special pains should be taken to make their stay here happy and interesting. It would certainly give great pleasure to Parliament and to the British public to know of the presence of these Russian sailors here and to be assured that they are being suitably entertained. Publicity regarding the transfer of the ships and the entertainment of the Soviet sailors would no doubt be of general propaganda value as a practical example of the co-operation and friendship between our two countries. We propose, therefore, to arrange for a visit of Press correspondents, Press and film photographers and wireless broadcasting experts to attend whatever ceremony may be agreed with the competent Soviet authorities to mark the formal handing over of the warships.

He concluded: 'I should be grateful if you would let me know as soon as possible your Government's views on this matter.' He did not have to wait long! Less than a week later he got a brief letter back from the Soviet Embassy. It is reproduced here in full:

In reply to your letter No. N 2698/25/G of the 13th May, 1944, I would like to inform you that the Soviet Government urgently request the British Government that no publicity whatsoever be given to the fact of the presence of Soviet sailors in this country until the warships reach Soviet ports.

And that was that! Meantime Russian intransigence was being uncounted further down the line aboard the *Royal Sovereign* as, what Royal Marine officer Major Wray himself delightfully recorded, 'The Tiddly Quid' painfully transformed herself into 'The Regal Rouble'.

The Soviet crews who were to man the British battleship *Royal Sovereign*, the American cruiser *Milwaukee* (which the Soviets were to rename *Arkhangelsk* and *Murmansk* respectively) and the other warships, were in April 1944, embarked aboard a number of empty Allied merchant ships awaiting return to Britain after unloading their cargoes in Russian ports. The 2,300 men were distributed among these sixteen merchant ships and this convoy sailed from the White Sea ports under escort of the destroyers *Gremyashchi* and *Gromki* and a minesweeper. They all arrived at the Kola Inlet on 27 April. There they joined the twenty-nine other merchantmen to form the homeward Convoy RA59.

For the first part of the passage the Soviets added the destroyers *Grozny*, *Kuibyshev* and *Razyarenny*, three minesweepers and six submarine chasers. After they turned back, the close escort consisted of the 8th Escort Group, the British destroyers *Beagle*, *Boadicea*, *Inconstant*, *Keppel*, *Walker*, *Westcott*, *Whitehall* and *Wrestler* and four Canadian frigates. To give air cover to the convoy, Rear Admiral McGrigor sailed from Scapa Flow to Kola with the cruiser *Diadem*, escort carriers *Activity* and *Fencer* (which had the Soviet Admiral A. Levchenko taking passage aboard her, together with his staff, which included his naval officer son), the destroyers *Matchless*, *Marne*, *Meteor*, *Milne*, *Musketeer*, *Ulysses*, *Verulam* and *Virago*. More powerful distant cover and protection against any attempts by the German surface fleet to intervene was provided by the Home Fleet with the battleship *Anson*, aircraft carriers *Furious* and *Victorious*, escort carriers *Emperor*, *Pursuer*, *Searcher* and *Striker*, cruisers and destroyers.

The Germans concentrated twelve U-boats in the Bear Island area to intercept this convoy, and they first gained contact on 30 April, despite the appalling weather conditions prevailing at the time. They stayed in touch until 5 May but were largely ineffective. Their only success was the sinking of the 7,167-ton freighter, *William S. Thayer* on 1 May, but they lost no fewer than three of their number, the *U-277*, *U-674* and *U-959*, in achieving this one hit. B. McDermott was serving aboard *Fencer* at the time:

> We brought back to Blighty with us the Russian Vice-Admiral Levchenko with some of his staff who were posted to the *Royal Sovereign*. Unfortunately some of his ship's company was lost when one of the Liberty ships they were taking passage on in our convoy was sunk. There were very few survivors.

When the British officers aboard *Royal Sovereign* later commiserated with their Soviet counterparts on the loss of some of their comrades aboard the ill-fated *Thayer*, they got their first inkling of the Russian character. 'Their reply, "No matter, we still have enough", shook us.'

The remaining forty-four merchant ships arrived safely at Loch Ewe on 6 May in time to celebrate the news of the D-Day landings at Normandy. The Russian crews were accommodated in a large merchant liner lying close by, gradually taking over jobs on *Royal Sovereign* and moving aboard. The ship in question was the hilariously named Canadian Pacific steamer *Empress of Russia*. The flash of inspiration behind this inspired choice turned out to be Captain Peter Skelton, as he recently revealed to me. After leaving the ship he had gone to a desk-bound job at the Admiralty Trade Division, which dealt with merchant shipping and war demands for their services:

> After I arrived at the Admiralty I very soon found on my desk a paper asking me to arrange accommodation for the Russian sailors in the Forth. I had the choice of three spare ships, but I had absolutely no doubts about the correct vessel to assign. For those taking over my *Royal Sovereign* it had to be the *Empress of Russia*.

At Rosyth the team assembled to aid the handover was headed by Admiral Archer. (He had three daughters named Faith, Hope and . . . Olive!.) The ship had been moved into the basin earlier, and a large working party of 'very ordinary' seamen arrived from Chatham. Stores were loaded aboard and repainting began. All the various departments prepared comprehensive notes for translation into Russian, and there were countless day-to-day problems associated with this chore.

The interpreter officers were supplied by the Royal Naval Volunteer Reserve Special Branch, and there was also a WRNS officer aboard, Elizabeth Hurst, and a Canadian lieutenant. The principal interpreter was an older man, who was bilingual and had been to Kiel University. All aboard called him 'Samovar', but what his real name was, other than unpronounceable, they never knew. This latter worthy briefed the British officers before the Russians came on board to be accommodated.

Major Wray remembers some gems of 'what-to-expects' from this source, such as, 'In Russia we are used to baths – where are the bathrooms?'

> Samovar explained that of course they were NOT used to baths. (Or plumbing – their ratings managed to block the

shore-side heads in one day – at that time we were in dry dock.) Samovar was right. The first day a party of Russian officers appeared, having asked the question, and occupied the wardroom bathroom till you could not see the bathroom for steam. Mind you, though there were Russians living on board for the next month, we never saw one in the bathroom.

The Communist party commissar was a mere lieutenant-commander, called Gordyev. He had what had been the paymaster commander's cabin, which had an adjoining bath and toilet. One day, the keyboard sentry came on deck to say that the Russian in the paymaster's cabin wanted to see me. Remembering to be 'correct', I went below (I was on watch). Gordyev said, 'Run me a bath.' Now the ship was of the vintage generation where, to get hot water, steam was blown through a water jacket. Simple, but I knew something he didn't. That afternoon, the fresh water was turned off, as it often was. The arrogance of the man to demand that the officer of the watch should run him a bath infuriated me, but I remained 'correct'. I told him that you turn that valve and then the tap, and left him to it. The fascinating thing is that he never complained about it, but he could not possibly have had a bath in anything but neat steam. On the same note of personal hygiene, it was interesting to note that the officers used (presumably on issue) a perfectly awful scent. Their ratings were not so issued. We could never make up our minds which was the worse smell. And their being Communists, full of comradely equality, we were surprised to find that the officers' cigarettes were of a far superior quality to those issued to the ratings. Mind you, both of them were awful!

With Russians on board, life was never the same! One stoker, who was a declared supporter of 'Uncle Joe', after two weeks had had enough and made a public denouncement (in the traditional manner) of Communism. I think the fact that the Russians had posted armed sentries at the bottom of the brows to stop their comrades going ashore may have had more than a little to do with his abrupt conversion.

Stan Amesbury adds some comments on the lower decks appreciation of the situation thus:

> All the Russian officers had servants, junior officers had one and senior officers had two. They always used a lot of perfume and scent and their clothes were of far superior quality than their sailors.

On the first day that the Russian officers came aboard, the Marine detachment, by now only thirty NCOs and Marines, whose chores included service in the wardroom, were told to expect about twenty for lunch. After lunch had finished the corporal in charge of the WRAs went to his commanding officer in great distress and said that thirty-five had turned up instead, with the consequent problems in the galley and in serving them all. The officer duly checked his list and found that it was twenty! The penny dropped: the twenty had been 'going round the buoy' again. The solution was subtle but effective. The ship was a rarity in having a laundry (equipped by ship's non-public funds). The ship's officers, of course, had their own table-napkin rings. The correct number were therefore laid out and taken away when the Russian officers had finished their lunch. There were no complaints.

Major Wray remembers that the Russian officers all wore pistols. 'We told them that, in our Navy, to bring a weapon into the wardroom would cost a round of port. This did not alter their custom, nor did it produce a round of port!'

One evening, after the Russian officers had retired to their cabins, an RNVR officer arrived in the wardroom. He had clearly dined well, but not excessively well. He said that he had heard that there were Russians on board and he would like to meet them. He said his name was Romanoff! The Canadian interpreter was in the wardroom at the time and he quietly requested the officer of the watch to remove him from the ship. Not only did they get him away from *Royal Sovereign* in double-quick time, but he was posted out of Rosyth completely by lunch-time the following day!

The Russian officers did not merely wear their medal ribbons, they wore the medals – all the time. We were given to understand that, after the handover, we would be given the Order of Suvarov (*sic*) (admittedly only fourth class! – but none the less unusual) with a fetching green ribbon arranged in a sort of inverted 'V' with the medal underneath. (If they did state that, then it was just a cruel joke, or sly fun-making at the expense of the British, because the Order of Souvorov (to give it its correct Russian title) was strictly an *Army* order and has only three classes, not four. The Russian naval medals were the Orders of Nakhimov and Ushakov.) At that time, the war campaign ribbons had not been issued, and we all looked forward to this interesting adornment. Unfortunately this did not happen. The buzz was that, on their way to Russia after the handover, one of the submarines transferred to the Soviet Navy was sunk by the RAF. Whether this story is true I cannot say – all I know is that none of us received a medal! (But I did know a Dutch submariner, Lieutenant-Commander Geys, who always ended his ETA signal by adding 'RAF permitting'!)

This story *was* true: the *B.1*, ex-*Sunfish*, commanded by Captain Fisanovich, was sunk with all hands by a Coastal Command Liberator on 27 July.

Admiral Levchenko complained to Captain Peachey that we were removing from the ship stores to which they were entitled. (Observing that the handover was a loan, how cheeky can you get?) In fact we had been disembarking old and damaged midshipmen's chests and replacing them with new ones. No doubt that creep Shandabuilev had reported to the Russian Naval Mission. As a sideline to this, the ignorant Russians asked for spare barrels for the 15-inch guns. Observing that the life of a 15-inch barrel was 200 full-charge rounds and that ours had fired fewer than fifty equivalent full-charge rounds, the request was ludicrous and – happily – treated as such, since the Russians were unlikely to shoot at anything, let alone hit it.

The Russians then (and do we not wish still?) knew almost nothing about seafaring matters. For example, the Russian gunnery officer was holding forth that, 'In Russia from the moment we see an enemy ship till we open fire is only ten minutes.' Our reply was that for the Royal Navy, twenty seconds was par for the course. Apparently the Russians had asked for *Vittorio Veneto*, but were told firmly that she would not be at all suitable for northern waters. So they asked for *King George V*, but were offered the equally regally named *Royal Sovereign* as being the best of the older battleships.

On his next visit to the ship Admiral Levchenko refused the Captain's hospitality because of these midshipmen's chests. Captain Peachey wasted no time on words. He got Samovar to write on his peculiar Cyrillic-charactered typewriter to the Russian Naval Mission to the effect that he would not have Admiral Levchenko on board his ship until – and I'm pretty sure I'm quoting correctly – 'he has been instructed in the common courtesies of Naval etiquette; I will not have him on board my ship.' As usual with Russians, firm words bring results – no further problem. As a postscript it did my black heart good to read some months later in the Monthly Intelligence Review that Admiral Levchenko had been executed for collaborating with the British!

In fact Admiral Levchenko was one of the most controversial, mysterious and 'dirty' figures in Stalin's Navy, according to some Russian sources, He was imprisoned in 1942, but not as a British spy. Six years later, in 1948, he himself judged 'so-called' British spies – Admiral Galler and others.

The actual tuition was conducted in a painstakingly comprehensive manner and was designed to ensure that the new crew could fully understand each separate part of the ship before taking it over from their British opposite numbers. As each section was mastered, the British ratings were disembarked and the Russians took their place.

One eyewitness recalls:

One of the best entertainments was to see a British gunnery instructor (GI) teaching Russian ratings 4-inch gun drill. Neither the GI nor the Russians could speak the other's language. But by sheer personality and the use of a good deal of basic Anglo-Saxon epithets, the Russians eventually cottoned on.

Captain Peachey revealed to Robin McGarel Groves some of the difficulties he faced in making the turnover work:

The Russians when they came on board *Royal Sovereign* were intensely suspicious, and found it difficult to accept anything they were told. Any discussions were through interpreters, which can add a dimension of its own if oriental custom is observed and the interpreter says what he thinks ought to have been said rather than what was actually said.

What of the British crew's impressions of their guests? The Russians were clearly hard workers, and their officers were very abstemious, possibly by order from on high. Major Wray again supplies some answers:

We all had an absolutely open mind about them when they arrived – after all, they were our Allies. After a very little while our experience led us to realise that the Russian was a peasant in nature, with a peasant's mentality. That is to say, politeness was not in their vocabulary – if there is a Russian word for 'please' I'll be surprised. Force is the only thing which underwrites their code, and not just Communists but over many generations. Hence the seriousness behind Stalin's famous question, 'How many divisions has the Pope?' Bullying is the name of their game – and bluff. Let nobody in the West forget that chess is their national game.

For example: towards the end of the turnover, by which time the Russians had a large contingent living on board, they needed to go inshore for various items of stores. On one occasion, when I was on watch, they asked for a boat to go ashore to collect some musical instruments for their band. I told the cox'n to come straight back – boat routine was hellish at that time. The boat took some two hours to return. The cox'n, Leading Seaman Dennis, a super cox'n, when asked why, said very properly that the Russians had told him to wait and he therefore did so. I was furious and told the Russian officer to wait on deck. I sent for one of our interpreters, and the Canadian appeared. I asked him to translate exactly what I had to say. This little homily of mine concluded with the exhortation to take his bastard accordion off my quarterdeck. The Canadian assured me it would be a pleasure. He did so. Big joke was we found out later that the Russian spoke fluent English, so he had it both ways. Thereafter, whenever this particular Russian saw me, he scuttled away.

Another example was on the day before the turnover, when I was officer of the watch. I needed to have the port boat-boom 'afted' so that, after the turnover, a vessel could come alongside to take the remaining British ratings and marines off. For some little time, the Russians, besides doubling up with a gangway staff, had been running one of our boats. I asked, through one of our interpreters, that they move their boat round to the starboard side. Nothing happened. Even a slack boat's crew could get down into their boat within ten minutes; a good crew, very much quicker. After ten minutes, I asked again ('correct' as usual!). Again nothing happened for another ten minutes. So I lifted up my voice and said that if they didn't move the boat at once, we would move it for them, permanently! It was moved almost instantly.

Despite all the irksome differences in temperament, attitudes and knowledge, both sides undoubtedly worked very hard to make the change-over a success. And this hard work was rewarded. Eventually came the day when the official handover was to take place and 'Tiddly Quid' was to become a part of the Soviet Northern Fleet.

Although *Royal Sovereign* was denied a chance of landing a last blow on the enemy, one of her sister ships, *Ramillies*, was destined to be right at the sharp end of the action during the climax of the European War, the invasion of Normandy, D-Day itself. Here she distinguished herself once more in her shore bombardment role. The historian Commander Kenneth Edwards made the assertion that, 'Curiously enough, the first nation to use large naval forces, including battleships, in this war for the bombardment of shore positions were the Japanese.' But of course this is wrong; the bombardment of Narvik in Norway by the Home Fleet, the bombardment of Cherbourg on the night of 11 October (ignored in the Official History), the bombardment of Bardia, 20 June 1940, Valona in Albania on 18 March 1941 and Tripoli on 20 April 1941 by the battleships of the Mediterranean Fleet and the bombardment of Genoa and La Spezia in northern Italy by Force 'H' on 9 February 1941, all predate the Japanese entry in the war by many months. However, undoubtedly the bombardments carried out by *Ramillies* and other battleships between June and July 1944 were the largest and best rehearsed in the European theatre of war.

It was recognised that in duels between ships and shore batteries the advantage would always lie with the latter, and the failures at the Dardanelles in World War One meant that not much thought had been put into this method of naval support between the wars. However, once accepted, a great deal of work was put in to perfect the method between the miserable failure of Dakar in 1940 and the brilliant work done at Normandy four years later.

The Germans had constructed particularly strong positions near Le Havre and on the Cotentin Peninsula which could dominate the landing beaches and create havoc in the mass of landing craft and supply ships destined to congregate there. It was known that they were well emplaced under eight or twelve feet of reinforced concrete and that only direct hits on the barrels of the guns themselves would permanently disable such weapons. None the less, if the guns could not be fully knocked out by naval bombardment with heavy armour-piercing shells, such a pounding would eventually break up the concrete. Equally importantly the huge concussion effect of salvoes of such enormous missiles falling in the immediate vicinity was expected at the same time to seriously demoralise the gunners themselves and force them to seek shelter in deeper bunkers, abandoning their guns for critical periods of time.

The heavy bombardment squadron which covered the eastern (British) area of the Normandy beachhead was under the command of Rear Admiral W.R. Patterson, and in addition to the *Ramillies* herself it consisted of the battleship *Warspite*, the monitors *Erebus* and *Roberts* and the 6-inch cruisers *Arethusa*, *Danae*, *Dragon*, *Frobisher* and *Mauritius*.

This squadron had assembled in the Clyde after carrying out a period of intensive shore bombardment practice at Scapa Flow.

The original plans were for them to sail from there three days prior to the actual landing so that they could synchronise their arrival off the beaches in time for 'H-Hour' and the opening bombardment. When the weather brought out the postponement of the invasion date to 6 June 1944, this squadron had already been at sea for two days. In order to kill time for an additional day while they awaited the next decision, the big ships had to reverse course for twelve hours and then resume their journey south again. This was done, but in the treacherous North Sea conditions they ran into one of the numerous coastal convoys that plodded up and down the swept channels between the minefields off the east coast. Moreover, this encounter took place in thick fog, which could have caused all manner of complications. Luckily all the ships escaped this close encounter unscathed.

By 0515 on 6 June *Ramillies* and her consorts had reached the allocated positions, and anchored to the east of Sword beach.

Each ship was allocated one heavy German battery as her particular target to silence. But of course they could switch from their allocated target to 'targets of opportunity' as the need arose, and they were helped in their work by special Royal Naval spotter aircraft based at Lee-on-Solent airfield.

The heavy German guns around Le Havre were dug in deeply under layers and layers of reinforced concrete and could thus take an enormous amount of punishment without being put of action for a length of time. Even the one-ton projectiles of the battleships required direct hits to silence such guns permanently. The best they could hope for was to make the German gunners keep their heads down while the troops got ashore, and then maintain such a constant rain of high explosives as to render them ineffectual in the days that followed.

Such a policy called for a high expenditure of ammunition of all calibres, but especially of the 15-inch projectiles, the ones that really shook the enemy up. Even as the first salvoes roared out from assembled ships, the German Navy put in a brief and fleeting appearance out of the early morning mists and smoke-screens at 0530. These German destroyers seemed to be amazed at finding the whole vast concourse of the Invasion Fleet spread before them rank on rank. They looked, fired one hasty salvo of torpedoes and fled back to port again, vanishing into the murk almost as quickly as they had come. As they disappeared, followed by gouts of water from the return fire, their torpedoes sped right at the bombarding force ships. One was observed to pass between *Ramillies* and *Warspite*, and others sped by other ships equally closely, but their only victim was the Norwegian destroyer *Svenner* (formerly the British *Shark*), which was hit and broke in half immediately.

After this lucky let-off, the battleships got down to their work in earnest. *Ramillies* experienced great difficult in suppressing one German battery located at Benerville. The battleship's firing was extremely accurate, but no direct hits were scored. By 0930 all the main German batteries had been reduced to silence for a while, although mobile guns continued to prove troublesome and difficult to pin down. However, further shoots had continually to be made against these most resilient German gunners as the day wore on. Between them the two battleships and the two monitors fired 218 rounds of the heaviest shell into the Houlgate battery and scored one direct hit on a gun. The *Ramillies* and other ships also directed some 284 rounds of heavy shell at the two guns sited at Benerville without destroying either gun.

Counter-battery work was gradually supplanted by longer-range bombardment of more diverse targets as the campaign wore on. The *Ramillies* and the other battleships were particularly useful to the land forces in this respect because they could engage targets some seventeen miles inland. Thus, surprised German divisions assembling in what they thought were safe or zones far from the coast, immune from artillery, would suddenly find heavy shells descending on them out of the blue, causing casualties and much consternation at the Royal Navy's reach.

Almost all of *Ramillies*'s shoots off Normandy were conducted against hidden targets; firing by map reference was the name of the game. Such blind bombardments brought no visible reward for the toiling gunners, their only consolation being the stream of congratulatory signals coming back from the Army as German tanks, guns and motor transport were pulverised from afar by an unknown hand of great power. The many factors involving accuracy, which in the climax of a naval action at sea are compressed into an hour or so, were made more difficult by both the nature of the target and the hazards of coastal navigation in mine-infested seas, and the effects of wear and tear on both guns and men alike as the days passed into weeks of continual action.

A large number of shoots were carried out thus, and shore-based Forward Officers, Bombardment (FOB), directed *Ramillies*'s guns onto hidden targets behind hills or in woods to great effect. All manner of enemy targets were thus engaged, from the dug-in batteries to armoured columns, supply depots, and even infantry. Ten per cent of all the 15-inch shells fired in the first month of operations at Normandy were against enemy infantry concentrations. The average range the battleships provided 'deep support' for during this period was found to be 17,000 yards (8½ sea miles), which was still well within their compass. The average distance of the first ranging shot at such extreme and unseen targets was found to have been only 146 yards, and subsequent salvoes were quickly dropping much more precisely than this.

Such prolonged bouts of firing by the heavy guns naturally soon emptied the ship's magazines, and when this happened they returned to Portsmouth to replenish. Prolonged work of this nature, as they followed the Army's advance along coast, also wore out the *Ramillies*'s 15-inch barrels. Life-expired heavy gun barrels had to be changed every 200 rounds or so, and the procedure adopted was for the battleships to sail back to Rosyth to have this done and then resume their work down south after a short interval. While they were away other battleships took over their role.

The *Ramillies* herself remained off the Normandy beaches throughout June and July. Commander Edwards makes the following often forgotten point:

> This bombarding and provision of deep artillery support called for great endurance on the part of the officers and men of the bombarding ships. When they were in the assault area or its vicinity they had to be ready for action at an instant's notice both day and night. Many of the officers in these ships did not take their clothes off for seventeen

days and nights, yet the enemy never tried to profit by their weariness, which he could easily have deduced. It was also very trying to the nerves. Imagine being in a ship, which fired one 15-inch or 16-inch gun regularly once a minute, as did the battleships *Nelson* and *Ramillies* when they bombarded Caen throughout the night of June 12/13th. They ensured that the Germans got no rest, but the crews of the ships got no rest either.

As to the effectiveness of *Ramillies*'s work, we need go no further than to quote from German reports of the time which tell what it was like to be on the receiving end of a British battleship's anger. On 16 June the Wehrmacht issued an analysis of this issue which concluded uncompromisingly that: 'It is no exaggeration to say that the co-operation of the heavy naval guns played a decisive part in enabling the Allies to establish a bridgehead in Normandy.'[1]

Although the naval historian Captain Stephen Roskill was later to cast doubts on the authenticity and validity of such statements, there seems no reason why the Germans on the receiving end should not give a truthful summary of what it was like and how it contributed to their eviction from the coastal region. Moreover the totally unbiased joint Technical Warfare Committee carried out a thorough investigation in 1945, which reached similar conclusions to that of the Germans. They studied both air and sea bombardments fully, and at the end of it they stated bluntly that during the Normandy operations 'the only weapon which was capable of penetrating the strong concrete protection of casemated guns was the armour-piercing shell from the main armament of battleships and monitors. None of the bombs used was adequate.' They concluded that 'naval gunfire was the only means available for producing a further appreciable but temporary reduction in enemy fire'. These statements seem unambiguous enough for anyone.

The commander of the German 7th Army spoke more with gut reaction than with critical study when he told General Rommel that, 'Coast defence guns were in most cases put out of action by direct hits on casemates.' He added that his own counter-attacks 'suffered very heavy casualties in the neighbourhood of the coast through enemy naval artillery fire'. And if anyone should know it was this worthy!

Aboard the *Ramillies*, although they were pleased with the effect of their work, living conditions were very poor. One officer, who had spent an exciting commission as a junior gunnery officer aboard the *Duke of York*, including her sinking of the *Scharnhorst*, was later transferred to *Ramillies*, were he found a very different state of affairs. He was later to recall she was 'a truly filthy ship. Every time they'd fire the main guns, roaches, mice and various sundry creatures would fall!'[2] A legacy of her time laid up idle, no doubt. Her 15-inch guns did their job none the less.

Towards the end of July *Ramillies* sailed for the Mediterranean. Another invasion was planned to take place in the bay between Cannes and the French naval base of Toulon in the south of France. Although the bulk of the troops were American, the need for an experienced and battle-hardened bombardment battleship led to the call for *Ramillies* to join the covering force under the American Vice-Admiral H.K. Hewitt, which included the US battleships *Arkansas*, *Nevada* and *Texas*.

She arrived in August and went into action again on the 15th of that month as part of 'Alpha' Force under Rear Admiral F.J. Lowry USN. The initial target allocated to *Ramillies* here was a battery of heavy guns located on the strategic island of Fort Cruos to the east of the beachhead. She conducted several shoots at this target, which proved effective, and the island itself was captured soon afterwards. The next objective was the heavy guns located to the south of the Gulf of St Tropez, which she was effective in silencing.

Again shifting her anchorage on the 25th, *Ramillies*, the American battleship *Nevada*, and the French battleship *Lorraine* took on in succession further German heavy guns mounted in former French fortresses in the vicinity of Marseilles and Toulon, particularly the St Mandrier battery. Again, despite good work and prolonged firing, some 147 separate shoots were conducted by the bombarding squadron as a whole up to the 28th, as these coastal guns proved very hard to silence. Both places duly fell to the Americans on 28 August. *Ramillies's* final work was done, and she returned home to Portsmouth.

Here she spent the final days of the war in retirement, becoming an accommodation ship attached to the *Vernon* mining school there. In a similar manner her other two sisters had been reduced to a humble role. The *Resolution* and *Revenge* had carried out their last important duty in February 1943, when they both protected the huge convoy that carried the Australian Division home from Suez to Australia. After further escort sorties in the Indian Ocean, both these battleships returned to home waters in September 1943, and despite the need for bombardment ships, they lay idle until May 1944. Again it was decided to reduce them to accommodation ship status, and together they became the HMS *Imperieuse* stokers' training establishment. Initially they were moored in Gairloch to perform this duty, but later they sailed south to Southampton, and they finished the war anchored at Devonport. And so only *Royal Sovereign* remained in active service as a fighting ship for the last year of World War Two and beyond, but not as part of the Royal Navy.

Notes:

[1] Edwards, Kenneth, *Operation Neptune*, Collins, 1946
[2] ARFHB to the author, 8 April 2008

CHAPTER TEN

Journey's End

R ight up to the time of the final handover ceremony there were problems and difficulties. As Robin McGarel Groves later was to recall:

The handover started with a most detailed tour of inspection of the ship with Captain Peachey and a number of British technical officers in attendance. Every time the party came to a place where something appeared to have been removed, detailed questions were asked what had been removed, why was it not still there, why was this piece of equipment part of what had been promised to the Russians being denied to them. When you consider the changes that had taken place in gunnery fire-control equipment, to name but one area, since the ship was launched in April 1915, you will realise that the bridge, spotting-top, fire-control directors, transmitting station and turrets had many empty screw holes, though in many cases these were covered by newer equipment. These Soviet equivalents of Captain's Rounds took over two weeks to complete, and periodically high officials were summoned from London to add weight to the complaints that the British had stripped the ship of equipment vital to her efficiency, before handing her over to their Allies.

One particularly vexatious problem was a number of holes in the bulkhead of the captain's after cabin. The Russians simply would not believe that these had been made to hold in place pictures of Their Majesties the King and Queen. Only when the photographs of King George VI and Queen Elizabeth were withdrawn from store and the bracket holes matched against the holes in the bulkhead was grudging acceptance given. Alan Peachey also arranged for the supply of more than adequate supplies of vodka to be available, and did his best to lubricate the situation and to overcome final hurdles. He claimed that this experience had put him off vodka for life!

In one respect the Soviets *were* right to be suspicious. There was simply no way that they were going to be allowed access to the very latest British radar secrets, although many of the older sets were freely made available and retained. Among the sets removed before their appearance was the Type 273 QR, it being noted that this 'should not be released at present. USSR have applied for a set, but agreement has not been received from US and release cannot be authorized without US concurrence.'[1] It was also noted that while it was not necessary to remove any of the W/T installations, 'All recognition apparatus will have to be removed.'

Although the Soviets had become reasonable conversant with most of the elementary functions of the ship and thus would be able to raise steam and sail her back to Murmansk, they were hardly in a position to take her into battle. A strong British escort would obviously have to be provided for her to give her protection against the U-boat packs, and should the threat of a surface engagement develop with the appearance of the *Tirpitz* (or something similarly large and aggressive) from one of the German fleet anchorages in the Norwegian fiords, then the *Royal Sovereign* would have to be able at least to manoeuvre out of harm's way while the Royal Navy tackled the problems. It was clear that such complex tactics, even the basic Allied convoy routines, would be beyond the Russian signals and communications crews, and so arrangements had to be made to provide a Royal Navy team to take passage in her for the journey north.

To illustrate this point, Captain R.H. Bevan, principal naval liaison officer at the Admiralty, submitted a report on the results of a fortnight's anti-submarine training course given to eight Russian officers and sixteen ratings at HMS *Osprey*. They were to man the anti-submarine equipment of the old Town-class destroyers being transferred with *Royal Sovereign*. Their competence and attitude was given as follows:

> The technical ability of the class was high in questions of electrical material, but the standard of operating was deplorable. At the start of the course the class was under the impression that the A/S problem ended with perfect knowledge of the Asdic set. It was finally realised how little they knew of the science of U-boat killing. The ratings seemed to assimilate knowledge quicker and more thoroughly than the officers.

Initially quite large parties of British officers and men were envisaged, but as time went on it became increasingly the concern of the British authorities that any such Royal Navy team would be at a grave disadvantage, and every opportunity was therefore made to keep their final numbers to an absolute bare minimum. The only time this question had come up was at a meeting between the Deputy First Sea Lord and Admiral Kharlamov on 15 May, when the Russian was asked what officers and ratings were required to go in ships to Russia. Kharlamov at that time requested that this should be held in abeyance until the arrival of Admiral Levchenko, but nothing had been done since.

Admiral Archer spelt out his worries on this score in a signal to the Admiralty on 27 May. In it he stated that for some time it had been becoming apparent that 'the Russians intend to exploit the British personnel left in *Royal Sovereign* after transfer' and that 'their position will become even more difficult than it is at present'. As an indication of 'the way the wind is blowing', the Admiral mentioned that the Russian captain stated that a writer rating would be unnecessary 'as all correspondence between British authorities and their higher authorities would be required to be submitted through the Russian authorities'.

Archer therefore stated that, to avoid a situation which 'might lead to not only unpleasant but serious incidents' he was telling the Soviet Admiral that British servicemen still aboard as instructors and demonstrators would be sent on board by boat each day instead of remaining aboard as hitherto. The C-in-C Home Fleet was being advised to make similar arrangements for the British party during the battleship's working-up period at Scapa Flow. He concluded by stating that Captain Peachey had 'previously expressed an opinion that no British personnel should be allowed to accompany the ship to Russia'. Admiral Archer now urged that this advice be followed.

The Admiralty considered what to do about the British residential party, then numbering twelve officers and seventy ratings. They concluded that:

Unless Senior Officer remaining (G) Lieutenant F.C. Reseigh RN is given honorary rank or some other status it is doubtful if Russians will recognise his authority in matters outside his direct technical province. A high authority who will sponsor the British party and ensure their well being is also much to be desired, judging by the present Russian attitude. This attitude also militates strongly against retention of any British personnel on ship's final departure for Russian waters.

Just prior to the handover, the command of the British Residential Party was taken over by Lieutenant-Commander W.R.T. Clements RNVR, and he had twelve officers and sixty-eight ratings.

The final British position was embodied in a message dated 21 July which stated that suitable opportunity should be taken to confirm that the Russian Authorities understood that, 'No British personnel will accompany ships to Russia except such communications personnel and accompanying interpreters as may be agreed.'

Meanwhile the final preparations for the handover were almost complete. A 'Most Secret' OTP ('one-time pad') signal in Naval Cypher A.1 was sent to the Admiralty from Admiral Archer, C-in-C Rosyth on 26 May. It read:

Agreement has been reached that transfer of HMS *Royal Sovereign* and the S/Ms will take place Tuesday May 30th ceremony being held on board HMS *Royal Sovereign* between 1030 and 1130. It is understood Soviet Ambassador will be present at ceremony.

The Admiralty replied next day:

Ceremony will be attended by DFSL (Deputy First Sea Lord) representing the 1st Lord and the Board of Admiralty and he will carry out the transfer of the ships to the Russians in their name. He will arrive Waverley Station at 0750 Tuesday 30th accompanied by his Secretary. Request onward transport may be arranged.

The Deputy First Sea Lord was Admiral Sir Charles Kennedy-Purvis, of whom Admiral Cunningham later wrote: '. . . whose wise mind, great ability and knowledge of Admiralty departments and methods were invaluable in relieving the First Sea Lord of much of the administrative work'.

In order to work out the handing-over ceremony, Captain Peachey and Marine Captain Wray went to the HQ of the Flag Officer, Rosyth. Captain Peachey wanted to know what to order to bring down (for the last time in twenty-eight years' service) the White Ensign. He already had a suggestion: 'Strike the British Ensign.' The Admiral said he didn't think that a very good order, as it suggested surrender. With more passion than tact, Captain Wray burst out, 'Well, isn't it, sir?' and was duly given a blistering reply, which 'left me feeling like the dormouse being put into the teapot'. The phrase they eventually settled upon was, 'Haul down the British Ensign', which was bad enough. Major Wray continues the tale:

For the ceremony I had managed to borrow from a County-class cruiser in the harbour (it may have been *Berwick)* her Royal Marine band, for, of course, we hadn't had one for a long time. The ship was in the stream. I went ashore and into Edinburgh for what I hoped was some pretty comprehensive dalliance with a WRNS officer of my acquaintance.

I was late back, slept aboard an escort carrier and rejoined the ship by way of the ratings' drifter first thing. I had the Confidential Book keys in my pocket, and this resulted in an interview with Captain Peachey when I came inboard that morning.

The handover was, one might say, a potential shambles engineered by the Russians. Their picket boat, carrying their Ambassador, the nonentity Gusev, and the liaison officer, Shandabuilev – an oily, smarmy man who looked like pictures of Napoleon – arrived twenty minutes before the scheduled time and, of course, hidden till the last moment by the still persistent mist. My braves were already on the quarterdeck, as was the borrowed band. We just had time to get fallen in before the party came on board, Shandabuilev smirking.

Another boat arrived with the Deputy First Sea Lord aboard, along with the C-in-C Rosyth and senior Russian naval officers, including Rear Admiral Ivanov, the ship's new captain, and finally the Soviet Ambassador himself.

Gusev, clearly with no idea how to inspect a guard, did not wait after I had reported the guard to him at the Slope, and pushed off to 'inspect' them. Hence the fact that, quite incorrectly, the guard was 'inspected' at the Slope rather than at the Order. Hence also my cross expression in the official photographs!

This done, the whole official party assembled by 'Y' turret. The Russians had present their own band, which had been practising assiduously with British instruments in the ship's chapel, which their musicians also used as a storehouse! The Royal Marines then took up positions aft facing forward, and the various dignitaries made speeches of varying quality and length. Admiral Kennedy-Purvis stated, presumably with tongue firmly in cheek, that, 'We know we turn these ships over to a gallant and high-spirited navy, and I am sure they will be used against the common enemy with full effect.'

In turn the Soviet Ambassador formally accepted the ship into the Soviet Northern Fleet, assuring them that the Russians sailors would use them to good purposes, along with the submarines *Sunfish, Unbroken, Unison* and *Ursula*, which were lying alongside.

The order was given to haul down the White Ensign, and the bugler sounded 'Still' as it came slowly down, while the National Anthem was played. The Russians then struck up their own National Anthem as their ensign was raised, bringing to an end twenty-eight years of continuous service for a battleship first commissioned on the eve of Jutland. Then it was over and the VIPs descended below for liquid refreshment. Major Wray:

> The ceremony over, the official party left the quarterdeck for the wardroom, leaving me, my guard and Captain Peachey. I reported to him for permission to march off the guard. As we turned forrard and started marching off, Captain Peachey called out, 'Well done, soldier – but that'll teach you to sleep with your Wren officer girlfriend in Edinburgh.' My braves could hardly keep their faces straight. (It still rankles – she *wouldn't!*)
>
> Although now officially named *Arkhangelsk*, the quarterdeck still retained the heavy brass nameplates by the gangways proclaiming her to be *Royal Sovereign*. The ship's crest – the Imperial Crown – was still to be seen adorning the tompions. But aloft was the indisputable fact. No longer the White Ensign, but the pale blue and white flag with the red hammer and sickle and star was above.
>
> Then came the party in the wardroom. Up to the change of flag the Russian officers had been abstemious, presumably by order of the ghastly Gordyev. But after the ceremony, it was different. Their commander, Chincheradze, a splendidly extrovert Georgian, clearly took a fancy to me and offered me a pat of butter, hugging me closely at the same time. *Ugh!* My party piece for a long time – well before 'Regal Rouble' days – had been to do a Russian dance. I was prevailed upon to do this. The Russians were as sick as the proverbial parrots, for, when called upon to do it properly, none of them could do it at all.
>
> One of my corporals then asked to see me, and 'would I come down to the messdeck'. Wondering what on earth

had gone wrong, remembering that the paymaster had issued 'neaters' rum instead of grog to celebrate the occasion, I went down to the messdeck in some trepidation. However, all the boys wanted to do was to offer me 'sippers all round'. Then the sergeants' mess invited me to join them. This took in a bottle of gin between all too few of us. Frankly I don't remember leaving the ship!

We were to be accommodated in HMS *Cochrane*, the ancient base ship at Rosyth. I awoke in the upper berth of a strange cabin, naked but covered by a blanket, to find a Wren sitting on the lower bunk. I asked – really wanting to know – what she was doing there. 'Cleaning your buttons, sir', she said. Ah well.

For me the main thing was that *Royal Sovereign* had been my home – my first ship – for over two and a half years. I wouldn't have minded the turnover if the Russians had had any feelings for her as a ship. To use the ship's chapel – refurbished with love and kindness by friends in Philadelphia – as a musical instrument store hurt awfully. When I went to Pitreavie to return the Confidential Books, there was, to me, a very ancient Royal Marines officer in charge. He asked me, 'What ship?' and I said *Royal Sovereign*. He said something to the effect, 'What a funny thing – I was her first OCRM, and I said, 'What a funny thing – I'm her last.'

The battleship remained at Rosyth for some time after the ceremony. Mr K. Simmonds, serving as a young AB aboard the battleship HMS *Howe*, then preparing to sail for the Pacific war, remembers seeing her off the Firth of Forth on his 19th birthday, on 12 June 1944. She was kept at least twelve miles downstream so that no detailed inspection of the radar outfit of Britain's newest battleship could be conducted by our Allies with their powerful telescopes and binoculars. He recalled to me:

We left Scapa Flow and carried out various exercises with ships of the Home Fleet and then moored in the Firth of Forth. Shortly afterwards another ship arrived, the *Arkhangelsk*, and moored out towards the mouth of the Forth, much further out than was considered normal. We could just see her, and she us. The generally accepted view was that the Admiralty did not wish to give the Russians an opportunity to study our most modern ships' radar arrays, etc.

It was soon after this that she finally sailed to Scapa Flow to carry out gunnery exercises on the Home Fleet ranges, and generally work up. J. Morris, an ex-CRS, wrote:

Those who were in Scapa Flow in the spring and summer of 1944 will recall seeing the 'Tiddly Quid' in Russian livery. Our liaison parties sent over told us of being isolated in their guarded messdeck with no contact with the *Arkhangelsk*'s crew except in the line of duty, to ensure presumably that no Capitalist Woodbines or nutty changed hands.

On 16 August, just before *Arkhangelsk* sailed from Scapa Flow, Admiral Sir Charles Kennedy-Purvis received a letter from Vice-Admiral Levchenko. In it the Russian expressed satisfaction at the way things had gone and gratitude to those who had assisted his crews with their difficult task. It was an extremely friendly letter, and, no doubt, sincerely meant.

Levchenko wrote, 'As I am leaving your country I would like to express to you and to all your officers my deep appreciation and thanks for all the assistance and attention which has been afforded to me and to my officers and men personally by yourself, and your admirals, officers and ratings who have taken part in the turnover of the ships.' He expressed the opinion that the hard work all concerned put in 'turned their duties during the transfer into a cementing of our Service friendship, in order that this should always serve as a remembrance of days of co-operation and as a strengthening for the future.' He particularly singled out Lieutenant-Commander Reseigh, whom 'especially it is desired to commend'.

He made absolutely no mention of Admiral Archer or Captain Peachey, and there were other omissions, which led Kennedy-Purvis to comment wryly:

While I do not doubt that these officers are deserving of his commendation, I am not sure that to do so would be a very wise thing, particularly as Admiral Levchenko has excluded from his list some of the officers . . . who, in my opinion, worked the hardest to ensure that the ships were ready for sea in the shortest possible time.

There remained the question of getting the Soviet battleship back to Murmansk in one piece. Churchill had been somewhat hoist on his own petard on the issue. Like all politicians he had wanted his cake and eaten it. Having castigated the Royal Sovereigns mercilessly, he then convinced himself that he was doing 'Uncle Joe' a favour by loaning him 'Tiddly Quid'. 'It is for the Russians to show gratitude rather than for us to show deference', he hectored Alexander and Cunningham on this issue. However, he was worried about the Marshal's reaction should the *Royal Sovereign* not make it back to Mother Russia with all her admirals intact. He therefore was firm in his insistence that the Navy should provide strong protection, as he duly informed Sir Alexander Cadogan at the Foreign Office on 18 April 1944.

The decision was made to sail the Soviet Force in conjunction with the next convoy operation, in the hope that the Germans would concentrate on the latter and enable the Russians 'a free home run', which, considering the Soviet warships were supposed to be for the protection of the convoys and not the other way round, was a pretty ironic situation. In addition, the Home Fleet put out in some force under Admiral Sir Henry Moore, operating in two task groups and conducting air strikes against the *Tirpitz* in her lair to keep her quiescent.

Thus it was that the full panoply of the Home Fleet's strength put to sea on 15 July 1944. Many of the big ships, as we have seen with the *Howe*, had already sailed for the Eastern theatre, but enough remained to assemble a powerful force. The only battleship was *Duke of York*, but there were three fleet carriers, *Formidable*, *Furious* and *Indefatigable*, two 8-inch cruisers, *Berwick* and *Devonshire* and fourteen modern fleet destroyers. Another group, comprising the escort carriers *Nabob* and *Trumpeter*, escorted by six Captain-class frigates, operated in conjunction with the main force. The convoy itself, JW59, consisted of thirty-three merchant ships and one rescue ship. It was escorted by the escort carriers *Striker* and *Vindex*, the 6-inch cruiser *Jamaica*, seven destroyers, two frigates, four sloops, five corvettes and eleven submarine-chasers, themselves on their way to be handed over to the Russians under Lend-Lease arrangements.

Two days later, on the 17th, the *Arkhangelsk* and destroyers *Derzkiyi*, *Deyatelnyi*, *Doblestnyi*, *Dostonynyi*, *Druzhnyi*, *Zharkiy*, *Zhivuchiy* and *Zhguchiy* sailed independently. One of those Russians serving aboard the destroyer *Zhivuchiy* later wrote in his memoirs[2] that the British were so much impressed by the knowledge and skill of the Soviet sailors that many newspapers wrote that they believed that there were no ordinary seaman among them, but only disguised engineers! Self-delusion or propaganda, it matters little.

Aboard the battleships was a small party of British W/T and signals ratings under Lieutenant-Commander Clements. One of these ratings was a young W/T trained operator, Len Thomas. The viewpoint of him and his handful of colleagues was a unique one of the Russian Navy at work, and is worth placing on record in full:

> I was 'on loan' from my ship, the heavy cruiser *Devonshire*, and the others came from other ships. It was a quiet run, though the Russians tended to be trigger-happy and to blaze away at imaginary U-boats. Maybe it was just gunnery practice!
>
> Our small messdeck on the *Royal Sovereign* was *not* guarded, and Russian ratings would sometimes sit with us and try to communicate; not easy, as we had no Russian and they had learnt only the much-used four-letter Navy words while at Rosyth and Scapa! However, they were keen to show us their family snaps, etc., and were fond of saying 'War no bloody good!' At least two were keen to swap complete uniforms with us for souvenirs, but we had no spare items with us. I was given a Russian sailor's cap by one friendly soul, but when I was back on the *Devonshire* it was stolen from my locker, together with my wristwatch.
>
> When off duty, we roamed about the ship as freely as if on any RN ship, and no one seemed to mind. We could not

eat the greasy Russian stews, and after the first day had tasty egg and chips type of food specially prepared for us.

There seemed to be rather a large number of high-ranking Russian officers on board, with plenty of gold rings and 'scrambled egg' on their caps, and others who, I thought, were 'political' officers – usually two-ringers – who were treated with marked respect and deference by officers of much higher rank.

There were regular political meetings, which the off-duty crew seemed bound to attend. Pictures of Stalin and other Russian leaders, and political (I suppose) banners and posters, festooned the ship below decks.

There were film shows on two or three occasions, Russian of course, which seemed to please and amuse the crew, who were, on the whole, a cheerful crowd and very much as on an RN ship.

My duty was to stand my watches in the main WT office and pick out any signals concerning the *Royal Sovereign* or the convoy as a whole. These were passed (decoded) to our flag officer. Our signalmen, of course, could communicate by flags or lamps with the RN convoy escorts. We had a Russian who spoke English to translate for us in the WT office. He was not prepared to talk about Communism, Stalin or the war, though a pleasant chap to be with.

The ship was handled well, and the Russians seemed have no particular difficulties. Maybe they were used to merchantmen, if not big warships, at that time. Also, they had probably had training from RN officers.

I had only one unpleasant experience on board. We were told to use the officers' heads near the WT office. Late one night a drunken officer – one of the politicals, I believe – was there when I went in. He could speak some English, and began to work himself into a rage because, when at Scapa, he claimed that the Russians had not been allowed to field a football team against an RN team. He blamed the British C-in-C. I told him I knew nothing about it, but he became aggressive, and I had to push/punch him away to leave the heads. I told our officer about this, but nothing was said to the Russians afterwards.

Apart from that incident, the Russians were friendly and always ready to wave and smile and say 'Good day' as we went about our business. The actual creation of the Soviet Northern Fleet Squadron was approved under the Order 00156 of the *Narkom VMF* and of the 00463 Order of the Northern Fleet War Council.[3]

Having got wind of the handover, the Germans were eager to cause an upset by sinking the Anglo-Soviet battleship if they could. They had sunk her sister ship *Royal Oak* easily enough in the assumed safety of her own fleet anchorage at the beginning of the war and were eager to repeat Prien's success at sea . There is no doubt that to have torpedoed another R-class battleship at this stage of the war would have lifted morale again back in the Reich. Accordingly they massed nine U-boats in two groups to oppose these squadrons, but apart from sinking the frigate *Bickerton* and the sloop *Kite*, and damaging the escort carrier *Nabob*, they failed in their attacks and lost two of their number, *U-344* and *U-354*, for their pains. A determined effort was made to sink the *Arkhangelsk* by the *U-711*, commanded by Lieutenant-Commander Lange on 23 April. He fired a salvo of two torpedoes at her and another at the *Zharkiy*, but all these torpedoes, which included the T-5 'homing' type of underwater missile, failed to hit, and exploded prematurely before the end of their runs.

Another former member of the *Royal Sovereign*'s ship's company from many years ago was E.S.W. MacClure, who had known her as a young midshipman. He was now serving as first lieutenant and torpedo officer aboard the escorting light cruiser HMS *Jamaica*. His memories of the voyage are as follows: 'My old ship was now crammed with Russian sailors and we kept a safe distance as they were constantly training their close-range weapons in all directions during the passage.'

It was with great relief, therefore, that the Admiralty received a signal from the Senior British Naval Officer North Russia, dated 24 April, which stated, 'IMPORTANT. U. S. S. R. ARCHANGEL (sic) and escort of 8 repeat 8 *Destroyers* arrived Kola Inlet 033011.'

Aboard the battleship the safe arrival of the whole force was celebrated by the Russians and the little band of Royal Navy communications men, as Len Thomas recollects:

> When we finally anchored at Murmansk, the Russian who had given me his spare cap stood beside me, looking around. He pointed all around and then said in English, 'Russkie Scapa – *no bloody good!*' We were thanked by a Russian officer before we left the *Royal Sovereign*, and were given a bottle of vodka each – a greenish bottle, with a black wax seal.
>
> We had been in convoy with the cruiser *Jamaica*, and it was she who brought us back home from Murmansk afterwards.

Lieutenant MacClure has similar memories:

> When we arrived at Kola the Russian pilot was down in *Jamaica*'s wardroom, eagerly studying the English glossy papers, as was their wont. I remember saying to him, 'What do you think of your new battleship?' to which he made the non-committal reply, 'You mean our old battleship!' Incidentally, it is interesting to note that the first Soviet captain of the *Arkhangelsk*, Rear Admiral Ivanov, had been the captain of the old battleship *Marat* at the Spithead Review of 1937. His Soviet rank was Fleet Flag of 2nd Ran (Rear Admiral), exactly the same in 1944 as it had been seven years earlier.

While the war lasted, men of the Royal Navy serving on the Russian convoys occasionally caught glimpses of the former British battleship. One such was former crew member Tom Pope, at this stage of war serving aboard the escort carrier *Queen*. He not only saw his old ship but actually went aboard her again briefly, as he explains:

> Reaching Murmansk after a convoy run, HMS *Queen* had the good fortune to be in harbour with the *Royal Sovereign* and I had the opportunity of visiting her, being invited by the Russians to a film show on board her. A party of us

went over. We were not allowed to see around the ship, but were taken straight to the forrard messdeck where the film was shown. We noticed the untidy dress of the crew and generally the lack of smartness, as opposed to the Royal Navy. I did notice, however, that the officers were not given priority for seats; they sat or stood with the sailors. But even the officers looked untidy.

According to M B Lebedinskiy,[4] because of the danger the Northern Squadron moved into the White Sea in the summer of 1945, the destroyers being based in the Northern Dvina river, while *Arkhangelsk* and *Murmansk* anchored in the deeper road-stead. By September, however, all had returned to Vaenga in the Kola Inlet.

Arkhangelsk never seemed to go far from the confined waters of the Kola Inlet after that, probably because she remained a prime target for every U-boat skipper in North Norway eager to get her scalp while there was still the chance. But, however much Len Thomas's Russian friend might disparage Murmansk as a base compared with Scapa Flow, it certainly seemed far more secure. Although several determined attempts were made to sink her there, none of the German U-boats managed to penetrate the net and boom defences, and so *Royal Sovereign*, if not contributing much to the Allied war effort in the Arctic, at least survived the war.

During the period 14 to 24 September, the German submarine *U-315*, commanded by Lieutenant Zoller, made persistent efforts to penetrate the Kola defences and get in an attack on the *Arkhangelsk*. Fitted with the schnorkel device that enabled her to stay under water for longer periods than normal, she made several probes towards her anchorage, but always the compre-hensive series of net and barrages made any approach both dangerous and difficult. In the end Zoller was forced to admit defeat. A second submarine skipper, Lieutenant-Commander Schweiger of *U-313*, attempted to succeed where he had failed. He sailed from his base on 28 September and also made a submerged approach using his schnorkel gear. He also returned, totally thwarted, on 10 October without achieving anything at all. The 'lucky ship' reputation of the *Royal Sovereign* evidently survived her change of ownership and name!

In any event, in November 1944 there was little movement of the battleship, apart from some training exercises. Indeed, for the whole of that year *Arkhangelsk* spent only twelve full days at sea! This picture was reflected in the following three years as follows:

1945: Forty days at sea, steaming 2,750 miles in total

1946: Nineteen days at sea, steaming 1,491 miles in total

1947: Twenty-one days at sea, steaming 1,826 miles in total

Again, these were mainly periodic forays into the Barents and White Seas for training, plus an anti-submarine exercise conducted in May 1946. This was to war-game the repulsing of an enemy (presumably her former owners) attempt to break into the White Sea, and *Arkhangelsk* served as the Exercise Staff HQ Ship. During these years she never appears to have been docked or undergone any maintenance. One Soviet historian claimed that her main function appeared to be as an experimental test ship for the embarked British radars. In this role she carried out some 150 radar-assisted gunnery shoots, with ratings who had undergone a special course in Glasgow learning how to work the sets. Although some British sources claim the Type 273 was removed from *Royal Sovereign* before the handover, a few Soviet sources are adamant that she retained this set for the main armament, and that her Russian crew paid special attention to this equipment.

Rear Admiral Vadim Ivanovich Ivanov served as her captain from 30 May 1944, being relieved on 15 March 1945 by Captain Nikolay Andreevich Petrishchev. While in Soviet service, the *Arkhangelsk* received many 'nicknames', one of which was 'Prisoner of Nations', which expression was itself a paraphrase of Lenin's famous words, 'Tsarist Russia was the prison of nations'. Three different post-war legends appertained to this epithet. Firstly, *Arkhangelsk* was used as a floating prison for dissident sailors; secondly, its compartments were small, low and cramped by Russian standards; and thirdly, the battleship didn't actually *do* anything, just stayed in one place.

A new enemy ploy was attempted in January. Following the Royal Navy attack on the *Tirpitz* earlier, when midget submarines or three-man 'X-craft' had been towed from Britain to off the Norwegian coast by conventional submarines, and had then penetrated the German battleship's defence nets and severely damaged her, the Germans mounted a similar operation against *Arkhangelsk*. The German equivalents of the British 'X-craft' were the *Biber* (Beaver) one-man midget subs designed by Kapitanleutnant Bartels. They were so slow and low-lying that they stood little chance of success against anything but a 'soft' target like a merchant ship. Against a battleship's protection, even an old one, they stood little chance of inflicting meaningful damage. None the less, the attempt was made, and six *Bibers* were attached, in pairs either side of their conning towers, to the submarines *U-295*, *U-716* and *U-739*. This made the U-boats highly vulnerable, but nevertheless they sailed on 5 January and headed north. *En route* bad weather was encountered, which caused damage to the midgets. So many problems were found with them, in fact, that the whole operation was aborted on the 8th, and the submarines and their cargoes returned to base. Although further attempts were mooted from time to time, this audacious plan in the end never ever took place. Lucky ship again!

Although the Germans never came close to sinking her, the *Arkhangelki*s demise was almost brought about by the Soviet Navy itself. On 3 September 1944, during a test firing of her torpedo tubes, the destroyer *Razumnyi* launched two live torpedoes in the direction of *Arkhangelsk* and *Murmansk*. Luckily both missed, and exploded ashore. The *Razumnyi*'s captain was dismissed from his ship (but survived without execution!)

So it was that not until the war in Europe was over and it was safe for her to venture forth did the *Arkhangelsk* actually put to sea again. She had two trials voyages, of short duration, in June 1945, carrying almost twice her normal RN complement. Great difficulties were encountered in handling her, but the Soviets tried once more in July of the same year, when she sailed on an extended voyage of two months around the perimeters of the White Sea before returning to Murmansk before the ice came too far south.

Here she remained throughout the winter, and in 1946 two further short trips were made, without any great improvements being noticed. In the autumn of 1947 she was reported as having run aground, but was eventually refloated after determined efforts. All this took place in secrecy, as the Iron Curtain had descended between the two former Allies, and all the brave words and promises of the handover period had been lost in the post-war harshness of British wholesale disarmament and Soviet expansionism into Poland, Czechoslovakia, Hungary and Rumania. As the nations Britain had gone to war in 1939 to defend against one dictator were swallowed up by another, there remained only hostility and rancour where once there had at least been the glimmerings of friendship and co-operation.

Meanwhile events had moved on, and the Italian battleship *Giulio Cesare* (renamed *Z.11*) had finally been prepared for the handover to Russia in the Black Sea. The actual transfer took place on 15 December 1948, and she received the Russian name *Novorossiisk*. It was therefore high time that the old *Royal Sovereign* returned home.

Notes

[1] The final tally of radar sets that remained aboard when the Soviets took over appears to have been one Type 279, one Type 284, one Type 273, two Type 285s and two Type 282s.

[2] Polyakov, G.G., *V Surovom Barentsevom* (*In the Stormy Barents*), Murmansk, 1978

[3] The fleet came into being on 10 September 1944, with *Arkhangelsk* as flagship. Orders with numbers beginning with double-zero were Top Secret (00 – hi hi), which may be where Ian Fleming got the idea for his James Bond creations code

[4] Lebedinskiy, M.B., *Povest' o Syl'nom* (*The Story of the destroyer Syl'nyi*), Vyborg, 1995

Epilogue

On 4 February 1949, the Soviet Navy's battleship *Arkhangelsk*, soon once more to be HM Battleship *Royal Sovereign*, returned once more to Rosyth. A small Royal Navy party was aboard her to assist in navigation, one of which was Chief Petty Officer Coxswain Priest. His son recalled: 'I have a superb brass plate giving the ship's name, engineering officers and engine room artificers of the day, with slots for their names in the plate. My father found it lying on the deck and brought it home as a souvenir.'

Major Wray knew she was on her way back, but, much as he loved her, did not see her homecoming:

> My friend Nowell Hall, then the Naval Correspondent of the *Daily Telegraph*, asked me, when the ship was due to return to the UK, if I would like to go with him, but I said no. I said that, to start with, the ship would not return on the date the Russians said she would, and to go on with, she would look superficially clean but would smell awful. Furthermore, I said that I loved that ship and couldn't bear to see her again. Needless to say I was right – she didn't, was and did!

Des Whitby *did* see her arrive back in the United Kingdom from the deck of HMS *Boxer*, a former landing ship, tank, being used for radar training:

> She came in to the anchorage under her own steam, along with a Russian merchant ship sent to take her crew home, and this is when the Russian crew left her. The weather was fairly murky. We looked through binoculars at the Russian ship and saw that some of the crew looking back at us were female. We didn't see any of the Russians ashore in Rosyth, Edinburgh or Dunfermline over our short stay of two or three days.
>
> From discussions with naval personnel who had supposedly been on board *Royal Sovereign* shortly after her return, she was in a pretty shocking state.

That was putting it mildly. According to some reports she was returned covered in rust, but worse, her guns were found to be loaded with *live* ammunition, some of it rusted in place! She officially became HMS *Royal Sovereign* again on 9 February, but there was no ceremony this time. All her sisters were already at the breakers' yards, the government of the day having taken the decision some time before that mass disarmament would mean that the scrap-metal value of the Royal Navy was more worthwhile to the austerity-ridden Britain of the post-war era than its limited fighting value. This recommissioning and the hoisting once more of the White Ensign was therefore nothing more than a mere formality on the part of the Admiralty. With little more ado, the faceless men in Whitehall placed her on the Disposal List, and she was sold on 5 April 1949, for breaking-up at Inverkeithing, the sad end of so many proud warships.

All smaller guns and equipment had been removed by the time she arrived at T.W. Ward's dismal graveyard. Here she found the remains of her proud sisters already well on the way to destruction and only partly retaining any semblance of identity as warships. The barrels of the mighty 15-inch guns were flame-cut off a few feet from the turrets, funnel and superstructure was lifted out by floating cranes, and then the superstructure and hull was steadily demolished deck by deck.

Few items were salvaged to preserve even the slightest part of their huge bulks for posterity. Two 15-inch guns on the lawn of the Imperial War Museum are about all that remain.

Revenge and *Royal Sovereign* lay briefly side-by-side for the last time in March 1950, and the 'Tiddly Quid' was the last to go completely. In all, ten proud capital ships were scrapped between 1948 and 1951. There should have been an eleventh, but *Warspite* put up a fight and was wrecked off Cornwall while under tow to Inverkeithing, and had to be broken up *in situ*.

Finally *Royal Sovereign* was gone for ever. Few artefacts remain of her outstanding thirty-four years of service. Major Wray was told, long ago, that one of her turret swash plate engines drives the Jodrell Bank telescope[1].

Her name could have lived on. However, when the five (later reduced to four) Polaris nuclear submarines built in the 1970s were given traditional R-class battleship names, *Royal Sovereign* was omitted from the list. The nuclear submarine was regarded as the modern-day equivalent of the battleship for some time, and nearly all the names were former battleship ones. Recently this has gone by the board, and traditional submarine names have reappeared, like *Talent*, *Tireless* and *Torbay*, which have no capital-ship connections at all. Before this reversion, however, one class of nuclear attack submarines was built which carried stirring names: this was the Swiftsure class, one of which, launched on 17 February 1973, was named *Sovereign*.

Not only can she fairly claim to be the direct successor of the 'Tiddly Quid', but she can also trace her ancestry right back to 1509 when the *Grace Dieu* was rebuilt and renamed that year as the *Sovereign of the Seas*. Lest anyone doubt that the direct line of descent via all three versions of the name is authentic, let them turn to Appendix One and the correspondence therein to set their minds at rest.

In November 1987, while in the process of researching the history of *Royal Sovereign*, I was fortunate enough to receive permission to visit HM Nuclear Attack Submarine *Sovereign* at Plymouth from her captain, Lieutenant-Commander Colin Stockman RN. I found her to be a most impressive vessel. From her deadly Mk 24 'Tigerfish' wire-guided torpedoes and 'Harpoon' guided-missile system to her sophisticated sonar and radar displays and nuclear-reactor power plant, she was in every inch the modern-day 'capital ship' in every sense of the word: an impressive vessel, fully worthy to carry on the torch of the Royal Navy's deterrence and attack capability. She served the Royal Navy for over thirty years. Any ex-member of the 'Tiddly Quid's' many ship's companies down the years would be proud of her.

Note

[1] Bernard Lovell recorded how:- " . . . Blackett himself suggested that the naval gunnery experts might help us with the problem of steering the telescope and the Admiralty Gunnery Establishment in Teddington was one of the many places I visited with Husband. This visit in time led Husband to the breakers yard where he secured the 15-in. gun turret racks of the *Royal Sovereign* and *Revenge* battleships at a bargain price. They were dismantled and stowed in our workshop at Jodrell . . . " Bernard Lovell, *The Story of Jodrell Bank*, Oxford University Press, 1968, pp29. Sir Bernard Lovell was the originator and driving force behind the construction of the 250ft. Mk. I telescope, now known as the 'Lovell Telescope', which is commonly misidentified as 'the Jodrell Bank Telescope'. H. C. Husband was the projects Consulting Engineer and P. M. S. Blackett, OM, CH, FRS, Nobel Laureate, was a Government Scienfic Adviser.

Battle Honours

Letter from MOD dated 11 June 1976:

Cdr P.R. Compton-Hall MBE RN (Rtd)
HMS DOLPHIN
Gosport
Hants
P012 2AB

Dear Cdr Compton-Hall

1. I write with reference to your letter of 21 April 1976 concerning the Battle Honours accorded to the present HMS SOVEREIGN.

2. The matter has been given careful consideration. I am pleased to be able to tell you that it has been agreed that the present SOVEREIGN should inherit all the Battle Honours of her ancestors. One wonders why these Battle Honours did not come with the badge so to speak but that is water under the bridge (or should I say over the fin!) and I do not propose to worry further about the reasons behind that decision because all that matters is that SOVEREIGN is now entitled to the following Battle Honours:

1642	KENTISH KNOCK
1666	ORFORDNESS
1672	SOLE BAY
1673	SCHOONEVELD
1673	TEXEL
1692	BARFLEUR
1702	VIGO
1794	FIRST OF JUNE
1795	CORNWALLIS'S RETREAT
1805	TRAFALGAR
1940	CALABRIA
1941	ATLANTIC

3. So far as the Honours Board is concerned I will make arrangements for a new one to be manufactured at Chatham. It will list all the Battle Honours and will be supplied to SOVEREIGN as soon as it is available.

4. Sorry it has taken a little while to get the answer on this one but I am sure you will agree good news is worth waiting for.

Yours faithfully

[signed]

for DIRECTOR GENERAL SHIPS

APPENDIX TWO

Ships of the Name

1. GREAT SHIP: 800 TONS, 108 GUNS, OF WHICH 20 WERE HEAVY

1486: Began building as the *Sovereign*. Some of the timber of Edward IV's *Grace Dieu* was used in her construction, which may account for her having been confused by the chroniclers with the *Henry Grace A Dieu* of 1512–14. Her building was supervised by Sir Reginald Bray, the famous architect, and there is reason to believe that she was an experimental ship in which new features were introduced. Her armament varied from time to time, and in 1495 consisted of 31 stone guns (short pieces of wide bore), and 110 serpentines (long guns). It is impossible to say how many of these were heavy pieces, for not all stone guns threw heavy shot, nor were all serpentines of small bore. Partially rebuilt and rearmed in 1509.

1526: Laid up without shipkeepers and reported unserviceable without great repair. Not mentioned again, i.e. was broken up soon after.

2. 1ST RATE: 1,522 TONS, 100 GUNS, 1635–7

Built at Woolwich by Peter and Phineas Pett. Launched 14 October 1637 and named *Sovereign of the Seas*.

1649: On the establishment of the Commonwealth it was

proposed to rename her *Commonwealth*, but the change was not made, and she became simply *Sovereign*.

1651: She was taken in hand for alterations, and is often stated to have been 'cut down a deck'. This was not so; her upper works were lowered to improve her sailing, but she remained a three-decked ship.

1659/60: Rebuilt at Chatham, 1,607 tons. After the Restoration she was more commonly called *Royal Sovereign*.

1685: Rebuilt at Chatham.

27 January 1696: Accidentally burnt at Chatham.

3. 1st rate: 1,883 tons, 100 guns

25 July 1701: Launched at Woolwich as *Royal Sovereign*.

1710–28: Laid up. Taken under great repair.

September 1763: Requiring great repair again. It was proposed to cut her down to an 84-gun ship, but after a survey in dock it was decided to break her up, which was done at Portsmouth.

4. 1st rate: 2,175 tons, 100 guns

January 1774: Began building at Plymouth.

4 September 1786: Launched as *Royal Sovereign*.

26 August 1790: Completed and sailed.

1806: Repairing after Trafalgar.

27 May 1825: Ordered to be renamed *Captain* and to be fitted as a Receiving Ship at Plymouth.

August 1841: Broken up at Plymouth.

5. Royal Yacht: 2nd rate, 278 tons

12 May 1804: Launched at Deptford as *Royal Sovereign*.

1806–32: In commission as yacht.

1832–49: Depot Ship at Pembroke; commanded by the Captain

Superintendent of the Yard. January 1850: Broken up at Pembroke.

6. 1ST RATE: 3,765 TONS, 120 GUNS

25 April 1857: Launched at Portsmouth as *Royal Sovereign*.

1864: Cut down and converted to an armoured screw-ship (800 hp) mounting 5 heavy guns in centre-line turrets.

1864–73: Tender to *Excellent*.

1885: Sold.

7. BATTLESHIP: 14,150 TONS, FOUR 13.5-INCH GUNS, TEN 6-INCH GUNS, 17 KNOTS

30 September 1889: Laid down at Portsmouth.

30 February 1891: Launched as *Royal Sovereign*.

31 May 1892: Commissioned for service as flagship of C-in-C Channel Squadron.

23 May 1905: Paid off at Devonport.

February 1907 to September 1911: In Special Service Squadron, Devonport.

1913: Sold.

8. BATTLESHIP: 25,750 TONS, EIGHT 15-INCH GUNS, FOURTEEN 6-INCH GUNS, 22 KNOTS

1 January 1914: Laid down at Portsmouth.

18 April 1916: Commissioned for Grand Fleet as *Royal Sovereign*.

May 1944: Loaned to Soviet Union and renamed *Arkhangelsk*.

February 1949: Returned to UK, resumed name *Royal Sovereign*.

1949/50: Scrapped at Inverkeithing.

9. Nuclear Attack Submarine (ASW) (SSN): 4,200 tons, Harpoon anti-ship missiles, Tigerfish anti-submarine torpedoes and Mk 8 Harpoon anti-ship torpedoes, 25+ knots underwater

17 February 1973: Launched as *Sovereign*.

11 July 1974: Commissioned.

1987: Visited by author at Devonport.

January 1997: Re-emerged after refitting at Rosyth. Cracks in tailshaft meant return to Rosyth for fourteen weeks' emergency repairs. Training.

March 2000: Onboard fire at Faslane.

May 2000: One exercise in Bay of Biscay, then used for training purposes. Potential reactor fault.

November 2001: Berthed Faslane, inoperational.

July 2005: Listed as operational, thirty-one years in service.

September 2005: Decommissioned at Devonport.

Battle Record

1490	Lord Willoughby's Expedition to Brittany
1512	Operations off Brest, 1st French War
1652	Battle of the Kentish Knock
1666	The St James's Fight
1672	Battle of Solebay
1673	First Battle of Schooneveld
1673	Second Battle of Schooneveld
1673	Second Battle of Texel
1690	Battle of Beachy Head
1692	Battle of Barfleur
1702	Expedition to Cadiz
1702	Attack on Vigo
1794	Battle of 'The Glorious First of June'
1805	Battle of Trafalgar
1918	Surrender of the German High Seas Fleet
1940	Battle of Calabria
1940/41	Battle of the Atlantic

Index